One-Hundred-and-One
African-American
Read-Aloud Stories

One-Hundred-and-One
African-American
Read-Aloud Stories

Edited by Susan Kantor

Tess
Press

Published by Tess Press, an imprint of
Black Dog & Leventhal Publishers, Inc.
151 West 19th Street
New York, NY 10011

Manufactured in the United States of America

Design by Liz Trovato

ISBN: 1-57912-530-1

b d f h g e c a

CONTENTS

INTRODUCTION

One-Hundred-and-One African-American Read-Aloud Stories is the next volume in the popular Read-Aloud series. Volumes one through four were created under the premise that there is value and significance in reading stories and poetry aloud to children. *One-Hundred-and-One African-American Read-Aloud Stories* was compiled in response to the great need for more anthologies on this subject. The demand for a collection of stories in this format further confirms that children love the sound of language and benefit from being read to.

We all remember being read to as children. These memories are indelible for many reasons. The companionship and security of being read to by someone else, the escape of exploring new adventures through these stories and the priceless excitement of learning to love books are all poignant moments for a child. Reading aloud together not only bonds reader and listener, but teaches and reinforces patience, attentiveness and curiousity—not to mention whetting the child's appetite for reading on his or her own.

Between the ages of four and nine many children begin to recognize and learn how to read words on a page. Reading aloud can help demystify the reading process. By reading stories that are on their interest level, but beyond their reading level, you can stretch your young readers' understanding and motivate them to improve their skills. No method better prepares children for that moment when "reading" clicks. Reading to children effectively builds and reinforces vocablulary as well. The relationship between the printed word, the spoken word and the meaning of words moves from the abstract to the concrete. Reading aloud contextualizes words that are often taught in isolated instances. Many of the stories in this collection may be beyond your child's reading level, but not beyond his or her listening level, and they are bound to introduce a plethora of new words.

More and more studies have proven that home reinforcement of concepts learned in school is an invaluable and effective educational step. Parents and readers of these stories can give children the attention and guidance that a teacher in a classroom cannot provide. Most importantly, children learn to look forward to these moments of reading together and ultimately anticipate reading for themselves.

ABOUT THE SELECTIONS

One-Hundred-and-One African-American Read-Aloud Stories contains traditional fairy tales, myths, fables and folk tales as well as selections from historical, biographical and contemporary works. And, as befits a culture with a special talent for storytelling, the classic tales are filled with wise chiefs, beautiful maidens, talking animals, inspiring heroes, some frightening monsters and, of course, astonishing feats of magic. Whether you choose to read a selection that will take ten-minutes or several of the shorter pieces, there are appropriate stories to satisfy the attention span and interests of both reader and listeners of almost any age.

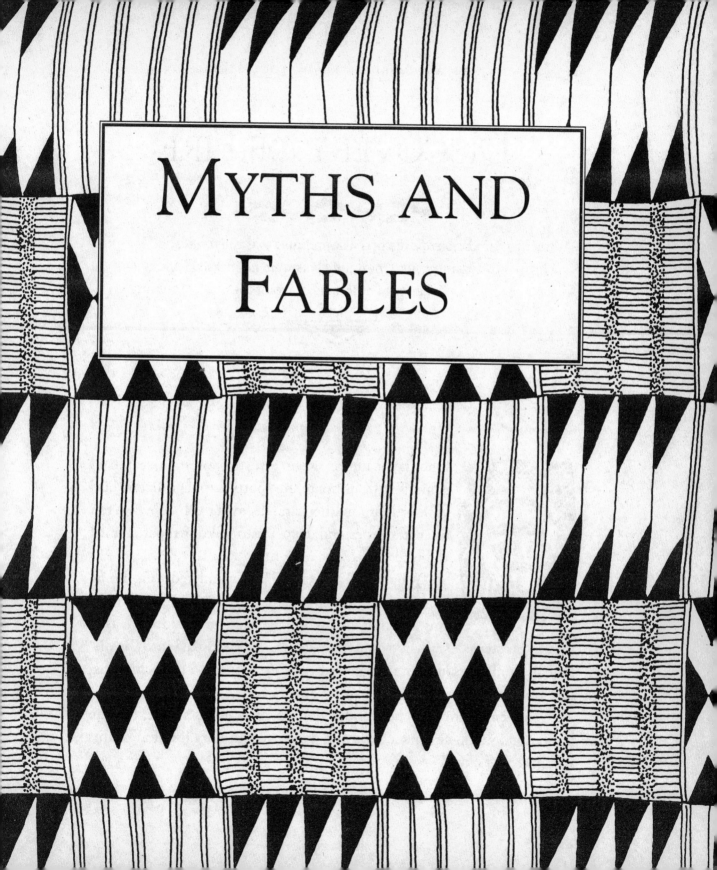

MYTHS AND FABLES

DISCOVERY OF FIRE

Before the discovery of fire, food was eaten raw,
iron was not forged, and pots were not baked.
The origin of this tale is unknown.

One day a hunter went into the forest in search of game. Far from home, he spotted a magnificent bird with brilliant feathers and decided to chase it. He ran after it, deeper and deeper into unknown parts, until the bird soared out of sight.

"What shall I do now?" he wondered. "Go home or continue hunting?" Then the hunter realized he was so far from his village that he could not easily retrace his steps. As he thought about what to do, he looked into the distant sky and saw something he had never seen before—a thin cloud rising straight up into the air.

"What could this be?" he wondered. Of course, it was smoke, but the hunter had no name for such a thing. He set off in the direction of this rising wisp of cloud.

It seemed that he had gone many miles but was getting no closer. The hunter did not know that a column of smoke may be visible from a great distance. When the sun disappeared, the hunter could no longer see the smoke, but just as he was about to abandon his search, he spotted a strange light below the horizon.

"How strange," thought the hunter. "Is it a fallen star?" Now, people who have never experienced fire know nothing about artificial light, for without fire it is impossible to burn a candle or a torch. The only night lights this man had ever seen were from the heavenly bodies, but none of them had ever glowed below the horizon. So he went in the direction of this extraordinary sight to find out what it was. As he came closer, he noticed that the light, which actually was a flame, flickered and flashed with the brilliance of a star.

"But it is not at all like a star," he thought, "for sparks and tongues shoot up from it and out of it issues a swirling cloud." When he approached it, he noticed that the fire gave off a strong heat which prevented him from touching it. The hunter concluded that this must be the revelation of a powerful spirit.

With considerable caution, he walked as near as he could to the flames and spoke the following: "Greetings to you, great Master! The sun has now set. How do you fare?"

The fire responded to these courteous remarks in a crackling voice. "Welcome, traveler! I invite you to keep me company this night. Come closer and make yourself warm. But first you must provide me with wood —trees, shrubs, trunks, branches, reeds, and dry grass."

The astonished hunter set off to gather up all he had been asked for, which he then tossed onto the fire piece by piece as he was instructed. As he fed the fire, he noticed that the flames increased in size very quickly. Indeed, the more branches he added, the larger the blaze became.

"You, too, have need of food," said the fire. "Look behind you at this moment." The hunter did so and saw a hare sitting nearby staring at the fire, seemingly transfixed by its glow. Quickly, the man fitted an arrow into his bow and let it fly. Once he had skinned his dead prey, the hunter prepared to eat it raw, as was his custom. But the fire stopped him with the following words: "Come here, young man, and cook your food so that you may savor its fragrance and enjoy its taste. Meat is much more delicious when it is roasted."

Never before having heard the word "roast," the hunter had no idea of what to do. Following further instructions from the fire, he learned that he should skewer the meat onto the blade of his spear. When he had eaten the cooked meat, he promised himself that he would never again eat meat raw. He was also determined to find a way to take the fire back to his village with him. Light, warmth, and roasting were now three comforts he could now no longer do without.

The hunter summoned up his courage and made an offer to the fire: "If you allow me to take you back to my village, I promise to keep you very well fed, and to look after you for as long as I live," said the man. However, the fire politely, and quite firmly, declined this offer.

"It is impossible for me to travel so I must forbid it. Such an act would be extremely dangerous, not only for you, but for all other living creatures and for the land. Better that I stay here where the gods have placed me. Although you must never attempt to take me away, you are always welcome to come here whenever you wish to warm yourself, to feed me, and to roast your meat. One more thing," said the fire. "Never tell anyone about my existence for they might find me and steal me."

The man honored the fire's wishes and that night he rested cozily near its flames. In the morning he rose refreshed and rested, and bid the fire farewell.

"Good-bye to you, fire, and thank you. I shall be glad to come back one day."

The hunter eventually found his way home. Upon his arrival, he gave his wife some of the roasted hare which he had so enjoyed out in the forest. This act of generosity, however, turned out to be a terrible mistake. For having tasted the succulent cooked meat, the woman asked for more.

Consequently, the man was obliged to go back again to visit the fire. There he not only made himself comfortable and warm, but also roasted meat for himself and his wife. The fire was not only accommodating, but was happy to have the hunter's company. In return, the hunter willingly fed the flames with dry sticks and branches. Gradually, he learned how to keep the fire burning nicely with big logs, and how to rekindle it with dry leaves when he had been absent for a long time and found it smoldering in its ashes.

In time, the hunter's wife told a friend about her husband's long absences and the delicious meat he brought home. This aroused the friend's curiosity, so he decided to follow the hunter the next time he went into the forest. He kept behind the hunter at a safe distance until he saw the wisp of rising smoke and then the fire.

As darkness fell, the spy crept up closer and closer to see what the hunter was up to. Following his usual routine, the hunter placed branches and logs on the fire before settling down for the night's sleep.

After he dozed off, the friend silently drew near. He took hold of a branch poking out from under the fire and ran off with it, unaware that he was leaving behind a trail of glowing sparks. The thief also was unaware that the flame at the top of the burning branch was eating through the wood. Suddenly, he let out a shriek for the fire had burned his hand. Immediately, he dropped the branch and, in great pain, ran for home.

He had not gone very far, however, when he heard a roaring sound behind him. Turning around, he saw he was being followed by tall flames, much larger than the cozy fire fed by the hunter. Screaming with terror, the man ran even faster.

As the fire spread over the savanna, it devoured everything in its path: the grass, the shrubs, and even entire trees. A massive curtain of flame seemed as if it would set the sky on fire and even threatened to devour the stars. The fire easily caught up with the fleeing man, completely surrounding him with a ring of flames. As he watched the fire continue to burn, he noticed that it never returned to any places it had already burned, and so was able to save himself by jumping onto a piece of scorched earth.

The fire continued to spread until it finally came to a halt by a river. Villagers along the fire's path had managed to save themselves by jumping into the river, but their homes and food supplies were destroyed.

Once the fire had burned itself out, the people cautiously returned to inspect the damage, and to wonder at this terrible and mysterious disaster. While searching in the rubble for something to eat, they found some food that had not been completely burned. And when they ate it, they discovered that it tasted better than the raw meat they used to eat. They also discovered that their clay pots, instead of being destroyed in the fire, had been baked hard and now were more durable than they had been before.

But what of the hunter and the original fire that he had so carefully tended? No sooner had the new fire begun its raging than the hunter awoke. He was horrified at the sight ahead of him. Meanwhile, the first fire burned on as before, gently consuming the logs that the hunter provided for it.

This fire began to speak: "The destruction you see in front of you is the result of a man attempting to steal me. Now you can see what happens when a fire is removed from its resting place. Here I am obedient, beyond I turn into a monster, destroying everything in my path. But I can also help you create useful things. I can bake your clay pots. I can roast your prey. I can fire and forge metals. When treated with respect, I am man's most valued friend."

ANANSI GETS WHAT HE DESERVES

Anansi thought he knew just the trick for making Guinea Fowl his dinner, but he wound up as hers instead.

Anansi lived in a country that had a queen who was also a witch. She decreed that whoever used the word *five* would fall down dead, because that was her secret name and she didn't want anyone else using it.

Now Brer Anansi was hungry because there was a famine and it was very hard to find any food. But Anansi was also a clever fellow and he had an idea. He made a little house for himself by the side of the river near where everyone came to get water.

And when anyone came to get water, he would call out to them, "I beg you to tell me how many yam hills I have here. I can't count very well." So, one by one he thought they would come up and say, "One, two, three, four, *five*," and they would fall down dead. Then Anansi would store them in his barrel, and that way he would have lots of food during hungry times and also in times of plenty.

In time he got his house built and his yams planted, and along came Guinea Fowl. Anansi said, "Excuse me, miss, please tell me how many yam hills I have here." So Guinea Fowl went and sat on one of those hills and said, "One, two, three, four, and the one I'm sitting on."

Anansi said "Cho! You can't count right." And Guinea Fowl moved to another hill and said, "One, two, three, four and the one I'm sitting on."

"Cho! You don't count right at all!"

"How do you count, then?" Guinea Fowl said, getting a little annoyed with Anansi.

"This way—one, two, three, four, FIVE!" Anansi fell dead, and Guinea Fowl ate him up.

WHY THE CHAMELEON SHAKES HIS HEAD

*In many parts of Africa the dog, though used for hunting, is not treated
as a worthy helper, but is left to scrounge around the village for scraps to eat or
bones to gnaw on. This tale from Northern Rhodesia shows how
selfish and ungrateful man can be.*

The dog and chameleon were friends. One day man, the hunter, was returning from hunting game, and the dog was trotting behind. The chameleon called to him, "Where are you going and why do you trot at the hunter's heels?"

The dog said, "The man and I are partners. We go hunting together. I catch game for him, he kills the animals for meat, and we share together."

The chameleon said, "Is this really true? I did not know man shared his meat this way."

"It is true," said the dog. "When the food is cooked, each of us takes what he needs."

The dog followed behind the hunter and the chameleon followed the dog. When they arrived at the village, the hunter's wife cooked the meat.

When it was cooked, she put some in a bowl and set it on the ground by her husband. The man took some and put it in his mouth. Then the dog trotted up and took some food from the bowl. The chameleon said, "It is true, they share the food."

Just then the hunter picked up a large stick and hit the dog on the head, making him drop the meat. The dog let out a surprised yelp and ran off into the bush.

The chameleon was so shocked by what he had seen that he went away shaking his head, saying, "It is unbelievable! The dog is his faithful friend. He helps him catch meat! Yet the hunter struck him on the head! Unbelievable! Man is a selfish ingrate. I will not live near man. I will live in the bush."

The chameleon went into the bush and stayed away from man. And whenever he thinks about how the hunter struck the dog for taking a piece of meat, he moves his head up and down as if to say, "It is unbelievable!"

TWO
CREATION MYTHS

Olodumare is the most important god of the Yoruba. It is believed that He is the owner of life and directs all things. There is a proverb saying, "Whatever Olodumare approves of is easy, but if he does not like someone's plan it is impossible to carry it out."

 In the beginning, there was only Olodumare, god of the sky in his heavenly abode, and below there was nothing but water. To create the world, Olodumare emptied out a snail shell full of earth. A pigeon and hen scattered the earth far and wide and it became land. Olodumare then created the oil-palm for food, the coconut tree for drink, and the kola nut tree for food.

Next, sixteen human forms were molded from earth and Olodumare breathed life into them—which only he can do. Then he ordered Orishanla, king of the forest, to lead the people to earth.

CREATION MYTH FROM KENYA

In the beginning, God created light. That was the first morning. Out of this light, God created the souls of all the human beings who would ever live. First, souls of the prophets were created, then the souls of holy men. After these, the Lord created the souls of ordinary people. Angels, too, were created out of this light. Because their bodies are transparent, they contain only purity, and have no desires other than to worship God and to help people.

After the light, God created seven other great things: the Canopy, the Throne, the Pen, the Book, the Trumpet, Paradise, and Hellfire. The Canopy is like a tent above the Throne upon which God lives. The Pen reaches from sky to earth and writes, day and night, the fate of all people. In the Book are all the events that will ever take place. The Trumpet of the Last Day will announce the end of the world and God's final judgment over all the souls He created. God then created Paradise, where the good and obedient souls will live in eternal bliss. Finally, God created Hellfire, the place for the wicked.

Beneath His Throne, God fashioned a giant tree, the Cedar of the End. On this tree are millions of leaves, some fresh and green, others old and withering. On each leaf, God has written a name. When he wills it, a leaf comes floating down, but before it reaches the earth, an angel reads the name on the leaf, and tells the Angel of Death who is ready to leave the earth.

At last, God created the earth out of one ocean, and the sun to rise above it. The warm sun made the mists rise up and form themselves into clouds that travel from one end of the sky to the other. Then God called the continents to rise out of the ocean. Next, He called the islands and they rose up quietly in the midst of the foaming waves. God caused green vegetation to sprout. Trees formed forests, grasses decorated the hills, and palm trees waved along the seashore.

When God made the sun set in the west, He painted the sky red and gold. He filled the night sky with bright lights, which He called stars.

Next, God created animals in four classes: those that swim, whose king is the whale; those that creep, whose king is the python; those that fly, whose king is the eagle; and those that walk on four legs, whose king is the lion.

Four classes of creatures with intelligence were also created: angels made out of the light; jinns or wind spirits made from the air; evil spirits made from fire; and human beings made from the earth.

All of the Lord's creatures are born and so they all must die, for nothing will live forever except God.

NINE WILD DOGS AND ONE LION

The lion has his own way of dividing equally.

One day nine wild dogs were on their way to hunt. Before they had gone far, however, they came upon a lion lying in the sun.

"Where are you young fellows going," he said.

The dogs hesitated before replying, "We are on a hunt."

"On a hunt? Why, let us go together," suggested the lion.

The dogs gave one another worried looks, and then stammered out, "Whatever you wish, king of the world."

Soon they had caught ten antelopes. Then the lion said, "Let us find some wise person to come and divide the meat for us."

Without thinking, the youngest wild dog remarked, "Well, we are ten, are we not? And we have caught ten antelopes. Let each of us take one."

In an instant the lion was up and with a big rough paw struck the outspoken dog in the face.

"No, no," the leader of the pack responded, "I know how to divide the meat: The king of the world is one, so he should have nine of the antelopes and that will make ten. For us, we are nine—if we take one of the antelopes, then we will be ten."

The lion lifted his tail and strutted about looking very pleased with this arrangement. "You are a wise dog," he said. "When did you learn such wisdom?"

"When you slapped my brother," was the truthful reply.

A HOME FOR SUN AND MOON

This myth from Tanganyika shows how an inability to admit a mistake leads to unforseen, and unintended, consequences.

At the beginning of time, Sun and Water both lived on the earth and were the dearest friends. Sun frequently visited where Water lived, and they spent many hours chatting together.

But Water never visited Sun where he lived, and Sun started to wonder why. One day, Sun finally asked his friend: "How come neither you nor your family ever come to pay me a visit? My wife, the Moon, and I would be very happy to offer you our hospitality."

Water smiled and said: "I do apologize for not having visited you, but the fact is that your house is far too small for me and all my relations. I fear that we would drive you and your wife out of doors."

"But we are about to build a new place," said Sun. "Will you come and visit us if it is big enough?"

"It would have to be very large, indeed, for me to come in," explained Water. "My people take up so much space. What if we damaged your belongings?"

Sun thought Water was just making excuses for not visiting him, and his disappointment was noticeable. To make Sun feel better, Water promised to visit him when his new place was ready.

So Sun and Moon started to work on their new home. With the help of many friends, they built an enormous mansion.

When it was completed, Sun said to Water: "Surely you can visit us now for our new place is large enough to hold many, many visitors."

But Water was not convinced. Nevertheless, because a visit meant so much to Sun, Water began moving toward Sun's new home. Through the enormous front doors he flowed, bringing with him thousands of fish, water rats, and even some water snakes. By now the water level was knee deep.

"Do you still want my relatives and me to enter further into your home?" Water asked politely.

"Yes, of course," replied the silly Sun, "bring them all in!"

So Water continued to flow into the new house until finally Sun and Moon were forced to climb onto the roof to keep dry.

"Are you sure you still want my relatives and me to come into your house?" Water asked again.

After insisting for so long that Water come to visit, Sun was too embarrassed to admit that it was not a good idea. Instead, Sun said, "Yes, of course. I want everyone in. Bring everyone in."

Finally, Water rose to the very top of the roof, forcing Sun and Moon up into the sky where they have remained ever since.

THE SHEEP

Sheep are rare in tropical Africa and so are highly prized. Berber sheep-shearers still sing a hymn to the rising sun which they call "Our great Ram."

 A chief named Muy and his wife had many fine sons. All were born strong and healthy except for the last one. This one was born a lamb. After his birth, the father called his sons together and said, "You have seen that your youngest brother is a sheep. We will never again eat mutton for it would be a crime to eat one's own brother."

From then on, sheep were the friends of the family. One day a stranger arrived. He had a young ewe which he offered to sell. Muy bought the ewe which he gave to his youngest son as a wife. They lived together happily and had many lambs.

But a wicked king also lived in that country. Each year he demanded an animal from every hunter and farmer. Whenever a man brought him an animal, the king would ask, "Where is my girl?" For in addition to the animal tax, every family also had to offer a girl to the king—not for him to marry, but for him to eat because he was a horrible cannibal.

When Muy arrived to offer the king a magnificent leopard he had shot, the king demanded a daughter from him as well.

"But I have no daughter," Muy protested.

"Then I will eat all the sheep on your farm!" shouted the king.

Muy was so frightened for his children's safety that he raised his spear and stabbed the king to death. Of course, he had to flee to escape the king's son who was now king. With his family, including a flock of grandchildren, they ran for their lives. Exhausted, they reached the bank of a river, but no bridge or boat was in sight.

Chief Muy bowed down in prayer to a very tall tree that grew on the bank. Slowly the tree bent down until it reached all the way across the river and they all then scrambled across to safety. As soon as they were across, the tree righted itself.

In pursuit, the king and his men rushed into the water, determined to swim across. Just then, a flood swept down the river and they all were drowned. Chief Muy and his family returned to their home and lived in peace and prosperity.

THE SUSPECT

In this Nigerian folktale, an innocent man is misjudged by his neighbors.

There was once a king who had a beautiful inlaid knife. It was forged by the finest craftsman of Benin and decorated with inlay of brass and copper. It was the king's most prized possession.

One day, a big carnival was held in his village. People came from far and wide to join in the festivities. There was dancing, and singing, and feasting, and the king gave out gifts. But when the carnival was over, and everyone had gone home, the king discovered that his precious knife was missing.

He looked all over for it but couldn't find it anywhere. He suspected that someone from the carnival had stolen it.

Word was sent out all over the country that the king's inlaid knife was missing, and a reward was offered to anyone who could find the thief. People were astonished.

"Who could be so foolish as to steal the king's knife?" they said. The thief must be found and punished.

There was a certain village called Gbo. When the people of the village heard the news they looked around suspiciously. In the village was a hunter who lived alone. His neighbors questioned him.

"Weren't you at the king's carnival?" someone asked him.

"Yes," he replied. "I went there and ate and danced just like everyone else. What of it?"

"You're a hunter, aren't you, and you use a knife?"

"I have many weapons," he answered. "Why should I want to steal the king's knife? I wouldn't want to skin my animals with a knife belonging to the king."

The hunter made it clear that he did not intend to waste his time answering any more questions and went off to hunt.

"Just see how he answers so sharply," the people of the village said among themselves. "He cannot be trusted. If he is innocent, why does he look so angry? And he didn't want to talk about it and turned his back on us. Surely he has a guilty conscience. He must be the thief."

As days and nights passed, the people watched the hunter with growing suspicion. When he went out into the forest in the morning, they watched him. And when he returned at dusk, they watched him.

"See how he walks, as if he had something to hide. He spends all his time in the bush and does not want to be seen. What does he do there all day?"

As more time passed, the villagers became more convinced that the hunter was the thief, and no one would even talk to him anymore. When he had skins to sell, no one would buy them from him, so he had to take them to other villages. This made the villagers even more suspicious.

It seemed that whatever he did only made his neighbors mistrust him more. He started to spend days at a time in the forest, and to come home after dark and not show his face in the village. Now they were absolutely certain that he was the thief.

"We should tell the king that we have found the one who stole his knife," somebody said.

"But that would bring shame on our village," said another. "We should drive the hunter out first, then we could report him." And so the villagers argued about what to do.

One day a messenger arrived from the king's village. The knife inlaid with copper and brass had been found. It seemed that it hadn't been stolen after all. For safekeeping, the king had hidden it in the rafters of his cottage before the carnival, and it had fallen down inside the grass wall.

Everyone was relieved that the king's knife had been found again, and that it had not been stolen. The people of Gbo were especially pleased. Now they looked at the hunter with new eyes.

"Just see how hard he works. He spends all day in the bush and wastes no time. He is so determined that he will not return from the hunt until he has some game," said one.

"He doesn't talk much, because he is so serious," said another.

"And the way he walks—you can see he is afraid of nothing."

"Anyone could tell by looking at him that he is an honest man."

THE SPIRIT TREE

In Africa, angels are good spirits who come to earth, appearing in any shape or form, to help ease human suffering. Often, they are the spirit of a kind relative who has died but who still wants to help loved ones left on earth.

 There was a sweet and gentle girl in Zaire whose mother had died. Her father then married a woman he thought was kind to his daughter, but he was rarely at home and so did not know how cruel the woman really was. The stepmother did not give the girl enough food, so the hungry child often sat weeping on her mother's grave.

One morning, a beautiful tree had grown up from the grave. It was laden with the most delicious fruit, providing the girl with as much food as she wanted. But the wicked stepmother had the tree cut down.

Once again, the girl did not have enough to eat, and again she cried upon her mother's grave. Soon, she saw a fabulous pumpkin growing from the earth which completely satisfied her hunger. A new pumpkin appeared each morning to feed her, but when her stepmother found out, she dug up the vines.

Then a stream appeared, with water that was fresh and nutritious. The stepmother discovered it, and filled in the stream with earth.

In despair, the girl went back to her mother's grave. As she wept, a hunter appeared. The girl hurriedly dried her tears so that he would not see her crying.

"May I make arrows from the wood of this dead tree?" he politely asked her.

"Yes, you may," the girl replied.

The good spirit of the girl's mother was in the wood. When the hunter made his arrows, her spirit was released, causing the girl and the hunter to fall in love and get married. And the mother's spirit protected them from harm for the rest of their lives.

THE QUARREL BETWEEN EARTH AND SKY

There are many stories to explain how the earth became separated from the sky. In this Yoruba story from western Nigeria, the consequences of the sky withdrawing explain why there are periods of drought and famine.

Long ago, Earth and Sky were the best of friends. They considered themselves equals in everything, and never quarreled. They often spent all day together, which they greatly enjoyed, especially when hunting.

One day they went into the bush to hunt. They followed the trails of antelope and deer, they tracked wild pigs, and they looked for birds, but their hunt was not successful. As the day wore on, they got more and more hungry, and they became rather irritable. Finally, at sunset, they caught a little bush rat. It wasn't really enough to feed two hungry hunters, but it was all they had. They made a fire and roasted the bush rat, but when it was ready to eat, an argument broke out.

Earth said, "I will eat the first portion because I am senior to you. In the beginning, Earth was there before the Sky came into existence."

"That's not true!" Sky retorted. "Sky was here long before Earth was formed so I should be given the first portion."

They continued to argue about who should be given the first portion, neither giving in to the other, and the more they argued, the more bitter their feelings became. At last Sky said, "This is no way to treat me. You aren't my friend anymore, so why should I be yours? I don't want your company any longer. Keep your bush rat—I hope you enjoy it!" And Sky stormed off. He went high up, far above the Earth and stayed there. Earth was angry, too, and left the place, leaving the bush rat lying there uneaten.

Before this quarrel, when Earth and Sky were close friends, rains were plentiful, rivers were always full, and the earth was always fertile. Vegetables and green things grew, the bush was abundant with game, crops flourished, and harvests were good. All creatures lived an easy life.

But once Sky moved far away, rains became scarce, the rivers dried up, the Earth turned dry, and deserts spread across the land. Wells dried up, crops failed, the animals of the bush began to die out, and people began to starve.

A meeting was called of all the creatures of the bush to see what could be done. The dead bush rat, the cause of all the trouble, was brought before them. They decided to appease Sky. A messenger would be chosen to carry the bush rat to Sky as a present, and beg Sky to come back down near Earth.

The birds were asked to select one of their own to carry the gift. One of them was chosen, but he was unable to carry the bush rat high enough to reach Sky. Another one tried and also failed. One after the other, all the strongest fliers among the birds were sent, but none of them were strong enough to carry the bush rat to Sky. At last Vulture spoke.

"I can fly higher than any of you. Let me carry the bush rat to Sky."

The other creatures laughed, for Vulture was rather clumsy.

"If our best fliers can't do it, how do you suppose you can?" they demanded.

But Vulture insisted, and since everyone else had tried, they gave him the bush rat to carry. As he flew up toward the sky, Vulture sang:

Earth and Sky went hunting,
Killed a bush rat for their meal.
Earth claimed he was senior
But Sky did not agree.
Sky went far up high above
Then Earth became quite dry.
Yams stopped growing in the fields
And maize lost all its grains.
Mothers searched for water
While their babies cried with thirst.

As Vulture sang this song, flying higher and higher, Sky heard him. Sky was sorry at what was happening and decided to forget his anger. He accepted the gift of the bush rat from Vulture and in return gave Vulture a bag of magic red powder. Sky explained to Vulture that whenever rain was needed, he had only to scatter a tiny amount of this magic powder in the air, and rain would fall in abundance.

Vulture gladly took the bag of magic powder and began his long descent back down to earth. On the way, however, he became more and more curious to see the powder, and couldn't stop himself from opening the bag to have a look. Suddenly, a gust of wind blew the powder everywhere, scattering all of it into the air at once. Instantly the light faded, big black clouds covered the sun, and strong winds whipped through the air. The powerful winds broke the trees and blew down the houses. Then torrents of rain came crashing down and great floods surged across the land, washing away crops and villages and leaving behind ruins.

When the storm was finally over, the creatures of the Earth looked for Vulture everywhere to ask him what had happened. At last they found him. He told them about his meeting with Sky, and the magic red powder he had been given. Then he explained his unfortunate accident. Everyone was furious. They attacked Vulture and beat him severely around the head.

As a result, Vulture, who used to have a beautiful set of head feathers, wound up with a bald head, which he has had ever since. The others, however, never got over their anger, and Vulture has never again been welcome among other animals. He has had to live apart from them, and is not allowed to share their food, but must wait until they are finished before eating their left overs.

WHY PEOPLE FIGHT

Many misunderstandings can be avoided if people do not
jump to conclusions.

No matter what some people may believe, the hyena does not like to fight unless he is attacked. So, why, he wondered, do people fight? He asked all the animals this question, but none gave him a satisfactory answer. When he happened upon the hare one day and asked him, the hare said, "Come with me and see what sort of thing can make people fight."

The hyena followed the hare to a game snare which a man had set. Here they found a small antelope caught and they took it out of the trap. Then they went to the river and found a fishing net. The hare said, "Let us take out all the fish and put the antelope in." Then they put the fish in the game snare.

The hare then said to the hyena, "Let us hide here, and you will soon see what causes people to fight." So they hid themselves in the bushes near the snare and fishing net.

When the owners of the snares came, the one went to his fish trap and found an antelope in it. The other went to his game snare and found the fish in it. The man who had laid the game snare said to himself, "What nerve! The owner of the fishing net has taken my antelope and replaced it with his fish." He went to the owner of the net and said, "Why do you put your fish into my snare? Do you think I do not know?"

The other replied, "Is it not *you* who put the antelope into my net?"

"Why would I put my nice antelope into your net, and take your small useless fish? It is you who put your fish into my snare." Thereupon they began to argue louder and louder until they finally came to blows.

Then the hare said to the hyena, "Have you seen what causes people to fight?"

The other replied, "Now I have seen." And they both went on their way.

WHY ELEPHANTS ARE AS INTELLIGENT AS PEOPLE

In African myths, the elephant is depicted as a wise chief who settles disputes among the forest creatures. The Wachaga in Tanzania believe that the elephant was once a human being, but was cheated out of all his limbs except for his right arm which now serves as his trunk. An Ashanti myth explains that in the past, elephants were human chiefs: When Ashantis find a dead elephant in the forest, they give it a proper chief's burial. This Kenyan myth tells how elephants originated.

A very poor man heard of Ivonya-Ngia, which means "he that feeds the poor." Though it was a long journey, the poor man decided to go and find Ivonya-Ngia. When he finally arrived, he saw more cattle and sheep than he could count, and in the midst of the lush green pastures, was Ivonya-Ngia's sparkling mansion.

Ivonya-Ngia received the poor man kindly. Without being told, he understood the man's need, and ordered that he be given a hundred sheep and a hundred cows.

"No," said the poor man. "I want no charity. I only want the secret of how to become rich."

Ivonya-Ngia thought for a while, then took a flask of ointment and gave it to the poor man, saying, "Rub this on your wife's pointed teeth in her upper jaw. Wait until they have grown and then sell them."

The poor man returned home and carried out the strange instructions, promising his wife that they would become very rich.

After some weeks, the wife's canine teeth began to grow, and when they had grown into tusks as long as his arm, the man persuaded his wife to let him pull them out. He took them to the market and sold them for a flock of goats.

After a few weeks, the wife's canine teeth had grown again, becoming even longer than the previous pair. But this time, she would not let her husband touch them. Not only her teeth, but her whole body became bigger and heavier. Her skin became thick and gray. At last, she burst out of the door, and walked into the forest, where she lived from then on. She gave birth to her son there, who was also an elephant.

From time to time, her husband visited her in the forest, but she would not be persuaded to come back.

This was the origin of elephants and explains why they are as intelligent as people.

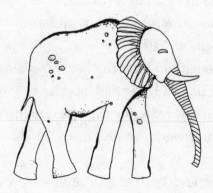

MOSES IN PHARAOH'S COURT

Episodes from the Bible were commonly used to explain miracles, reproach the wicked, or express a moral. In this familiar story, Pharaoh's court sorcerers are seen as hoodoo practioners who lose their power, known as their "hand."

 The Israelites were captured and carried down in bondage to Egypt. And Moses was born there. To keep the Hebrews from multiplying so fast, Pharaoh told his soldiers to kill all the little Hebrew boy babies. So when Moses was born his mother kept him hidden for three months. When she couldn't hide him any longer, she made a basket of bulrushes, and put him in it. Then she carried him down and put him in the river where Pharaoh's daughter went to bathe.

When Pharaoh's daughter found the baby, she carried him to her daddy and begged to adopt him. So he agreed, and he told her, "Go out and find you a nurse, an Israelite woman, for they'd know how to take care of this baby." And the daughter went out and hired an Israelite woman who was the baby's real mother.

The baby grew fast, and learned all the Egyptian words and languages.

So Pharaoh made him a ruler then, because he saw how smart he was. One day, Moses walks out and he sees a Hebrew and an Egyptian fighting. And he kills this Egyptian, and then buries him in the sand.

A few days later, he sees two Hebrews fighting again. He said, "Why do you all strive against one another?" "Aren't you brothers?" One said, "Are you going to kill one of us like you did that Egyptian the other day?"

Moses didn't think anyone had seen what he did, and he got scared and ran away into Middin. He stayed there forty years and married an Ethiopian woman.

One day he was out minding his father-in-law's sheep, and the Lord spoke unto Moses and said, "Pull off your shoes, for you are on holy ground. I want you to go back and deliver my children from Egypt." Then the Lord said, "Moses, what is that in your hand?"

"It's a staff," said Moses.

"Cast it on the ground," said God.

The staff turned into a snake, and Moses was frightened and drew away.

The Lord said, "Go back and pick it up." So Moses picked it up, and it turned back into a staff. The Lord said, "Go back and wrought all these miracles in Egypt, and deliver my children from bondage."

So Moses goes on back. He goes in to see Pharaoh and tells him what the Lord said. Pharaoh said, "I never heard of this God. Who is he?"

"I can show you what he has the power to do," said Moses. And he cast his rod on the floor, and it turned into a serpent. Pharaoh said, "That ain't nothing. My hoodoo magicians can do that." He brought in his magicians and soothsayers and they cast their rods on the floor, and theirs turned to snakes, too.

But when Pharaoh's snakes crawled up to Moses' snake, Moses' snake swallowed up their snakes. And that's where hoodoo lost his hand, because theirs was the evil power and Moses' was the good.

HUNGER, RICE AND CASSAVA

*When Rice and Cassava appear in a village, the people are
always happy to see them.*

On the day God created people, He also created food in two forms—Rice and Cassava. Then He told them: "Remember, Cassava, the people must eat you properly cooked, otherwise you will make them sick. And you, Rice, must be boiled or eaten in soup or gravy, but never raw. Go now to the villages of the people and be their food so they may live."

Rice was ready to begin the journey, but Cassava said, "You have made my brother Rice and I the keepers of people's lives. What will happen if we are not treated with proper respect?"

God answered, "My son Hunger, who you will soon meet, has been created to teach gratitude. He will accompany you on all your journeys."

Hunger arrived. His skin was as dry as a drum-skin, and his bones were sticking out. God told him, "If the people do not show proper appreciation for their food, and do not carefully cultivate Rice and Cassava, you will make them as thin as yourself."

So the three of them set out on their journey. Whenever they approached a village, Hunger would blow in first. A terrible wind would dry the leaves and stalks, and people would become faint with their need for food.

But as soon as they could see Rice and Cassava coming down the path, the people would rush towards them, offer them water, beg them to stay forever, and thank God for sending them.

INDAJI, THE RECKLESS HUNTER

In Africa, successful hunters were highly honored, and many were believed to possess magic. The following tale is from northern Nigeria.

There was once a very skillful hunter named Indaji. His arrows never missed. His spear always found its mark. No animal he aimed at had any chance of escape. When he whistled the animals would come to him, for he possessed magic power. At first, he killed 10 animals a day, then 20, and then 100 animals every day.

He was the richest and most famous hunter in the land. He had many children and owned more horses, cattle, and goats than he could count. What more could he want? But still he killed animals.

Finally, the god of the forest became angry about this hunter's greed and arrogance. One day he appeared to Indaji in the forest and said, "Indaji, your fame as a hunter is known everywhere. There is nothing you need.

From now on, you may hunt no more than one animal each day. That will be more than enough to feed your family. If you go on killing animals like this, soon I will have none left. If you do not obey me, I promise you will surely regret it."

Not long after that warning from the forest god, Indaji shot three antelopes that were grazing peacefully together in the forest. Suddenly, he heard a voice, "This sin will cost you your life." And at that moment, the three dead antelopes changed into three fierce lions who sprang at Indaji. But Indaji, who possessed magic, turned himself into a songbird and flew away. The lions changed into hawks and soared after him. But the songbird changed into a tree. Then the hawks changed into a fire and burned the tree to ashes.

THE MOON KING

In this Angolan myth, a little frog plays matchmaker for the Prince of the Earth and the Moon King's daughter.

The King of the Earth had one son. When he came of age, his father told him, "You must marry. I will help you choose a wife." The prince replied, "I only want the Moon King's daughter for my wife."

The King asked each of the wise men and women of his kingdom how to find the path to the Moon, but no one knew. Just then, the Frog spoke up. "Sire," he said, "I will travel to the Moon for you." The King did not really believe the Frog could make such a journey, but decided to give him a chance. "All right," said the King. "Take this letter to the Moon King."

The Frog knew that the Moon King's water bearers came to Earth every morning before sunrise to fetch water from a hidden spring deep in the forest. The next morning, the Frog hid in the spring, and swam into the first pail they lowered for filling.

When the water bearers returned to the Moon, the frog jumped out and asked to be taken to the Moon King. When the Frog was brought before him, he produced the Earth King's letter. The Moon King read it, wrote a reply, and handed it to the Frog who was brought back to Earth in one of the empty water pails.

He swam out when the pail was lowered into the water, hurried to the court of the Earth King, and announced himself by saying, "The Ambassador to the Moon King's court is here with a message for the Earth King."

The Earth King read the letter. The Moon King had agreed to the wedding of his daughter to the Earth prince as soon as the bride price was paid. The Earth King gave the Frog a bag of gold to take up to the Moon. When the Frog arrived, he was treated to a fine meal of pork and chicken, and then carried the message back to Earth that the Princess of the Moon would arrive the next night.

Nobody really believed the Frog, but they put on their best clothes just in case. Sure enough, the next night, the Moon Princess descended along a silver cord woven by the Moon Spider, and was married to the Prince of the Earth.

A Quarrel Between Friends

In this Yoruba tale, a neighbor plays a trick on two neighbors in order to test their friendship.

Once there were two farmers, Olaleye and Omoteji, who lived next door to one another. They also were best friends. But one neighbor wanted to see just how important their friendship really was.

This man made himself a hat—red on one side and green on the other. He put it on and then strolled down a path between the two farms. When he passed Omoteji on his left he said, "Good morning, Omoteji."

"Good morning," the farmer replied. "What a nice red hat you are wearing."

"Thank you very much," the man answered. "Well, I will see you later."

Further down the path, he saw Olaleye on his right, weeding his yams. "Good morning, Olaleye. How are you this morning?"

"Oh, good morning," Olaleye responded. "My, that's a lovely green hat."

"Thank you. I made it myself, you know. See you later, Olaleye."

At lunchtime the two friends sat together by the path and ate. After chatting about many things, Olaleye said: "Did you see our friend's new green hat this morning? He said he made it himself."

"Don't you mean red hat," corrected Omoteji.

"No, it was definitely a green hat. Perhaps the sun was in your eyes."

"But I specifically remarked about the red color and he did not say it was green. You must be the one who is mistaken."

"But I also commented on the color. It most certainly was green."

Each continued to insist that he was right about the correct color of the hat. Soon, they had both become very angry and for the first time ever they were shouting at each other. Just as Omoteji was ready to grab Olaleye, the neighbor returned.

"Why are you arguing?" he asked. As he spoke, he walked between the two so that each farmer saw the other side of the hat from the one that he had seen that morning.

Immediately, the two stopped fighting. "Oh, my friend, I am sorry," said Olaleye. "You were right. The hat is red."

"No. You were right," said Omoteji. "The hat is green."

They might have started quarreling again if their neighbor had not taken off his hat and showed both sides to them.

"My friends, please don't fight," he said. "As you can see, my hat is both colors—red on one side and green on the other, but the color is not important. What's important is that you were about to let a simple thing like the color of a hat destroy your friendship."

"Omoteji," said Olaleye, "I have been very foolish. This will never happen again. From now on, all I care about is having a good friend like you."

"And I, too, have been foolish," replied Omoteji. "I promise to never fight with you again."

And they never did.

SOME AFRICAN PROVERBS

The wide appeal of proverbs seems to be their ability to express in a few words universal truths and undeniable wisdom.

An egg cannot fight with a stone.

If you stub your toe, go on.

When near danger, cry out early.

Helping me may help you.

If a crocodile deserts the water, he will find himself on a spear.

One does not become great by claiming greatness.

Giving something to a person does not insure everlasting friendship.

A wanderer cannot know the full meaning of a home.

I had wanted to bathe, but I did not expect to fall into the pond.

A rat is not afraid in the presence of a dead cat.

If there are no vines, where will the gourds grow?

The ashes are the children of the fire.

A turtle knows where to bite another turtle.

The things in the pond are different from the things outside of the pond.

Haste has no blessing.

To the person who grasps two things at once, one always slips away from him.

The path of falsehoods has seven endings.

Speak in silver, answer in gold.

A person used to a donkey does not ride a horse.

The prayer of the chicken hawk does not get him the chicken.

THE GREEDY WOMAN BECOMES A WOODPECKER

*Episodes from the Bible or the gospels were commonly used to explain
miracles, reproach the wicked, or teach a lesson.*

Once when the good St. Peter,
While traveling around the earth,
Lived in this world below,
He walked about here preaching,
Just as He did you know.

He came to the door of a cottage
Where a woman was baking cakes
In ashes on the hearth.
He asked her for a stovecake
To give him a single one.
She pinched a tiny scrap of dough,
She rolled and rolled it flat,
She baked it as thin as a wafer,
But could not part even with that.

She said, "My cakes may seem so small
Yet they are too large to give away."

So she put them on the shelf.
And then the good St. Peter grew angry
For he was hungry and faint,
And surely such a woman
Were enough to try any saint.

He said, "You shall get your food
As the birds do, by pecking and pecking
All day in the hard, dry wood."
Then up through the chimney she went,
Never speaking a word, and out the top
Flew a woodpecker—she was changed into a bird.

All of her clothes were burned black as charcoal
Except for the scarlet cap on her head,
And every country schoolboy
Have seen her up until this very day
pecking and pecking for food.

FAIRY TALES

BABOON SKINS

A SWAZI TALE
Terry Berger

A maiden's beauty causes her so many problems that she wraps herself in baboon skins and refuses to show her face.

Now in this story there is neither Fairy nor Inzimu; there is no one who wins a kingdom with secret spells. (Some little bags of pythonskin are mentioned, but you will see that they have no effect on anyone.) In fact the only magic used in this story is a woman's wit and kindness of heart; the oldest charms in the world.

Many years ago there lived a Chief who had many wives. Two of these were more distinguished than the others for each had a most beautiful daughter. In fact these two wives had families exactly alike, for each had a plain son too. I cannot tell you what became of the plain sons, though no doubt each had a history, for this tale concerns only the two beautiful daughters.

The name of one girl was Inkosesana, which means "the Young Lady." Her mother was very proud of her and expected her to marry a great Chief, and Inkosesana was as conceited as possible as a result of this.

The name of the other maiden was Lalhiwe, which means "Thrown Away." As you can imagine from her name, she was a much quieter and more modest girl than Inkosesana.

As time went on and both maidens grew into womanhood, suitors began to arrive. Each mother was hoping for great things for her daughter, and the rivalry between the two families became more and more bitter. It was all they could do to keep their constant quarrels from reaching the ears of the Chief.

Early one morning Lalhiwe's mother awoke and went to prepare corn for the day's food. To her horror, she discovered some animal blood and small pythonskin bags filled with charms, under the grinding stone.

"Lalhiwe!" she cried out, "come and see what bad fortune awaits us; cast your eyes upon this!"

Lalhiwe rushed to her mother and upon seeing the charms she nearly fainted. "It is witchcraft," she said. "It must be some wickedness devised by Inkosesana and her mother. They will never rest until we come to harm. I know in my heart that these charms are meant to cast a spell over us so that we may fall ill and die."

Lalhiwe's mother nodded her head in agreement. And after a minute she begged Lalhiwe to run quickly to a neighbor, who was a Wise Woman, and to bring her back with the charms necessary to undo the evil that their rivals had intended for them.

After this had been accomplished, Lalhiwe sat down and spoke to her mother, saying, "Mother, I am tired of all this. How can I care about beauty when it has brought us only endless quarrels and bitter jealousies? To end this constant fighting, I have decided to cover myself with baboon skins, the ugliest skins of all. I shall wrap myself up in them and remain that way until Inkosesana has married. In that way, we shall all have peace."

That very day she asked her brother to fetch two baboon skins for her and to bring them with the heads and the limbs still on them. As soon as they were brought, she joined the two skins at the shoulders and at the heads. Then she slipped into them so that the heads completely covered her own head. Only her two bright eyes peeped out through the eyeholes she had cut. The rest of her face was completely hidden, and all that one could see was the mask of a grinning ape. The two skins hung down from her shoulders to her knees, in the back and in the front, but one could still see her legs which were pretty and well-shaped. She looked like a person suffering from some great deformity of the head or body, who had hidden herself from the gaze of men.

As soon as her rival's mother heard what Lalhiwe had done, she laughed heartily and said, "This is the best news I have heard for many a long day. What a fool that girl must be! Surely she must be mad!"

And with this opinion, all of the women in the kraal agreed. For they had never heard of hiding a pretty face before, and it was impossible for them to believe that Lalhiwe would do this in order to find peace. But in spite of all their attempts to convince Lalhiwe of her error, she remained faithful to her idea. She wore the ugly baboon skins every day, and not once did she show her face, even to her dearest friends. Happily, her sacrifice proved to be worthwhile; for after the first few days, peace reigned in the kraal. There were no more quarrels, everyone seemed happier, and Inkosesana became the undisputed beauty of the countryside.

Then one day, many months after Lalhiwe had started wearing the baboon skins, there was a great stir in the kraal. Two ambassadors had arrived from a very mighty Chief, seeking not one bride, but two for their master. Both girls must be beautiful, for the Chief was very rich and he was prepared to give a magnificent marriage gift for each of the maidens. The two ambassadors sat and conversed with the head of the kraal, while the women stood in small groups talking excitedly. Finally they were asked to come forward and the request of the great Chief was made known to them.

The mother of Inkosesana was the first to advance. She moved forward with an air of triumph. "Here," she proclaimed, "is the bride that you are searching for," and she brought forth Inkosesana, who did indeed look beautiful. She had thrown aside her cloak, and she stood there decked in all her prettiest beads, which set off her lovely black skin and graceful figure to full advantage. The ambassadors both agreed at once. "This is the most beautiful girl we have seen as yet. We accept her with pleasure, for we believe that our King could not wish for a more lovely maiden." Then turning to the Chief they asked, "Have you another pretty daughter, so that we may see her too?"

The Chief did not answer, but the mother of Inkosesana, made bold with pride and longing to triumph yet further above her rival, called out, "Yes, there is another daughter, but she is always wrapped in baboon skins and she is of no importance at all."

"Let us see her anyway," insisted the ambassadors, whose curiosity was aroused by this bit of information.

And so Lalhiwe was brought forth, holding her skins tightly around her body. But though she was covered with baboon skins, nothing could take away from the grace of her movements; and the King's messengers walked around her, longing to see her hidden face.

"Why are you hiding underneath those skins?" they asked her. "You have very pretty legs and you walk gracefully. What is wrong with you that you do not wish to show your face? We beg you to let us see your true appearance."

"No," replied Lalhiwe. "He who marries me must marry me for myself alone and not for my beauty."

"Are you deformed then? Or are you so very ugly?"

"I did not say that," answered Lalhiwe. "All I said was that he who marries me must marry me for myself alone."

"But why is it that you behave so strangely?"

"To please myself," retorted Lalhiwe.

"I cannot believe that you are not deformed," said one of the men, hoping to arouse her anger.

"You may believe what you wish, but I tell you the truth," repeated the girl; and although the ambassadors did all they could to provoke her into throwing off the skins, she did not get angry nor speak rudely to them.

Finally they realized that they could not make her reveal herself, and they held a conference with each other. Should they take Lalhiwe as well as the beautiful Inkosesana and risk the King's displeasure? True, they had both admired her wit and her good temper, but what was to be found underneath the skins? In a moment of weakness they decided to take a chance, and they asked for Lalhiwe also, praying that all would be well in the end.

Before returning to their King, the ambassadors went to the brothers of both maidens. The brother of Inkosesana they instructed to make a big kraal to receive the cattle in payment for his sister, as there was no doubt that their master would be delighted with her. To Lalhiwe's brother they said very little, aside from directing him to send his sister to their master. This brother, fearing that his sister would not be welcomed, did not bother to make a kraal at all for a marriage gift.

The messengers then returned to their King, who was delighted with the reports that they brought of Inkosesana. However, when he heard the tale of the second bride, the one who wore baboon skins, he became enraged. "No girl," he shouted, "who has a pretty face would ever hide it. I am certain that she must be absolutely hideous; and remember, if that is the case, you shall both pay the penalty of death. I cannot believe that I sent such fools on such an important mission!"

The ambassadors now regretted what they had done. They were terrified lest the second bride be hideous, for the King always kept his word. And while he awaited the arrival of the brides, the King sent twenty cattle for each one of them, less than was suitable; "We can easily send more if both are acceptable," said he; "and if they should not be, for I will not have an ugly bride, we shall not have to ask for a return of the marriage gift. The forty cattle will be proper payment for Inkosesana."

At the appointed time, the two brides said farewell to their kraal and set out on their journey together. They walked for many days, each attended by her own bridesmaids. Finally they reached their destination and were brought at once to the great Chief. With Inkosesana, he was pleased immediately; but at Lalhiwe, who still remained covered in her baboon skins, he looked with puzzled eyes. Noticing her graceful bearing, he began to admire her, longing to know her secret.

"I beg of you, my maiden," said he, "please let me see your face."

"No, great King," answered Lalhiwe in her usual quiet voice; "I cannot show my face to anyone until the wedding morning." And that was her last word on the matter.

The two brides then retired with their maids, each to her own hut, until all preparations for the wedding feast were completed. Among the women in the King's kraal, there was great gossip. For Inkosesana there was nothing but admiration, while for Lalhiwe there was only scorn for one who could be nothing but hideous. "She is undoubtedly the most ugly of women," they decided, "or she would surely show her face."

When the day of the wedding arrived, each bride left her hut and went down to the river to bathe. Since they went to separate pools, neither one could see the other.

Lalhiwe and her maids descended to a deep pool underneath a great rock, where it was pleasantly warm from the morning sun. Tall white lilies grew on the banks and fresh green ferns peeped out of every nook and cranny. Slipping off her baboon skins, Lalhiwe rolled them into a tight bundle and buried them in an animal hole near the pool. Then she and her maidens laughed and chattered as they bathed in the clear pool, until the time came to array themselves for the wedding.

The bridesmaids decked themselves in their most beautiful beadwork; but Lalhiwe, as was the custom for a bride on her wedding morning, wore a skirt of deep black oxskins, the dress that was worn by married women. For an ornament, she wore just a girdle of bleached white beads encircling her waist, and in her hand she held an assegai. Though her dress was simple, when she stood there in the dazzling sun, her maidens cried out, "Lalhiwe! You are infinitely more beautiful than you ever were! Indeed, you are far more lovely than Inkosesana."

And they were telling her the truth. For all of the months that Lalhiwe had been hidden from the sun, her beauty had increased; her skin had become as smooth and soft as a lily petal, and her every movement was a joy to behold.

The bridesmaids gathered behind Lalhiwe, and together they started up the path toward the kraal. As they walked, they sang a song, a sad song of farewell for a friend that would be playing with them no longer in their old home.

As they approached the gate of the kraal, they met Inkosesana and her maidens, who proudly stepped in front so that they could meet the first glances of the wedding guests. All greeted Inkosesana with great approval, but in truth, their eyes looked beyond her, waiting anxiously to catch the first glimpse of her mysterious sister. When Lalhiwe finally appeared, perfect in every sense, loud shouts of surprise and joy came from all sides.

"She is so lovely!" cried all the guests. "There has never been one so beautiful in our land!"

At last the two brides appeared before the King and danced for him in the great cattle kraal, as was the custom. The King, dumbstruck with amazement, never once took his eyes from Lalhiwe. As soon as the wedding was over, he called his two ambassadors to him and gave each of them twenty beautiful oxen as a gift of appreciation. "You have shown yourselves to be wise and trustworthy men," he said, "for Lalhiwe is beautiful beyond belief. Choose all of my finest young cattle and send them as a marriage gift to her father. Let the first herd that I send be the marriage gift for Inkosesana, but make sure that Lalhiwe has a marriage settlement such as has never before been given."

The King's commands were carried out at once by his relieved ambassadors. Lalhiwe's mother, surprised and grateful, rejoiced for many days after the arrival of the marvelous herd of cattle. She, in truth, had never expected that such honor would come upon her child. Her rival, however, the mother of Inkosesana, hid herself in her hut, filled with bitter disappointment that she had not triumphed in the end. She sulked for many months and never again regained her old position in the tribe.

BATTLE BETWEEN THE BIRDS AND THE BEASTS

Frances Carpenter

In this story, being big and strong is not as important as being clever and brave.

 Birds and beasts were on this earth long before there were men and women. At least that is how one old African tale is told.

Sometimes the two, the birds and the beasts, were at peace. They lived together as brothers.

Sometimes, however, they quarreled. Then there was war between them.

It was a quarrel between an ostrich and an elephant that started the trouble this time. Oh, it was a famous battle. Many stories were told about it by the African grandmothers.

What was the quarrel about? No one knows surely. Some say the ostrich was annoyed with the elephant because that great beast did not look where he stepped as he ambled over the plain. Again and again his clumsy feet would spoil the round nest which the ostrich had dug in the earth for her eggs. It was because this happened so often that the ostrich went to the other birds. It was because she complained so bitterly that they agreed to make war on the elephant.

It was the chief of the ostrich tribe who delivered the declaration of war. With his head so high in the air, the ostrich could see far, far across the flat plain. He knew just where to go. And with his long, strong legs, he ran quickly to face his enemy.

"You have destroyed one too many of our nests, O Elephant," he shouted. "We declare war upon you. All the birds will fight with me. You, yourself, had better ask for help from the other beasts."

So the elephant called all the four-footed creatures about him. "Get ready, Friends!" he shouted. "The birds have declared war upon us."

How those animals laughed! Imagine birds, puny birds, trying to do battle with elephants! It sounded silly, indeed. But the birds did not laugh. "Wait and see who wins the battle!" they said.

It must have been a strange sight. On one side of the plain the four-footed creatures formed a long line. The monkeys were there, the leopards and lions, and of course the elephants. Great beasts and small beasts, they stood shoulder to shoulder.

On the other side of the plain were the creatures with wings. One would think that the birds would have been afraid. They were so much smaller. But size does not always mean courage, as you shall see.

"The lion and the leopard shall be my chief helpers," the elephant said. "They shall be my two generals. We three will lead the beast army in the battle."

So those three big animals took their place in the very front line.

"I choose the eagle, the falcon, and the stork to fight with me," the ostrich cried when the line of birds was drawn up.

"I myself cannot fly, for all I am a bird," the ostrich reminded his friends.

"But I have made a plan of battle that will win the victory for us."

"For our weapons we shall use these eggs which my hen has laid." He pointed to three giant cream-colored balls in a round nest in the ground. With its shell, each ostrich egg would weigh several pounds.

"First the eagle shall take one egg up in his claws. He shall fly toward the animal army. For a quick moment he shall light on the elephant's head. He shall break the egg there. Then he shall fly back again."

The birds looked at each other. They did not understand how ostrich eggs could win the battle. But they did not object, and the ostrich went on telling them of his plan.

"The falcon shall follow the eagle's example. Only, he shall break the second egg on the head of the lion. The stork will deal with the leopard."

The birds were still puzzled. But, after all, this was the ostrich's war. They would fight as he commanded.

"The eagle is coming!" The hyena, standing upon a high rock gave the warning to the beast army. But the animals were not worried. What harm could a bird do, flying up in the sky?

But before they could gather their wits together, the eagle had swooped down on the elephant. He lit on the head of the surprised beast.

Crack! Splash! The ostrich egg was broken upon the skull of the great beast. Its thick yolk was running down into the elephant's small eyes.

All the animals heard the elephant cry out.

"Oh! Oh! My head is broken open. It is bleeding and I am going to die." He had flung up his trunk to feel his head with its tip. And it had found the broken egg. The elephant, who could not see for the yolk in his eyes, thought the bits of shell were his crushed bones. The thick yolk felt like blood. And besides, the blow from the big, heavy egg had made his head ache.

"Oh! Oh! The elephant's head is broken. Oh! Oh! Our general will die."

The hyena ran with this message from one end of their battle line to the other.

"And now the falcon is coming!" the hyena scout cried out a second time. "He flies toward General Lion." You remember, this was the next part of the ostrich's plan of battle.

The lion roared. But this did not stop the fierce falcon from lighting upon his head.

Crack! Splash! The falcon flung the second ostrich egg at the lion's nose.

"The lion's head is broken, too!" the hyena screamed. "Another one of our three generals will die."

The paw of the lion went round and round, trying to wipe the egg yolk out of his eyes. He, too, was blinded. He, too, was sure the wetness he felt was blood.

"Yes, my head is broken," the lion roared. "It hurts. I shall surely die." Before the beasts had time to think clearly, there came the stork, flying over the head of the leopard.

The third egg was dropped from high in the sky. It landed between the small ears of the leopard. And now all three of the generals of the animal army were in a sad state.

The beasts, without their leaders, did not know what to do. And their troubles were not over. For the ostrich had called for help from the bees. To be sure, bees are not birds. But they are creatures with wings. And they were glad to fight with their feathered friends.

By the thousands, the bees buzzed round the heads of the beasts. On their tender noses, the lion and the leopard felt their sharp stings. The bees even found tender spots in the elephant's open mouth in which they could thrust their sharp stingers. All in the army of animals felt their attack.

The generals—the elephant, the lion, and the leopard—ran away to escape the stings of the bees. Who can blame the other four-footed creatures for doing the same?

"The victory is ours!" The ostrich flapped his tiny, useless wings in joy. "The battle is over."

But there was still one beast left on the plain. This was the hyena, truly a silly creature. He had crept up behind the ostrich and he had seen the patches of pink meat that showed between the giant bird's long, thin tail feathers. How good it would be if he could have just one bite! He leaped up off the ground, but the ostrich whirled around in time.

Oh, it was terrible, the punishment which the hyena had then. The angry ostrich struck the beast with his mighty feet. And an ostrich's legs are strong enough to knock down a leopard or a lion. The poor hyena was kicked about over the plain like a leaf tossed by the wind.

All the time the furious ostrich was pecking at the hyena's head. It was just by luck that the giant bird did not find the animal's eyes.

Now the hyena is known to be a coward at heart. As soon as he could, this one ran away. He crept into a hole between some rocks where the ostrich could not get at him. He hoped that, in time, the angry bird would go away.

At last all was quiet outside the hyena's den. The animal crept to its opening, and he stuck his head out of the rocks. Quickly he drew it back again. For the ostrich was still there, walking up and down, up and down. He was still waiting for the hyena to show himself.

A little later, the hyena peeked out again. That time he only just escaped a fierce peck from the bird's beak. The same thing happened another time, and another.

The hyena would never have come out again, perhaps, if the ostrich had not grown tired of the game. Oh, that big bird was clever. Before he went off, he pulled several long feathers out of his tail. And he stuck them into the ground so that they waved across the mouth of the hole in the rock.

Two or three times the hyena peeked out. Twice he went back again, fooled by the feathers into thinking his enemy was still there. But the third time, he was so thirsty and hungry, that he took a chance and slipped out of his den. And he saw how he had been tricked.

Is this story true?

Who can know?

What is sure, however, is that the hyena today makes his home in a hole in the ground, or in a den in the rocks. And he does not come out to hunt for food and drink until it is dark.

WHO CAN BREAK A BAD HABIT?

Frances Carpenter

Scratching and twitching come naturally to monkeys and rabbits, and there's just nothing to be done about it.

One day, in a West African forest, a rabbit and a monkey were sitting under a tree by a river. Every few minutes the monkey scratched himself with his long finger. First he scratched his neck. Then he scratched his ribs. Stretching his long arms around him, he even scratched his back. Scratching like this is a habit of monkeys.

The rabbit, close by, was no quieter. Every few minutes he sniffed the air. His nose wrinkled and twitched. His long ears flopped as he turned his head from one side to the other. This is the way of all rabbits. They seem always afraid that some danger is near.

Each animal noticed the movements of the other. And at last the rabbit could stand the monkey's scratching no longer.

"Why do you keep scratching yourself, Friend?" he said to the monkey who was then rubbing an ear. "You are not still a minute. Always, oh, all the time your nails are digging away at your hide. This is a most annoying habit you have."

Now nobody really enjoys being scolded. And so the monkey replied in the same tone of voice.

"My habit is no more annoying than yours, my good Rabbit. You do not keep still either. Your nose wrinkles and twitches. Your long ears keep flopping. Every few minutes you turn your silly head from one side to the other as if you were afraid."

"Well, perhaps I do twitch my nose and turn my head. But I can easily stop," the rabbit declared.

"I'll bet that you can't. Although I myself could easily keep from scratching, if I really wanted to." The monkey clasped both of his forepaws together.

They argued back and forth.

"I can stop my habit, but you cannot."

"If you can, I can." So it went until at last the monkey broke off.

"We'll make a test," he suggested. "We'll see which one of us is strong enough to break his bad habit. I'll bet you I can keep quite still for the whole afternoon. And I'll bet you cannot."

"Good!" There was nothing the rabbit could do but agree. "The one who moves first will lose the bet." He gave his head one last turn, and his nose one last twitch.

There they both sat, under the tree by the West African river. Not one move did either make. But each looked very unhappy.

Never in all his life did the skin of that monkey feel so dry and itchy. The rabbit's heart was cold with his fear of the unseen danger that might be behind him. But the monkey did not scratch. The rabbit did not turn his head.

It was not really very long. A beetle passing by had crawled only a few yards along the riverbank. But it seemed to the two animals that they had not moved for a whole day.

"What shall I do?" the poor rabbit was thinking hard. "I cannot keep still very much longer. If I could only sniff once! If I could but turn my head halfway round! Then it would not be so bad."

At the same time the monkey's hide was burning and itching.

"I cannot keep from scratching much longer," the beast said to himself. "If only I could rub myself without the rabbit seeing me."

It was the rabbit who spoke first.

"The time is long, Friend Monkey. Of course I am quite comfortable. I am entirely easy in my mind, Monkey. But the sun is still high in the sky. Why should we not tell each other a story to make the afternoon pass more quickly?"

"Well, why not?" The monkey suspected the rabbit was thinking of playing some trick. But he only added, "Yes, Rabbit, let us, each one, tell a story."

"I'll begin, Monkey. I will tell you of one day last month when I was far out of this forest. I was alone in a clearing, and there was not one bush to hide me."

Here the monkey broke in. He did not yet know what trick the rabbit had thought of, but he knew he should be prepared.

"Oh, Rabbit," he cried, "that very same thing once happened to me."

"Now don't interrupt." The rabbit was impatient to get on with his tale. "I heard a noise in the tall grass on this side of me." Like any storyteller he naturally turned his head to show how it was. "I saw some hyenas running toward me. One came from this side. One came from the other side." Again and again the rabbit's head was turned to illustrate his tale.

"Other hyenas came after them. From the right; from the left; from behind; and before me." Oh, now the rabbit was having a fine time, turning his head and twitching his nose. Anyone telling of so many dangers would have to do the same thing.

The monkey soon saw what his friend was up to. The moment the rabbit stopped to get breath, he began his own story.

"One day," he cried, "I went to the village on the other side of the forest. Some boys saw me there. And they began to throw stones at me.

"One stone hit me here." The monkey reached up and rubbed his neck to show where the stone hit. Oh, it did feel good to get in just that one little scratch.

"Another stone hit me here." The monkey rubbed his shoulder. "Another! Another! And another stone came." Now the creature's paw was flying from one itching place to another.

The rabbit burst out into a laugh. He laughed and he laughed. The monkey laughed too. Each guessed the other's reason for telling his story that way.

The two animals laughed so hard that they had to hold onto each other to keep from rolling into the river.

"Well! Well!" the monkey cried. "I have not yet lost the bet."

"No more have I," said the rabbit. "We were each of us only telling a tale as it should be told."

"But we must agree, Friend," he continued, "it's very hard indeed to break a bad habit. No one ever easily changes his ways. Let us worry no more."

So the rabbit's nose wrinkled and twitched again as often as he wished. His long ears flopped as his round head turned every few minutes from one side to the other.

The monkey's paws scratched his hide wherever it itched. And from that day to this no member of either of these animal families has kept still very long unless he was asleep.

Two Ways to Count to Ten

Frances Carpenter

Even King Leopard is surprised at the outcome of the contest he arranges.

"Old Tanko has come! The Teller of Good Tales is here!"

The news spread quickly through the Liberian village in the faraway back country. Men, women, and children came running to the Palaver House, the big "talky-talk" hut which had room for them all.

Everyone in that village knew Old Tanko, the Teller of Good Tales. Everyone there enjoyed his exciting stories. Whenever he wandered into their cluster of grass-roofed huts, they made him welcome.

"Ai, I'll sing you a story," Tanko said that day when he had finished the bowl of soup they set before him. "It will be a strange tale from the long ago." He arranged his white robe, and settled himself cross-legged on the earth floor.

The old man placed a very small gourd drum in his lap. And with his bony brown fingers, he began to tap lightly, lightly upon it.

"I had this tale from my grandfather," he began. "He, too, was a great Teller of Tales."

"What will the tale say to us, Tanko?" the headman of the village was speaking. He had squatted down on the ground, close to the old man.

"It will say there is more than one way to count to ten. It will also tell how, if you can guess the right way, you can get yourself a king's daughter for your wife."

The people in the talky-talk house nodded to one another. They smiled. It was as if they were thinking, "This will be another good tale." But no one spoke. In silence, they waited for Old Tanko to tell his story.

The little drum on the old man's knees soon began to whisper. "Tap! Tap! Tap-tap-tap!" And Tanko, in his soft singing voice told this strange tale.

In the long, long ago, animals were not so different, one from the other. Oh, they had different shapes, just as they do today. But they lived together in friendship and peace. Like people, those of one animal tribe sometimes took their wives from those of a different tribe. Like you and me, in those times the beasts could talk. And like people they had a king to rule over them.

In the place of this story, the leopard was King. Rich he was, beyond telling. Mighty was he in his power over the other beasts. All the animal obeyed him.

"Who shall I name to rule after me when I shall die?" King Leopard said one day to his pretty daughter. "I must find one who is wise enough so that he can rule well. Yes, my dear daughter, I must seek out the cleverest beast in our jungle land. I shall make him a prince. He shall have you for his bride. And to me he shall be a son."

King Leopard was pleased with his idea, and he planned a great feast. His royal drums carried word of it far and wide through the jungle. And all the animals came.

There were good things to eat. There was plenty to drink. The drums beat. And the guests at King Leopard's feast danced for three days.

At last the King called them to make a huge circle. Stepping into its center, he called his pretty daughter to come to his side. Then he spoke in a loud voice.

"Listen to my words, Friends!" he cried. "Someday I must die. Someday another king must rule in my place. I will choose him now from among you, so that he will be ready."

There was a murmur of wonder all through the crowd. The King had to order them to be quiet.

"I shall seek the cleverest among you, for your King must be wise. I shall name him Prince. He shall be to me a son, and to my dear daughter a husband. He shall share all my riches. And when I die he shall be your King."

Shouts came from the eager guests at the King's feast. No doubt each animal hoped that the good fortune would be his.

The King Leopard held up his hunting spear.

"Look at this; my people! Watch!" And he flung the spear far up into the air.

"With this spear I will test you," he went on. "He who would be our Prince must throw the spear toward the sky. He must send it so high that he can count to ten before it drops down to earth again."

There was a buzz of talk among all the animals then. This would not be so hard to do, they thought.

One after another, they came forward to try their skill. Each jungle beast danced before King Leopard and his pretty daughter. Each one sang a song that told how well he would rule, if he were chosen.

First to try his luck was the elephant. He was so big that he could push all the other beasts out of his way.

"I must be first," he said to himself. "This task is too easy. Almost any one of us can do it."

The elephant danced clumsily. He was very big and his body was heavy. Then, with his trunk in the air, he trumpeted all the fine deeds he would perform if he were Prince.

The great beast threw King Leopard's spear up into the air.

"One! Two! Three!" he began counting. But he spoke slowly, as he did everything else. An elephant cannot easily hurry, you know.

Before the elephant had said, "Four!" the King's spear had dropped to earth. The proud beast hung his head so low that the tip of his trunk dragged on the ground. He knew he had failed.

Next came the bush ox. His wide gray horns swept the other beasts to the side.

"I'll throw the spear up to the sun," the huge animal sang while he danced. "I'll be a strong husband for King Leopard's daughter."

The bush ox picked the spear up in his mouth. With a mighty toss of his great head, he flung it far, far above his spreading horns.

"One! Two! Three! Four!" the bush ox counted more quickly than the elephant. But he, too, was slow. Before he could say. "Five," the spear was down on the ground. And he went off, ashamed, into the deep jungle.

The chimpanzee was third. He jumped up and down in a merry dance, and King Leopard's daughter laughed at his antics. He beat his hairy chest with his two fists, and he sang of how much he would like to be King in the leopard's place.

The young ape rose up straight on his hind legs. He held the spear in one hand, just like a man. With a twist of his long arm, he threw it up toward the sky.

"One-two-three-four-five-six-seven!" He chattered as fast as he could. The watching animals held their breaths. Surely, with such a quick tongue, the chimpanzee would make the count.

But he did not! He had not even said "Eight!" before he had caught the spear once more in his hand.

One by one, other animals tried to count to ten while the spear was still up in the air. One by one, they all failed.

"It seems I must look somewhere else for a prince to rule when I am gone," King Leopard said sadly.

Then out from the crowd stepped an antelope.

Beside the elephant, the bush ox, and even the chimpanzee, the young deerlike antelope seemed puny and weak. His legs were long, yet so slender that it was almost a wonder that they would hold up his body. But the antelope spoke bravely.

"Let me try to throw your spear, O King," he cried. "I would like well to marry your pretty daughter."

Ho! Ho! The other animals burst into laughter. How could such a weak creature fling the King's spear high enough to say more than two or three words? However could he hope to count up to ten?

But the antelope would not be turned aside.

"I wish to try," he insisted. And King Leopard nodded his head. He had promised a fair trial for all who wished to take part in this contest.

"Who can say what any creature can do until he has tried?" The King spoke to the crowd. "The antelope may throw the spear." So the other beasts were moved back to give him room.

When the antelope, on his slender legs, danced before the King, the leopard's daughter cried out with pleasure. No one could deny that his steps were more graceful than those of the elephant, or of the bush ox, or the chimpanzee.

Then the antelope threw the spear. With a toss of his head, he flung it far up into the air. Before it could fall to earth, the clever beast called out two words. "Five! Ten!" he cried. "I have counted to ten. King Leopard did not say how the count should be made."

The leopard laughed then. He nodded his royal head.

"No, I did not say how the count was to be made," he agreed. "And as everyone knows, one can count by fives as well as by ones. The antelope has won the contest. He has proved he is the cleverest of you all. He shall wed my dear daughter. He shall be King when I am gone."

The other animals stared stupidly at the winner. They did not understand yet what had happened. But they could see that the antelope had outwitted the King.

At the wedding feast which King Leopard gave for his daughter, they all cheered for the antelope, their new Prince.

Old Tanko put his drum down in his lap.

"Remember this tale, Friends," he said to the crowd in the talky-talk hut. "Do not forget that it is not always the biggest nor the strongest, but sometimes the cleverest who wins the prize."

THE FAIRY FROG

A SWAZI TALE
Terry Berger

*Tombi-Ende's beauty makes her sisters so jealous that they
try to get rid of her.*

Tombi-Ende was the most beautiful of all the maidens in her father's kingdom. Her eyes were as brown as the eyes of the doe, and when she led the dance her feet were as quick as the feet of the gazelle. Her name, Tombi-Ende, meant "Tall Maiden," and she was indeed taller than any of her sisters. She carried her head high, like a true Princess, and her parents looked upon her with joy and pride. They expected that one day she would be a mighty Queen.

But no one has an altogether happy lot. It was true that Tombi-Ende was tall and beautiful, and that she had the gayest and most wonderful handkerchiefs with which to deck herself, and more beads and bracelets than any other girl in the countryside. But she also had sisters who were not so tall or beautiful or so greatly admired, and who grew more jealous of her daily. At last, this jealousy grew so intense that it made them quite forget their love for her, and they decided that Tombi-Ende must disappear or no one would ever notice them at all.

And so the jealous sisters worked out a plan to rid themselves of Tombi-Ende. One day they went to her and said, "Come with us. Let us go to the great pit to dig up red ochre, for there is none to be had in the kraal." So every maiden shouldered her pick, and they all walked together, singing and laughing, for many miles. At last they reached a great red pit, many feet deep, surrounded by tall grass on every side. There they stopped; and each girl leaped down in turn to dig out a lump of the precious red earth, and then jumped up again. But when it came time for Tombi-Ende to jump down, the others did not let her jump up again. Instead, each of the jealous sisters threw picks full of earth upon her, until the poor maiden was buried alive. This done, they ran back to their village leaving their sister behind.

When they arrived home, they told their father that Tombi-Ende had accidentally fallen into the pit and before they could help her to escape, she had suffocated before their eyes. But unfortunately for the girls, each sister told the story in a different way, and the King doubted their innocence in the matter. Ordering his servants to lock all of them into a hut, the King began to mourn for his favorite daughter, for Tombi-Ende the Tall Maiden.

Surprisingly enough, Tombi-Ende was not dead. Although the red earth was very heavy, she was able to breathe through the breaks in the great mound of red ochre that lay above her. And she began to cry out:

> I am Tombi-Ende,
> I am not dead,
> I am alive like one of you.

For many hours she lay in the red ochre pit, chanting the same call, though fearing more and more that she would never be rescued. When evening came, however, she thought she heard a croaking sound. And indeed she did for at the edge of the pit stood an enormous frog.

"Beautiful Princess," he croaked, "what has befallen you?"

Hearing this question, the lovely maiden cried out in reply, "Alas! My sisters are jealous of me and hate me, and they have thrown earth upon me and left me here, hoping that I would never get out."

"Do not grieve," said the frog, "I will help you." And with that, he jumped into the pit, tunneled through the earth to the Princess, opened his big mouth, and swallowed the Princess in one gulp. Then he jumped up out of the pit, landing directly on the path above, with the Princess safely inside of him.

From there the frog set out upon a long journey. He hopped all night, taking care to avoid any kraals along the way, for the people believed frogs to be an omen of bad luck and he would not have been welcomed. Whenever he passed a bird he sang out:

> Do not swallow me,
> I carry the Princess Tombi-Ende.

And no creature touched him. Though the next morning they very narrowly escaped a great danger, for they came upon a horrible ogress. This Imbula had heard that Tombi-Ende was still alive and had gone in search of her, but when she arrived at the red ocher pit, she had found it empty. Now she was looking for the Princess everywhere, dashing about in a frenzied state, but luckily she paid no attention to the big frog.

At midday the frog stopped hopping. He opened his large mouth, allowing the Princess to step out.

"Wait here and rest," said the frog, "and then we will go on." He croaked three times, and delicious porridge appeared in a little brown pot, all ready for the Princess to eat.

Tombi-Ende ate and soon fell asleep under the bushes, for she was very
tired. When evening came, the frog swallowed her once more and they continued on their journey. They had decided not to go to her father's kraal, for
fear of her jealous sisters, but rather to go to the home of her grandmother,
where Tombi-Ende was sure of every welcome. The frog hopped all through
the night, and when morning came he arrived at the grandmother's kraal.
Hopping up to the chief hut, the frog sang out loudly:

> I am carrying Tombi-Ende,
> The beautiful Princess
> Whom they buried in the red pit.

Out came the old grandmother, crying out, "Who is speaking? Who
knows what has become of my darling Tombi-Ende?"

"It is I that knows all about her," replied the frog. "Bring clean mats to
spread before me, and you will see." All the women hurried to get fine new
mats, and these they placed before the frog. When this was done, the frog
croaked loudly; and opening his mouth as large as before, he allowed the
Princess to come out. The women almost fainted as they saw Tombi-Ende
standing before them, as tall and beautiful as ever. But their surprise soon
turned to joy and there was not one among them who could hear the
Princess tell her tale often enough, or sing often enough the praises of the
wonderful frog.

"What can we do to reward your kindness?" the grandmother asked of
the frog. "There must be something that we can give you."

The frog thought for a moment. "I will only ask you to kill two oxen and
two bulls," he said, "and to lay a feast before me."

So a great feast was held, and the frog sat by the Princess's side and was
given great honor. He seemed very pleased by the many preparations that
had been made in his behalf. The next morning, however, the frog had dis-

appeared, and although the Princess searched for him throughout the kraal, he could not be found.

In the meantime, the grandmother had sent a messenger to the King, telling him of his daughter's safety. Upon hearing that all was well, the King was beside himself with joy. First, he released the jealous sisters from their prison, instructing them to prepare robes of state for Tombi-Ende. Then he dispatched his favorite son to bring the Princess home.

The boy arrived, rested a few days at the grandmother's kraal, and then the two set out for home. Great heat and dry earth were their companions on the journey, for the rains had been meager that year and the streams had dried up. The sun was very hot and after hours of walking, the Princess and her brother became very thirsty. Even the underground springs could not be found, for the earth was harder than brick that is dried in an oven, and the water courses were dry. After a time they began to feel faint from the intense heat.

Suddenly, as if in a dream, they saw a strange man standing right across their path. Except for his large size, he appeared to be like other men, and they greeted him with thanksgiving.

"What do you want?" he asked them in a voice that surprised them, for it was of the deepest bass and it rumbled like thunder.

"We are looking for water," said the Prince. "We find that all of the springs are dried up, and we are still many days from home."

"If I should give you water," bargained the giant, "what will you give me in return?"

"You may ask for anything in my father's kingdom," the Prince answered without thinking.

"I will take this beautiful Princess," said the giant, with a wicked smile playing on his lips. "If you do not give me what I ask for, you will die of thirst. All of the springs are dry within the next three day's journey."

The trials of the past were nothing to the grief and unhappiness that

Tombi-Ende and her brother now suffered. What were they to do? To grant the stranger's request might prove fatal for the Princess, but a further lack of water would leave them both helpless. The only solution was to accept the giant's offer and to pray that he would treat them with mercy.

When they agreed to the giant's terms, he chuckled for a few minutes and then led the way to a great fig tree by the side of a dry water course. As he struck his stick upon the ground, a fountain sprang from the very roots of the tree, and its water was as clear as the moon and as cool as the depths of the forest. The brother and sister plunged themselves into the water, allowing it to bathe their faces while they drank of it eagerly and long.

After some time, Tombi-Ende lifted her head, and as her eyes met with the giant, she let out a shriek, for the giant had turned into a most horrible Inzimu. He was monstrous and misshapen, covered with red hair. Behind him on the grass, lay his long tail, and his white pointed teeth forced his thick lips to remain open.

Frightened by his sister's screams, the Prince looked up. Seeing the monstrous Inzimu, he realized at once just how dangerous their situation was. The ogre was very powerful, and no fighting could possibly save them. He just kept glaring at them, through tiny eyes that radiated evil pleasure.

For Tombi-Ende and her brother, the end seemed to have come; but suddenly there was a loud croak, and out of the fountain sprang the giant frog.

"Save me!" cried Tombi-Ende. "Oh help us, frog! No one is as clever and as wise as you!"

The large frog hopped right up to the ogre. The ogre looked down at the frog with disdain and laughed at him with disbelief. The frog allowed the ogre to laugh in this way for a few minutes and then, opening his mouth as large as he could, he swallowed the ogre up, tail and all. At once the frog jumped back into the fountain, and there he remained until the ogre was drowned. Then he returned to Tombi-Ende.

"Ah, my frog, how can I thank you enough?" asked the Princess. "This time you must not disappear. You must come home with us, to be honored as is your due."

And so in three days, Tombi-Ende, her brother, and the frog reached the kraal of the King. As they arrived, they were greeted by the King's guard; beautifully arrayed in otter skins and holding shields and assegais. At their head stood the King, who hailed his two children with joy and affection.

"But why," he inquired, "is that horrible frog at your side? I cannot bear to look at him; let us have him killed."

"Oh, no, father," gasped Tombi-Ende, "do not kill him, for he is the best of creatures; twice he saved my life. If it were not for this frog, you would see your Tombi-Ende no more."

As she spoke these words, the frog suddenly turned into the handsomest of men, taller even than Tombi-Ende herself. He was dressed in a splendid array of skins and white ostrich plumes, and everyone could see that he was a Prince. Loud, happy shouts greeted him; but the Princess, herself, did not seem too surprised to see what had happened.

"I am no frog," said the Prince. "My father is a great Chief. The ogre, from whom I rescued the Princess, bewitched me in days gone by. But now that I have won the heart of a maiden, I am free once more. Please, sir, give me the hand of your beloved daughter in marriage, and one hundred cattle shall be yours."

And so a few days later, Tombi-Ende married the fairy frog, an end to the story that brought joy to them both. As for the wicked sisters, the King forgave them, and Tombi-Ende soon forgot all they had done and thought only of her happiness in her new home.

Pemba and the Python and the Friendly Rat

Frances Carpenter

A kind-hearted man and a hungry rat are justly rewarded for their good deeds.

One good turn deserves another!

Everyone knows that this is true. No doubt it is the rule among animals as well as among men. The python in this story acted as if it is.

This giant snake lived in a faraway part of Central Africa. It was long, long ago, in the days when animals talked with one another and with men, as well. It was, of course, in fairy-tale times.

The young man in the story was Pemba, a member of the Yao tribe. And he had a kind heart.

The python was Sato, whose giant body was three times as long as Pemba was tall. Oh, yes, Sato was big, and Sato was strong. The coils of his brown body could squeeze a man until he could not breathe. When his huge mouth opened wide, he could swallow a deer.

One day Sato was napping out in the African bush. This is to say he was in the wildest part of the land. He had found a dark hiding place in a thicket. And he was fast asleep.

There had been no rain for a long time. The plants were brown. So when someone built a cooking fire, its flames quickly spread through the dry grass.

It was the smoke of the fire that waked Sato up. The python at once saw the flames coming toward him. And he knew he was trapped. He never could crawl fast enough to get out of their way in time. So he called out for help.

A herd of bush buck came bounding over the plain. They kept ahead of the fire by running fast, fast.

"Stop! Bush Buck, stop! Save me from the fire." The python thrust his head out of the thicket. "Let me wind myself round your neck. You run much faster than I can crawl."

The leader of the herd stopped only long enough to cry out, "You would choke me to death, Python. Or you would swallow my wife. Let the fire get you. It is only what you deserve." And he went away, running as fast as the wind.

Next there came a hyena. And the poor python called out again.

"Stop! Oh, stop, Hyena! Take me along with you. You run faster than I can crawl. And the fire is near."

"Why should I save you?" They hyena laughed scornfully. "Only a short time ago you squeezed my brother to death. Let the fire come. It is what you deserve." And he, too, ran on.

Then Sato, the python, saw a young man nearby. This was the Yao youth, Pemba, who had a kind heart. He carried a digging stick over his shoulder. He had been working in his garden when the fire came.

"Stop, Young Man! I beg you. Do something to save me. The fire is coming this way and I shall burn to death."

Pemba halted to see where the voice came from. At first he was afraid when he saw the head of the python raised high off the ground.

"Oh, no! I will not stop," he cried. "I know your ways. You will wrap yourself round me. You will squeeze me and squeeze me until I cannot breathe."

"I truly will not harm you, Young Man. Indeed, I give you my promise. Save me, and forever I will be your good friend."

A kind heart had Pemba, as you have heard. The smoke was thick. The fire was racing close. But he took time to dig a round hole in the ground. With his digging stick he pushed the earth up all about the hole. He made an earth wall high enough so that the flames could not get in. Coiled up in this hole, behind the earth wall, the giant snake would be safe.

"One good turn deserves another, Friend." The python thanked Pemba. "Come back after the fire is out. I will have a gift for you."

Well, at the end of four days there was no more fire. The ashes had cooled. It was safe for Pemba to return.

"I hardly believe the python will still be where I left him," the good youth said to himself. "But snakes are strange creatures. I will just go and see."

When Pemba came to the hole he had dug in the ground, no python was there. "I was right," he said aloud. "The snake has not kept his promise."

There was only a young lad standing beside the hole. Pemba was about to go back to his home when the boy called to him.

"Welcome, Good Friend," he heard the lad say. "Today I am not wearing my python's skin. My magic allows me to take on a human shape once in a while. And magic is in the gift I bring for your reward." The lad handed the young man a little bottle-shaped gourd. It had a wood stopper fitted into its neck.

"This gourd will protect you, Pemba," the snake-boy explained.

"Someday it will save your life, as you saved mine. But do not pull out its stopper unless you are in real trouble."

Pemba wondered. How could such a small gourd save a man's life?

He soon had a chance to try its magic power, however. For when he went back to his village, he found that it had been attacked by an unfriendly tribe. His own people had run away. The enemies were gathering all the village treasures together, so that they might carry them off.

"Here is trouble indeed." Pemba at once thought of the words of the snake-boy. He pulled out the stopper, and a cloud of white mist came out of the gourd's mouth.

The white cloud spread over the heads of that enemy army. When it melted away, the strong magic of the python's gourd had made the attackers disappear.

"Oh, indeed, the python has done us a good turn." Pemba told his joyful people when it was safe to come out of hiding. And he put his magic gourd safely away in a far corner of his own hut.

The peace of his village was not to last long, however. The very next day that enemy tribe was back again. There was a bigger group of attackers than there had been before. The village people once more had to run for their lives. They hid themselves even further away in the forest.

Pemba tried to reach his own hut to get his gourd to help him again. But the enemies caught him. They tied him up tight. However, since it was dark by then, they decided they would not kill him until morning came.

Lying on the ground outside his hut, Pemba could not sleep. "If only I had the python's magic gourd," he thought, "I could save the village again."

Just then he felt something nibbling away at his toes. He could see, even in the dimness, that it was a rat. It was the very same rat which so often ate the grain in his storehouse.

An idea came into his mind.

"Friend Rat," he whispered. "You have had many a good meal in my grain storehouse. Now you can pay me for them.

"Creep into my hut. In the farthest corner you will find a little gourd shaped like bottle. Bring it here to me. But be sure that its stopper does not fall out on the way."

What happened then is one more proof that animals, too, believe "One good turn deserves another." The grateful rat crept inside Pemba's hut. He went to its farthest corner.

Quietly and carefully, the rat dragged the gourd over the earth floor of the hut. He rolled it within reach of Pemba's tied hands. Somehow the young man was able to loosen the cord. Perhaps the rat helped him, but the story does not say so. Pemba hid the gourd safely inside his gown. Then he slipped the cord back on his wrists.

Pemba's enemies did not notice the lump, made by the gourd, inside his gown. It did not fall out when they carried him off to the open square in the center of the village the next morning.

All the strangers were there. They were just about to cut Pemba's throat, when he brought forth the gourd and pulled out its stopper.

Again, at once, the magic mist settled over their heads. Like leaves from a tree, those men fell to the ground. When the mist cleared away, they had all disappeared. And this time they were gone for good.

"Friend Rat," Pemba said. "You have paid well for your grain. One good turn deserves another, and from now on you are welcome to feed in my storehouse whenever you wish."

So because of this excellent rule, all three were happy—the python and Pemba and the friendly rat.

THE THREE LITTLE EGGS

A SWAZI TALE
Terry Berger

With the help of three magical eggs, a young mother and her children begin a new life.

By the side of a great fig tree there was a poor little hut surrounded by a woven fence. Nearby was a small patch of cultivated ground, where a few dried mealie stalks were still standing. The sun had barely touched the top of the tree, when a woman hurried from the hut and passed through the kraal gate. You could see that she was married, by her full skirt of oxskins and her peaked headdress. Besides, she carried on her back a dear little baby girl, wrapped in a goatskin and half asleep, and by her side ran a jolly little boy. The mother, herself, was still young and pretty, though her face was worn and thin and if you looked closely you could see that her arms were covered with scars and burns, as if she had been dealt with badly.

She stood for a few minutes and looked toward the wide plains. Then she turned to where the great hills rose up, ruddy and golden in the early sun. She seemed to hesitate, but only for a time; at last she faced the mountains and entered a tiny pathway that wound its way into a wooded gorge and eventually led hundreds of feet above the plains. She did not sing as she went, but rather cast many frightened glances behind her, as if fearing that she would be seen. No one followed her, however, and as the little hut disappeared from sight, she grew less anxious and walked with a lighter step.

She was running away from her husband. For four years she had been married, and each year he had been more unkind to her. Not only had he demanded a great deal of her, but he had often beat her and scarcely given her or the children enough food to sustain them. She, being good and obedient, had tried hard to please him, but he had only become more and more cruel to her and the children. Two days before, he had gone off to a big dance in a faraway kraal, and the poor woman had so dreaded his return that she had decided to run away and beg her living as best she could. On the other side of the mountain were many kraals, and she was sure that she could find enough work to provide food for the three of them.

As she walked and thought about this, the baby girl awoke and started playing and laughing. They were following the course of a stream, where only a trickle of water remained and the thick bushes stood dry and leafless. As the mother chanced to look up, she saw a fluffy white nest, hanging from a long bough, which was otherwise barren.

"How pretty!" she thought. "That will be the very thing to amuse the baby."

Reaching up to the bough, she lifted the soft nest down, while her young son looked on with great interest. How surprised she was to discover that the nest contained three little eggs, for it was still many months before the spring would appear.

"Hold it carefully," she cautioned her little one, "so that you do not smash the tiny eggs."

The day had passed quickly and now, noticing that the sun was sinking and the air was growing colder, she began to walk more quickly; for they were on the hilltops, where there is a sharp frost every evening. Finally, not seeing a hut in sight, and having no covering except for one poor goatskin, the mother became distressed. "Where shall we rest tonight?" she asked herself. "There is nothing here but open country."

In reply, a tiny voice at her ear said, "Take the road to the right; it will lead you to a safe place."

She turned this way and that, looking for the one that had spoken to her, and discovered to her amazement that the voice belonged to one of the little eggs in the fluffy nest. Heeding its advice, she looked to the right and saw a tiny pathway, which to tell the truth, she had not noticed before. And so she took it at once, just as the sun was disappearing and the white frost was beginning to show. In a matter of minutes she had reached a beautiful hut, under the side of a great rock.

The hut appeared to be abandoned, but it was warm and comfortable within. On the walls hung karosses of oxskin and goatskin, and on the floor there were calabashes overflowing with delicious thick milk. There was food already prepared in little red pots: crushed mealies and monkey nuts. The little boy and the baby girl cried with delight, and the poor mother was pleased beyond measure.

First the little nest was carefully laid aside, and then both mother and children partook of a sumptuous meal; for needless to say, they were quite hungry. The little boy fell asleep soon after, wrapped in the warm skins, but his sister cried and would not lie quietly. So the mother tied the child on her back once more, and sang the Kafir cradle song, which is as pretty a song as you will hear.

Soon the tiny black head nodded forward, the little round arms relaxed, and the baby girl was fast asleep. The tired mother put her down, and in a few minutes, she too was dreaming by her children's side.

Early the next morning they set forth again, this time feeling refreshed.

They continued on the same path, the baby girl carrying the little eggs as she had before. Toward midday, they came to a point where there was a fork in the road. Not knowing which path to take, the woman stood for some time, looking confused. Then another tiny voice, much the same as the first, spoke in her ear. It was the second little egg this time, and it said, "Take the road to the left."

So she started down the left-hand path until she came to an enormous hut, three times as big as any she had ever seen. Full of curiosity, she went right up to the door, and there she discovered an unforgettable scene. The calabashes and pots within were all blood-red in color, and so thin that the breezes swayed them as if they were large bubbles, for they were as light as the air. One of the big pots was blown right across the room, and as the poor mother's eyes followed its course, she almost screamed aloud; for on the side of the hut where the pot came to rest, a huge monster lay fast asleep. He was most immense, both tall and stout, and his body was covered with brick-red hair. Two horns grew out of his head, and his long tail lay curled across his knees. Without any doubt, he was an Inzimu, an ogre if you will. Fear raced through the mother's body, knowing that the ogre would kill them all, if he should awake and see them.

"What shall I do?" she cried to herself as she rushed away from the door. "I am afraid that we will all be killed!"

It was then that the third little egg spoke up saying,"Do you see that great stone? Lift it and carry it with you to the very top of the hut."

Looking around the woman tried to determine which stone the little egg wanted her to take, for there were many in sight. But her eyes soon focused on one round white stone, the perfect size to drop through the thatched roof. Surely this one would kill whoever it fell on. But how could she lift it up?

"Do as I bid you," repeated the egg.

So the woman stooped down and attempted to raise the stone. To her surprise, she found it light enough to take to the back of the hut with little difficulty. There she was afraid to leave her babies alone on the ground, so she lifted them onto the roof first. Then she climbed up herself, clutching the stone in her hand.

"Now," said the egg, "you are ready to let the stone drop down on top of the monster."

Before dropping the rock, the mother peeped through the thatched roof to determine the exact spot where the ogre lay. She feared that any mistake might be fatal for them all. It was just as she was about to drop the rock, that she realized the door of the hut was opening; and to her horror, a second ogre appeared, dragging several bodies after him.

"Now we shall certainly be found out," said the mother. "All is over." But she managed to keep the children quiet while the second Inzimu prepared his evening meal. He was so engrossed in what he was doing, that he stopped only once to sniff the air.

"There is something tasty hidden in this hut, but I don't know where it is," he muttered to himself.

After finishing his preparations, the Inzimu looked around the hut, but fortunately he never thought of going up on the roof. He ate his dinner with relish and soon fell asleep next to the first Inzimu, while the mother watched in terror from the roof.

"Now there are two Inzimus," she gasped. "I cannot kill both with this one stone. What am I to do now?"

"You had better come down as quietly as you can," whispered all the little eggs at once, "and with your babies run as fast as you possibly can."

They had hardly finished speaking before she began to slip down very quietly, the little boy helping her with his baby sister. Although they were trembling in every limb, they managed to be on their way in the next few minutes. Luckily, the Inzimus did not awaken, and it was not too long before the big hut was out of sight.

The poor mother felt that she could take a deep breath once again. She walked along wishing that she would find a kraal and people that she could talk to. She was thinking of this as she wound in and out of the bushes, which grew thicker and more thorny. Then great trees began to appear and as the path gave a sudden turn, she almost collided with a huge evergreen tree, which seemed to spring up before them. To add to her astonishment, a horrible ogress lay sleeping under the tree. Hard to believe as it was, she was even uglier than the Inzimus, for she had a hideous snout, just like a wolf's, and between her eyes was one little horn. Her snoring was so violent that the very branches of the tree shook unceasingly.

Now the mother was sure that her last hour had truly come, for there seemed to be no means of escape. It was impossible to return to the hut of the Inzimus and she could not go forward, for the bushes were too thick to pass through. But the little eggs brought comfort to her once again.

"Look on your right; a big ax lies there."

She looked and just as the voices said, there lay a great ax, gleaming in the sunlight. It was so large that it must have belonged to the Ogress, but somehow the woman managed to lift it.

"That was good," the little eggs encouraged her. "Now put your little ones into the lower branches of the tree; and then when they are safe, climb up yourself. Creep along the great arm of the tree over the monster's head, and make sure that you hold on to the ax tightly."

Once again the mother did as she was told. She lifted her little son up into the branches and found that he was able to hold his baby sister among the leaves. Then mounting the tree herself, the woman crept forward with the ax in her hand As she reached the spot directly above the monster's head, she became so frightened that she almost toppled from the tree. Again the little eggs spoke:

"Aim the ax at the monster's head and drop it!"

She did as she was told, and the ax hit the Ogress just above the horn, but to her dismay, the blow did not kill the beast; it merely stunned her.

"Slide down the tree!" urged the third little egg, "and kill the monster before she revives."

In a moment the mother had slid from the tree and was running forward with desperate courage to kill the beast before she herself was the victim.

Finally she met with success; she finished the beast with one mighty blow. As soon as it was over, she stepped back to give thanks for her victory and to rest up from her ordeal. When she was standing several feet away, she glanced back toward the monster that she had slain. And she could hardly believe what she saw with her eyes, for out of the Ogress came an endless procession of men, women and children, as well as cattle and goats. One after another they filed out, spilling onto the already crowded path. There were actually hundreds of creatures, for the Ogress had eaten every form of animal life and whole families of men in her wicked lifetime. When all had been released, there were enough people and animals to start a great kraal. Each one of them approached the young mother to thank her for making their freedom possible. And when all were assembled, their leaders came forward, asking her to honor them by consenting to be their Queen.

"Thank you," she said, "but I must be truthful with you and tell you that I should not have been able to do it without these three little eggs." As she told them this, she turned to show them the little white nest. She had barely touched it with her fingers, when all saw it disappear. And in the place where it had rested, the earth began to tremble. The strange quakes kept up until three handsome princes rose up where the nest had been. The eldest of the three knelt before the woman, and taking her hand said,

"You, dear woman have freed us from the spell of a wicked enchantress by being so full of courage. I beg of you to agree to become my wife, in order to complete my happiness. There is nothing to stop you, for I have heard that your cruel husband is dead. Please do as I ask you, and we will rule together over this great kraal."

The young mother was delighted to accept the offer of so great and noble a Prince, and she did so happily. Now, both she and her children could have a happiness that they had never known before. And of course, all of the people rejoiced, too, for they were to have both a King and a Queen.

THE MAGIC BONES

Two brothers could have lived happily-ever-after if they had
not been so jealous and greedy.

There once were three brothers who were left orphans during a great famine. When the youngest of them became ill, the two elder brothers did not know what to do. Then one proposed, "Let us take him into the veld and nurse him. Maybe he will recover there." So they carried him far into the bush.

After some time the two elders again wondered what to do with their youngest brother as he was not getting better. "It is a time of famine," said one to the other. "We have no food. Let us leave him here and return home."

When the sick one heard this he pleaded, "Please do not leave me here alone." But they left him, and went on their way.

Eventually, the youngest brother recovered, and began to set snares to catch game. One day he set his snares on the site of an old village. The next morning, when he went to check them, he found an old man caught in one of them. He stood some distance away, afraid to go nearer, but the old man called out, "Come nearer, boy, come here to me!"

When the boy approached, the old man asked, "Who told you to set snares here?"

"No one," said the boy, "but I was hungry. How was I to eat?"

"Put your hand into my bag," said the old man, "and draw out my magic bones."

The boy did as he was bid.

"Do you want some porridge?" asked the old man.

"Yes," the boy quickly answered, "for I am very hungry."

"Throw the bones and say, "Let porridge come forth at once."

The boy did so, and behold, porridge came forth.

As the boy ate, the old man said, "I shall soon die. My name is Jirimpimbira (which means "jumping shin-bone"). Don't forget that name when I am dead, for I am leaving it to you. When you wander about you will reach a wide plain. Throw the bones and you will get a dwelling and all you desire." With that the old man died.

The boy wandered about and at last came to a wide plain. He threw the bones, saying, "Let there be a large village and lots of food." Instantly, a large village, full of people, appeared. Many came out shouting "Jirimpimbira!" begging for food for there was another great famine.

Now the two brothers who had left their brother in the bush heard from others that there was a chief named Jirimpimbira who had plenty of food, so they decided to go to him in the hopes of obtaining something to eat.

The chief saw them coming, clapping their hands in salutation, and shouting "Jirimpimbira!" He gave each a bowl of milk and asked them to drink, then said, "Have you forgotten me? I am your youngest brother, the one you left in the bush."

When they heard this they wept. "We left our brother in the veld when hunger overcame us. Please forgive us!" Then the chief gave wives to each and said, "My brothers, stay here and live with me. Look upon this place as yours."

At first the brothers were very happy, but after several months, they became envious, and said to each other, "Why should our younger brother be chief. We are the elders." They went to their brother's wife to find out the secret of how he had obtained so large a village. They flattered her until she told them the secret. While Jirimpimbira was away cultivating his fields, the brothers begged her to show them the bones.

"If I let you see them, what will you give me?" she asked.

"Whatever you desire," they said.

"If you bring me the flesh of a hare, I will show you the bones," she replied.

They readily agreed and immediately went away to hunt. Soon they returned with two fat hares for the woman.

She gave them the bones, telling them that when they reached a place they liked, they were to throw the bones and a village would appear.

The brothers ran away with the bones. When they came to a suitable spot, they threw the bones on the ground and asked for a large village with much food. Instantly, it appeared. Then they threw the bones a second time, saying, "Let Jirimpimbira's village disappear." Immediately it vanished, and Jirimpimbira found himself all alone.

Jirimpimbira lamented, "My brothers have got hold of my magic bones! Again they have left me all alone!" Just then, Gonzo, the rat, appeared. "Why do you cry, Jirimpimbira?" he asked.

"I cry for the loss of my bones which I know my brothers have stolen."

Then Ngabi, the hawk, who happened to float over him, asked, "Why do you cry, Jirimpimbira?"

"I cry for the loss of my bones which I know my brothers have stolen."

Then Gonzo and Ngabi said, "Do not cry. We will get the bones and bring them back to you."

Jirimpimbira rejoiced at this, and told them he would be most grateful for their help.

"What will you give us if we return the bones to you?" they asked.

"Anything you desire," he replied.

"I want chickens," Ngabi answered. "And I want nuts," said Gonzo.

The rat ran along while the hawk flew high in the air. When Ngabi reached the village of the two brothers he hovered in the air, waiting for Gonzo to arrive.

Gonzo was sure the bones were being kept in the largest house. He crept in and scurried up the wall. He nibbled through the string by which the bones were tied, and then carried them outside. Once outside, people began to shout, "The Chief's magic bones are being carried away by a rat!" But just then Ngabi swooped down, picked up Gonzo with the magic bones, and flew away. When the people saw this, they cried out, "Toko! (Well done!) The rat is being carried off by the hawk." Of course, they thought the hawk would eat the rat.

The hawk carried Gonzo and the magic bones to Jirimpimbira who thanked them for what they had done. He then threw the bones and said, "Let there be nuts and chickens for Gonzo and Ngabi."

Then he threw the bones again, saying, "I want my village and all I had returned to me." His village and its people appeared. He threw the bones again, saying, "May the village of my brothers be scattered and no trace of it remain." And no one ever heard of or saw the two brothers ever again.

TIMBA, THE DISSATISFIED BIRD

Timba gets everything he asks for, but it still isn't enough.

Strangely enough, two very different creatures of the wilds—Ngango, the mighty lion, and Timba, the little brown robin—had formed a friendship.

It began when Timba noticed that from time to time, the lion made kills that were too large for him to finish at one meal. This meant that part of the carcass was left to rot—and rotting meat meant big, juicy white maggots, which were Timba's favorite food.

It was, therefore, easy to understand why Timba took to following Ngango from one hunting ground to another, listening for his roar of victory each time he made a kill. *"This is my hunting-ground; this is my hunting-ground!"* the lord of the forest would roar, as he stood majestically on the top of the highest ant-heap to let all the creatures know that they were to bow down to him. Of course, no one dreamed of opposing him—especially the little brown robin.

The lion had no objection to Timba benefiting from his leavings. Day after day the big cat would chat amiably with the little bird who sat twittering in excited anticipation in the tree above him, waiting for the maggots to ripen.

"*Tii-tii-tii-tii-tii!*" trilled the robin, his song making the countryside glad with music. "Great is the strength of Ngango. Wise is the rule of his law!" Then one day he added, "But oh, *why* am I so small and insignificant?"

Ngango always enjoyed listening to Timba's flattering song, and he was in a particularly good mood that morning. "Yes, my friend," Ngango said, "all you sing of me is true, and it is indeed unfortunate that you are of so little account. If you were of greater importance, your song would carry more weight among my subjects. But why do you shame yourself by eating my rotten leavings, instead of hunting good, red meat of your own?"

"Indeed, wise Ngango, I agree with all that you say," answered the little bird sadly, "but I am too small to catch anything else. Oh, that I were bigger and stronger and fiercer!"

"I can help you to become so, should you wish," said the lion pleasantly.

"Oh, Lord of the Forest, Mighty One, please do so!" trilled the little robin.

"Then we must visit Fisi, the witch-doctor," said the lion. "Come, I will take you to him."

They found Fisi the hyena lying asleep at the entrance to his bone-littered cave. The lion's loud greeting sent the ugly creature scuttling into the shadows behind him. "Fisi, my brave fellow," laughed the lion, "I have some work for you to do. Our friend Timba is tired of being so small and insignificant that he is forced to eat the worms that live in the leavings of other people's kills. He wishes to be changed into a fierce animal who can catch and kill meat for himself. Please mix a suitable potion for him."

The hyena went back into the gloom of his cluttered cave. He soon returned with the desired mixture which he gave to the robin. No sooner had the little bird swallowed it, than he changed into Lilongwe, a fierce little gray mongoose. He was delighted, and immediately went into the forest to hunt rats, birds, and other small creatures.

Things went well to begin with, but after a while the lion and mongoose met. "Well, Lilongwe, how are you getting on?" asked the lion.

"Not so well as I could wish," grumbled the mongoose. "Birds are difficult to catch. Besides, it is the good, red blood of *animal* flesh that I crave. If only Fisi had mixed a little stronger potion for me," he added wistfully.

"Very well," said the lion with an indulgent smile, "we will visit him again and see if he will help you further."

They repeated their visit to the witch-doctor's cave, and Fisi mixed another magic brew at the lion's request. No sooner had the mongoose swallowed it, than in his place stood a sleek and velvety spotted leopard. Nyalugwe, as we now must call him, purred with pride and pleasure, and at once bounded into the forest to hunt small buck, hares, and baboons.

For some time the leopard was contented with his lot, but eventually he thought how very much more exciting it would be to hunt in the open by daylight, instead of keeping to the shadows of the dark forest. Besides, he wanted to kill big animals—zebra and buffalo—not little things like baboons and rock rabbits. The more he thought about it, the more dissatisfied he became with his present lot.

It was not long after this that Ngango saw Nyalugwe slinking along a path in the depth of the forest one morning just after sunrise. "Good morning, my friend," the lion greeted him, "I am sure you must be quite satisfied now."

"Not completely," replied the leopard irritably. "I wish I could catch big animals like you do."

"Very well," said the lion patiently, "we will visit Fisi once more." So they went to the witch-doctor's cave for the third time. When the hyena had prepared an extra large potion, the lion took it and, before handing it to Nyalugwe he said, "I must make one condition before your next change takes place. When you have made your kills, you are never, never, ever to roar like I do because, as you are well aware, all the hunting in this area belongs to me. In my roar I am entitled to say *'This is my hunting-ground; this is my hunting-ground.'* You must say, *'This is Ngango's hunting-ground; this is Ngango's hunting-ground!'* If you disobey this order, you will be punished. Do you understand?"

The leopard thumped the ground sulkily upon each side of him, with his elegant, yellow and black tail. After he had promised to follow the lion's instructions, Ngango handed the leopard the magic potion. Nyalugwe could hardly wait to gulp it down, and as soon as he did, a fine young lion appeared—strong and well-built, but smaller than Ngango. Soundlessly the young lion slipped into the tall grass at the edge of the forest, and at once began to stalk and hunt big game upon the plains.

His first kill was a buck, and the following day he killed a young kudu. This was life, indeed! How proud he felt as he dragged the various carcasses to the top of an ant-hill, as he had seen Ngango do, and from there to announce to all, *"This is Ngango's hunting-ground; this is Ngango's hunting-ground!"* before settling down to his meal. The big lion heard him, and was pleased.

The young lion went from one success to another, his kills becoming larger and larger, until finally he pulled down a big buffalo. "Surely," he said to himself with pride, as he dragged the body of the big beast to the highest point that he could find, "I am now a match for any creature living. I have as much right to this hunting-ground as any other lion." And he roared, for all to hear, *"This is MY hunting-ground; this is MY hunting-ground!"*

The king of the wilds heard the boastful roar, and hastened to where the young lion was tearing chunks of meat from his kill. "What did I hear you roar?" the older lion asked in an icy tone, as he bared his huge yellow teeth.

The young lion's heart skipped a beat or two. Perhaps, he thought, it had been unwise of him to declare his strength *quite* so soon. Maybe he should have waited until he had reached full maturity, and was certain that he could overcome the mighty Ngango. "I spoke without thinking," he said hesitantly.

"That is no excuse," growled Ngango. "Tell me," he continued in a more pleasant tone, "what were you before Fisi changed you into a lion?"

"I was a leopard," mumbled the ungrateful one. What happened then, happened so quickly that the young lion was not aware of the change until it had taken place. Looking down at his paws, he saw the earlier spotted fur of the leopard to which he had returned!

His head reeled, but he was brought back to his senses by the older lion asking him, "And before you were a leopard?"

"I was a mongoose," muttered the leopard, now very unsure of himself. He was startled to see how enormous Ngango had suddenly become, until he realized that it was he, himself, who had grown small again, for he was once more Lilongwe, a fierce little gray mongoose.

But the lion had not finished with him yet. "Yes," went on the Lord of the Wilds, "of course, a mongoose. I remember. And before that?"

"I was a robin," stammered the mongoose. The words had barely left his mouth, before he was once more Timba, the tiny little insignificant brown bird of the beginning of this tale. "*Tii-tii-tii*," he chirped, as he fluttered up into the tree above the lion, to begin once more, his permanent search for big, juicy white maggots.

Therefore, it is always wise to show gratitude for the good things that are given to you in life, for the Great One Who gives them, can also take them away from those who do not appreciate His gifts.

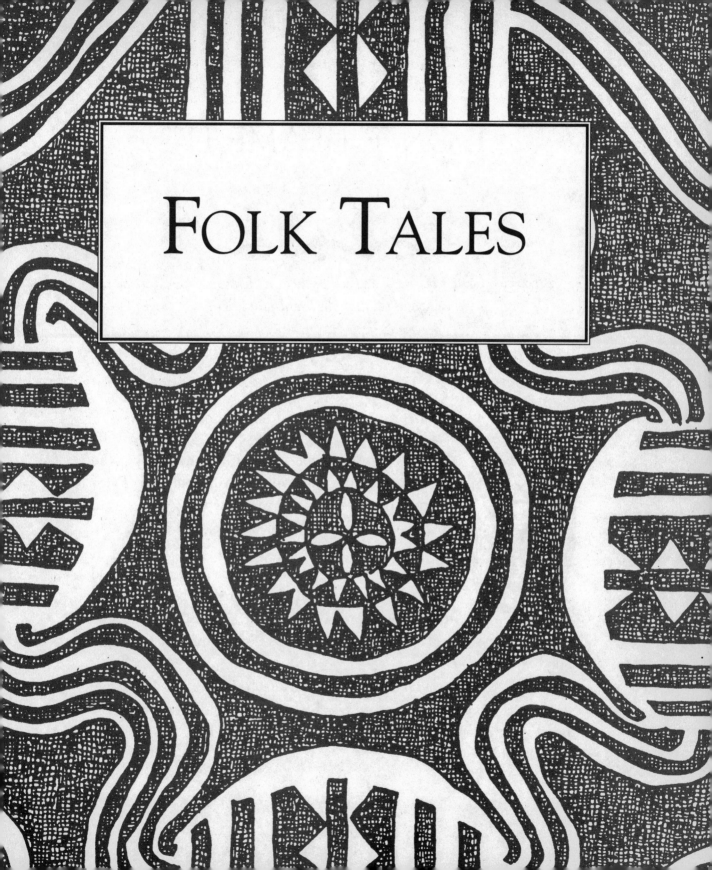

FOLK TALES

DON'T BLAME IT ON ADAM

A poor woodcutter believes he would be living a life of ease if Adam had not been banished from the Garden of Eden.

There once was a poor woodcutter named Iyapo who lived on the edge of a village in a small hut. Every morning he arose early and went deep into the forest to chop wood. Then he bundled it up, and carried it to town to sell.

He was not able to eat breakfast until after he sold some wood so he would have money to buy something to eat. "Wood, wood. Who'll buy some of my wood?" he would say as he walked up and down the streets. "It's all the fault of Adam. Good wood for sale."

One day as Iyapo was selling his wood, the king heard what he was saying.

"Who is this person?" he asked his chief adviser. "And why does he say that it's all the fault of Adam? If someone has wronged him, then I should know about it."

The chief adviser of the king asked the other officers but none of them knew who the woodcutter was or what he meant. So they took him to the king. The poor woodcutter fell on the floor in fear and respect.

"Now, woodcutter, what is your name?" asked the king.

"Sire, my name is Iyapo."

"Your name, Iyapo, means 'many troubles,' but why are you blaming Adam?"

"I have heard that long ago Adam disobeyed God and ate the forbidden fruit. If he had not, we would all now be living in the Garden of Eden and I would never go hungry. That is why I say it is the fault of Adam."

"I see," said the king. "You work hard yet you go hungry. It does not seem fair that you are suffering because of Adam's mistake. I will help you."

The king called his chief adviser. "Have Iyapo washed and dressed. Bring him to the palace and let him stay in one of the rooms there. Take his rags and wood away. He will have a new life."

Then he said to Iyapo, "From now on you can call me brother. We will share everything. You can do anything you like except for one thing—you may not open the green door at the end of the hall. That is the one thing you may never do. Do you understand?"

"Oh, my king," cried the happy Iyapo, "what reason do I have to open the green door? I have food, clothes, and shelter. What more could I want?"

And so the woodcutter began a life of comfort. He never had to get up early or work hard. He had so much to eat he was even starting to get fat.

He had forgotten all about the green door until one day he happened to pass by it, and as he did he remembered it was the door he was never to open. However, he couldn't help wondering why he, the king's brother, was not allowed to find out what was in the room behind the door. He sighed and walked on.

During the next few days, Iyapo seemed to be drawn to the green door.

Several times a day he found himself outside the door, and each time he was getting more and more curious as to what was behind it. Sometimes, without realizing it, his hand actually moved towards the handle but he managed to stop himself each time.

One day, the king said, "Brother, I have been called away to another town, and I will not be back until late today. I am entrusting the palace to you. Please take care that nothing happens."

After the king left, the woodcutter started thinking, "I am responsible for the palace so surely I also am responsible for the room behind the green door as well. I must be for I am the king's brother and have been left in charge. I am going to find out what is hidden there."

After checking that no one was looking, he put his ear against the door. He could not hear anything.

"I must know what is in there. I will just open the door a crack and close it again. The king will never know." And so he opened the door slightly. The room was dark, but after a while he could see that all that was in there were the old rags he used to wear and the wood he used to sell. Just then, a mouse ran out the door.

"Oh, no!" cried Iyapo. "The king was hiding a mouse in the room and now it has escaped. I must catch it." As he ran after the mouse, his shoes fell off. He tripped over the bottom of his long fancy robes, and had to take them off. Still, he could not catch the mouse, and he was now very hot and out of breath. Suddenly, the king appeared. He had returned early!

"What are you doing, Iyapo?" boomed the king. "Why are you running around the palace without your clothes?"

Poor Iyapo threw himself at the king's feet. "I'm sorry" he sobbed. "I did not mean to let your mouse go."

"What mouse?" asked the king. "I have no mouse."

"The mouse in the room. When I opened the green door . . ."

"You opened the green door?"

"I did not mean to. It was wrong, but my feet kept taking me there and I was curious and . . ."

"Iyapo, I am very disappointed in you. Opening the green door was the one thing I told you not to do."

"I know, sire, but I am the brother of the king and . . ."

"And now you want to be the king himself," shouted the king. "You are worse than Adam. You should have learned from his mistake."

"I am sorry, my lord. It will never happen again. I promise. What do you wish me to do?"

The king's anger had disappeared. Now he had tears in his eyes. "Go back to the room," he said sadly, "and take your rags and sticks. Return to the market and sell your wood."

"Yes, sire," was all the woodcutter could say.

"And remember this—others cannot make you happy. It is up to you and your fate. Go and work hard and know that your poverty is not the fault of Adam or anyone else."

And so Iyapo returned to the market. Once again he shouted, "Wood for sale. Who wants to buy good wood?" But he never mentioned Adam again.

THE BRAVEST OF ALL MEN

*Sedu brags and boasts so much that he cannot possibly
live up to his reputation.*

A man named Sedu lived in the village of Golo.
Whenever the men of the village went hunting and
returned with game, Sedu said to his wife: "Among all
the hunters, I was the bravest. By myself, I fought with
the leopard and chased the elephant. When I went
forward with my spear, even the lion fled. I am the
bravest of hunters."

His wife, Ladi, replied, "Did no one but you bring
back meat?"

Sedu said, "Because of my fearlessness, I brought good luck to others."

When it was said that the enemy was approaching, Sedu went into the
bush country with the men. When he returned, he hung his spear on the
wall and said to his wife: "When I ran at the enemy, they turned and fled.
My reputation has spread everywhere. I am the bravest of warriors. What
do you have to say to that?"

Ladi answered, "It is so."

There was a funeral one time in another village, and some of the women of Golo wished to go. But the men were working in the fields and could not accompany them. Ladi told the women, "My husband is the bravest of men. He will take us through the forest."

She went to Sedu, saying, "The women who are going to the funeral agree that you are the one to take them through the forest. Will you do it?"

Sedu said, "From one day to another no one mentions my courage. But when courage is needed, people ask, "Where is Sedu?" All right, I will do it."

He took his spear and went into the forest with the women.

There were warriors of the enemy in the forest hunting game. When they saw Sedu coming with the women they said, "Look how the man struts like a guinea cock. Let us strike fear into him."

They waited near the trail, and when the people of Golo were near, the hunters came out of the brush before them and behind them.

Sedu shouted, "We are surrounded! Run for the trees!"

The women ran among the trees and Sedu ran with them. But they were all captured by the enemy warriors.

The leader of the hunters said to Sedu's wife, "What is your name?"

"Ladi," she replied.

"Ladi is a name used by the women of our tribe also. Because you are called Ladi, we shall not hurt you.

To another woman he said, "What is your name?"

Seeing how good it was to be named Ladi, the woman replied, "My name is also Ladi."

The leader of the hunters said, "A good name—we shall not hurt you."

He asked another woman and she too replied, "Ladi."

All of the women were asked, and all of them answered "My name is Ladi."

Then the leader of the hunters spoke to Sedu. "All the women of your village are named Ladi. It is a strange custom. In our village each woman has a different name. But you, guinea cock who leads the guinea hens, what are you called?"

"I," said Sedu, "I too am called Ladi."

When the hunters heard Sedu's reply, they laughed. "No," declared the leader of the hunters, "it is not possible. Ladi is a woman's name. You are a man with a spear. Do not tell me the men of your village are also called Ladi?"

"No, no," said Sedu, "only the women are called Ladi."

"Then why are you called Ladi?" he asked.

Sedu looked around, but saw no chance of escape. "You see," he said, "appearances are deceiving. I also am a woman."

The enemy roared with laughter. The women of Golo laughed too.

Sedu's wife spoke. "He speaks modestly of himself. He is the courageous Sedu, the famous Sedu."

Sedu then said, "Yes, it is so."

A hunter said, "People say that Sedu claims to be the bravest of all men."

"No," Sedu replied, "it is no longer so. I *used* to be the bravest of all men. Now I am only the bravest in my village."

The hunters let them go. Sedu and the women went to the funeral, and they returned afterwards to their houses. When they arrived in Golo, everyone was laughing at Sedu. Instead of calling him by his name, they called him Ladi. He went into his house and closed the door. Whenever he came out, they laughed. He could not hide from the shame.

At last he sent his wife to tell them this: "Sedu who was formerly the bravest of men was reduced to being the bravest of his village. But from now on he is not the bravest in the village. He claims to be only as brave as other people."

So the people of Golo stopped making fun of Sedu. And thereafter he was no braver than anyone else.

Why Brer Wasp Never Laughs

It's hard to believe that a creature as bad-tempered as the wasp actually got that way from laughing too much.

God's creatures didn't always stay just the way they were when they were first made. With mistakes, and accidents, and one thing and another, they became different as time went by. Some became so different, they hardly looked anything like when they started out.

For example, at one time Brer Wasp looked and acted very different from how he is now. He loved to talk, and joke, and cut the fool. He just liked to laugh and have fun.

One day, while he was walking along a path, he met up with Brer Mosquito. Now, Brer Mosquito and his family weren't very big, but they took themselves mighty seriously. Brer Mosquito and his pa planted a little tiny patch of ground together, but they always called it the plantation. They talked so big about their crops and land and everything that you would have thought they had 1,000 acres.

That very week, there had been a heavy frost, and all the sweet potato vines turned black and died, and everybody was forced to dig for the early potatoes. So after Brer Wasp politely passed the time of day with Brer Mosquito, he asked him how he had made out with his crops.

"We made out fine, Brer Wasp, just fine," Brer Mosquito said. "We had the biggest crop you ever did see!"

"The potatoes were big then?"

"I tell you, sir, they were huge! You've never seen such potatoes!"

"How big were they, Brer Mosquito?"

"My friend," Brer Mosquito replied, puffing out his tiny chest and pulling up his little britches at the waist, "most of our crop came up bigger than the calf of my leg!"

Well, sir! Brer Wasp looked at Brer Mosquito's skinny little leg, and as he thought about those "huge potatoes" he had to laugh to himself. He tried to mind his manners, but his chest and face swelled up, and tears ran out of his eyes, and he burst out laughing right in Brer Mosquito's face. He laughed and laughed till his sides hurt him. Whenever he thought he would stop, he looked at that ridiculous little toothpick of a leg, and he laughed some more. His sides hurt him so much from laughing he had to hold them in with both his hands while he rocked back and forth.

"What's so funny?" Brer Mosquito asked him.

Brer Wasp gasped out, "Good Lord, Brer Mosquito, looking for the biggest part of your leg is like looking for the heaviest part of a hair. How big those potatoes must be, if you say they were as big as that!" And he laughed again until his sides hurt so bad that it wasn't enough to press them—he had to hold them in both his hands and squeeze.

Brer Mosquito was so angry that he felt like fighting Brer Wasp, but he remembered how Brer Wasp was kind of nasty when he got in a fight. So he just drew himself up, and stuck out his mouth, and said, "Go ahead and laugh, you no-mannered devil! But take care that the day doesn't come when somebody laughs at you the same no-mannered way."

But that didn't stop Brer Wasp. All the way to his house he had been laughing so hard that he had to stop now and then to catch his breath. At last he got home and started to tell his family about Brer Mosquito.

Just then his wife got a good look at him, and she hollered out, "For cry-ing-out-loud, Brer Wasp! What's happened to your stomach? "Brer Wasp looked down where his waist had been and he could hardly see it.

He lost all notion of laughing right then. He looked again and he saw what all that shaking, and pushing, and squeezing had done to him. He was almost in two! Even his little hand could reach around his waist. He remembered how big it had been, and he saw how much he had shrunk up, and he was afraid to so much as sneeze.

Then he remembered what Brer Mosquito had said to him. He remembered all those people he had been joking about and laughing at so hard and for such a long time, and he thought about how now the others were going to have their turn to laugh at that little waist he had now. And that is why he has so little patience. Everywhere he goes he thinks somebody is ready to laugh at him. If anyone so much as looks at him, he gets so mad that he's ready to fight.

And the worst thing is that from that day to this, he can't laugh any-more, because if he does, he will burst in two.

DIVIDING THE CHEESE

*When the monkey cheats the cats out of their cheese,
they've gotten just what they deserve.*

Two cats stole a cheese. Neither thought the other would divide it equally so they agreed to ask the monkey to do it.

"With pleasure," said the monkey. He sent the cats to fetch a scale. Then he got out his knife. But instead of cutting the cheese in half, he made one portion larger than the other. He put both pieces on the scale. "I didn't divide this quite right," he said. "I'll just even it up."

The monkey began to eat the cheese from the heavier side. As he ate, the heavier side became lighter than the other piece. Then he changed over and began to eat from the other side.

The cats, watching their snack disappear, said, "We've changed our mind. Please, let us have the rest of the cheese, and we will divide it ourselves."

"No, a fight might arise between you, and then the king of animals would be angry with me," said the monkey.

And he continued to eat, first on one side, and then on the other, until all the cheese was gone.

WHY THE HIPPOPOTAMUS LIVES IN THE WATER

The tortoise uses a clever trick to uncover the hippo's secret name.

Many years ago, the hippopotamus, whose name was Isantim, was one of the biggest kings on the land—only the elephant was bigger. This hippo had seven fat wives, of whom he was very fond, and they went everywhere together. Now and then he used to give a big feast for the people, but though everyone knew the hippo, no one, except his seven wives, knew his real name.

At one of the feasts, just as the people were about to sit down, the hippo said, "You have come to feed at my table, but none of you know my name. If no one can guess my name, you shall all go away without your dinner."

After some time, as no one could guess his name, they reluctantly prepared to leave. But before doing so, the tortoise stood up and asked the hippopotamus what would happen if he told him his name at the next feast?

The hippo replied that if the tortoise discovered his name, he and his whole family would leave the land, and for the future would dwell in the water.

Now, the tortoise knew that it was the custom for the hippo and his wives to go every morning and evening to the river to wash and have a drink. The hippo used to walk at the head of the line, and his seven wives followed behind. One day, when they had gone down to the river to bathe, the tortoise dug a small hole in the middle of the path, and then hid himself behind a nearby bush and waited.

When the hippo and his wives returned, two of the wives were some distance behind the others, so the tortoise came out from where he had been hiding, and crawled into the hole he had dug, leaving the greater part of his shell exposed. When the two hippo wives came along, the first one knocked her foot against the tortoise's shell, and immediately called out to her husband, "Oh!, Isantim, my husband, I have hurt my foot." As you can imagine, hearing this made the tortoise very glad! As soon as all of the hippos were out of sight, the happy tortoise went home.

At the next feast the hippo reminded his guests that they could not eat unless someone knew his name. The tortoise got up and said, "You promise you will not be angry if I tell you your name?" The hippo promised. The tortoise then shouted as loud as he was able, "Your name is Isantim!" When the hippo admitted that this was his name, a cheer went up from all the people, and then they sat down to dinner.

When the feast was over, the hippo and his seven wives, in accordance with his promise, went down to the river, and they have lived in the water from that day till now. And although they come ashore to feed at night, you never can find a hippo on the land in the daytime.

THE HYENA'S DINNER

The poor hyena is almost always depicted as cowardly, but in this story he is shown to be quite foolish as well.

In one of the animal kingdoms on the slopes of Mount Kenya, in the heart of this great continent of Africa, a committee of animal rulers once called a meeting of the inhabitants to discuss the lack of gratitude among many of the creature of the wilds.

"We must remember to give thanks to the Great Lord Ngai for all the food that He provides," said the leader of the meeting, "for how can we expect Him to satisfy our hunger if we do not show gratitude? Surely those who fail to praise His goodness will one day have these gifts taken from them!"

The animals nodded their heads in agreement, for the good Ngai was recognized as the Father of them all and, as food had been scarce for some time, they had begun to wonder if they had not taken His favors for granted. The meeting ended, and the animals returned to their homes, determined to mend their manners in the future.

Not long after this, the greedy hyena was walking along a path when he came upon a calf tied to a tree by a rawhide thong. "Surely," he said to himself, "the good Ngai has put this calf here for me to eat." He smacked his lips at the thought of the splendid meal ahead of him.

In his excitement, however, he forgot to give thanks to Ngai for leading him to such a wonderful meal. "Where," he wondered, "shall I begin my meal—by eating the tender calf first, and leaving the hard, dry thong that ties it until the end? Or, shall I begin by eating the thong first, and saving the calf for the end of my meal?"

After hesitating briefly, he decided to eat the thong first. This way, he reasoned, he would have more time to think of how much he would enjoy the tender second course. "Yes," he said to himself, "I will first eat the hard, dry hide, and then I will eat the calf."

He set to work with his powerful jaws, close to the calf's neck, and as he swallowed the lumps of indigestible rawhide thong, he got nearer and nearer to the tree to which the calf had been tied. And so intent upon his meal did the foolish fellow become, that he did not notice that the calf, now at liberty, had lost no time in running toward its owner's hut.

Having swallowed the last piece of the rawhide thong, the hyena looked around for the best part of his meal—but it had disappeared. He ran along the path, and in the distance saw the calf disappearing over the rise in front of him.

It was only then, that the greedy creature remembered that he had failed to give Ngai thanks for providing him with such a sumptuous meal. He thereupon hastily did so, and then called loudly upon The Giver to make the calf stand still, so that he could catch up with it.

But as so often happens in life, the hyena was not given a second chance. The calf reached the safety of its owner's hut, while the ungrateful hyena had to be content with the piece of hard, dry thong for his supper.

KIMWAKI AND THE WEAVER BIRDS

A young man squanders his inheritance until he learns that it is more satisfying to give than receive.

As an old man lay dying, he sent for his only child, a young man named Kimwaki.

"My son," the father said, "I have lived a long life, and the time has come for me to join my ancestors. My years have not been spent idly. I leave you the fairest fields in the village, and the largest herd of cows and goats. Now carry me beneath the stars, for I am ready to die."

After the burial ceremony, Kimwaki looked around him and counted his wealth. It was, he realized, great for such a young man. "I have no need to ever toil again," he thought.

Day after day Kimwaki lay dreaming in the sunshine. When the sun became too hot for comfort, he lay in the shade of a big tree that grew beside his hut. He let his lovely garden become overgrown by weeds and grass. His sleek and glossy cattle, with no one to drive them to their pastures, became hollow-eyed and thin. The little goats bleated in distress.

But Kimwaki did not care, because his wise and thrifty father had also left him overflowing food bins. He felt he would always have enough. Hunger would never touch *him*.

In a land where it is the custom for each neighbor to help the other, not a soul lifted a finger to assist this lazy youth who gave no help to others. Though things for Kimwaki went from bad to worse, no one cared. Kimwaki was shunned by all around him.

Kimwaki led this useless life for many months, until he began to tire of the loneliness.

Then one day in early spring, while Kimwaki was napping as usual beneath his tree, he was awakened by excited twittering and singing. Annoyed, he opened his eyes to see what had disturbed his pleasant sleep. Up in the tree was a flock of little weaver birds, darting here and there. They were all as busy as could be, for it was nesting time.

Spring was in the air, and the male weaver birds were building nests in which to raise their young. Their excited twittering and busy activity made Kimwaki open his eyes a little wider to watch the birds as they worked together. Before long, the lazy boy could not help noticing what joy the birds found in working together.

Chattering and singing, each male bird did his share to build the colony. One would bring a tiny piece of grass, another a little twig, while yet another added a feather to his nest. Busily the birds worked, as though their very lives depended upon the timely completion of their task—which, indeed, it did. When evening came, the frames of the little nests were completed.

On the following day the same activities took place. The clever birds used their tiny beaks to weave the grasses in and out, lining the nest with the softest down.

Kimwaki watched it all from beneath the big tree. By the time the second evening came, thunderclouds were gathering in the sky. Kimwaki thought how wise the little weaver birds were to provide shelter for their babies against the coming rains.

Every day Kimwaki watched the diligent feathered workers. In a short while, a whole colony of finished nests hung from the branches of the tree. And during all this time, the lesson of the birds' cooperation and their hard work had been making quite an impression on Kimwaki.

Finally, the young man said to himself, "I am a strong young man, while they are only tiny birds. I have two big hands with which to work, while each of them has only a little beak. They are safe and sheltered, and I am not. Surely the birds are wiser than I am!"

He thought the matter over that night, and the next morning he rose early. Taking his rusty hoe with him, he went to the field that belonged to his nearest neighbor. There Kimwaki began to dig and clear the weeds and grass away. When this was done, he started to hoe the ground.

All day long Kimwaki worked in a friendly way with others who joined him. When evening came, he found himself singing as he returned to his dilapidated hut. He felt as happy and lighthearted as the little weaver birds!

Day after day Kimwaki went unbidden, first to the garden of one neighbor and then to another, helping where he could and asking nothing in return.

Then one morning he awoke to hear cheerful chattering and laughter coming from his own overgrown garden.

He looked out and saw all his neighbors as busy as could be, clearing and hoeing his weed-covered fields. He joined them at once, and soon the plot of ground was ready for planting.

Later, when the rains came, his neighbors helped him plant his crops and repair his leaking hut.

The season progressed, and Kimwaki's crops grew. As the maize, beans, and potatoes grew, so grew his pride in achievement. The young man no longer wasted his days beneath the big tree, but continued to help those around him. He also saw to the comfort of his neglected flocks. He watched happily as the glow of health returned to the once-dull coats of his cows and goats.

Before long, Kimwaki's crops were ready to be harvested. His willing neighbors helped him in the fields, thereby returning the help that Kimwaki had so generously given them. And when all the grain had been winnowed and stored away, and his potatoes and beans sold at the market, Kimwaki found to his joy that once more his father's fields had yielded the highest return in the land.

Kimwaki gave thanks to the little weaver birds for showing him that only through hard work and sharing can peace, security, and happiness be found.

THE 'NSASAK AND THE ODUDU

The 'Nsasak bird wins a contest by cheating, but forevermore is destined to be hunted.

Long ago, the King of Calabar wanted to know how long an animal or bird could endure hunger. The one that survived without food for the longest time, the king promised, would be made a chief of his very own tribe.

The 'Nsasak bird is very small, having a shining breast of green and red, blue and yellow feathers, and a band of red around his neck. His chief food consists of ripe palm nuts. The Odudu bird, on the other hand, is much larger, about the size of a magpie with black and brown feathers, a long tail, and a cream-colored breast. The Odudu lives chiefly on grasshoppers and crickets.

Now, the 'Nsasak and the Odudu were friends, but since each desired to be made a chief, they both went before the king in order to be tested. The

Odudu was confident that he would win as he was so much bigger than the 'Nsasak. Therefore, he offered to starve for seven days.

The king told them both to build homes which he would inspect, and then he would have them sealed up inside, and the one who could remain the longest without eating would be made chief.

They both built their houses, but the 'Nsasak, who was very cunning, knew that he could not possibly live for seven days without eating anything at all. Therefore, he made a tiny hole in the wall and covered it very carefully so the king would not notice it on his inspection.

The king then came and looked carefully over both houses, but failed to detect the little hole in the 'Nsasak bird's house. He declared both houses safe, and ordered the two birds to go inside their respective houses. The doors then were carefully fastened on the outside.

Every morning at dawn the 'Nsasak would escape through the small opening he had left high up in the wall, and fly off and enjoy himself all day, taking care, however, that no one should see him. When the sun went down, he would fly back to his little house creep through the hole in the wall, and close it carefully behind him.

When he was safely inside, he would call out to his friend, the Odudu, and ask him if he felt hungry, and told him that he must bear it well if he wanted to win, as he, the 'Nsasak bird, was very fit, and could go on for a long time.

For several days this went on, the voice of the Odudu bird growing weaker and weaker every night until, at last, he could no longer reply. Then the little bird was sorry for he knew his friend must be dead.

When the seven days had expired, the king came and had both doors of the houses opened. The 'Nsasak bird at once flew out, and, perching on a branch of a tree which grew near, sang most merrily— but the Odudu was found dead, and there was very little left of him, as the ants had eaten most of his body, leaving only the feathers and bones on the floor.

The king, therefore, appointed the 'Nsasak as chief of all the small birds, and in the Ibibio country, even to the present time, small boys who have bows and arrows are presented with a prize, which sometimes takes the shape of a female goat, if they manage to shoot a 'Nsasak, as it is king of the small birds, and most difficult to shoot on account of its craftiness and small size.

Two Riddle Stories

*Riddle tales, widely known in Africa, usually have no clear answer but
result in many lively discussions.*

Who Shall Marry
the Chief's Daughter?

Three brothers all wanted to marry the same girl. She
was the daughter of a powerful Chief. The Chief called
the brothers to his house and said: "In the forest live
the Little People. My daughter wants one of them for
her servant. Whichever of you first brings her one of
the Little People shall be her husband."

The three brothers went away and talked about the
task the Chief had given them. "Wherever will we find
the Little People?" one of them asked.

Another brother said, "Many speak of the Little People, but I have
never known any one who has seen them."

And the third said, "Well, let us go into the forest and look."

Each of the brothers had a special magic. The first had a magical mirror. If he looked into his mirror, he could see things that were happening any-where in the world. The second brother had a magic hammock, which would take him anywhere he wanted to go. And the third brother had the power to bring the dead back—within one day of their death.

They traveled for months in the great forest looking for the Little People. Whomever they met on the trail, they asked: "Do you know where the Little People are to be found?" But no one knew.

One day, the first brother looked into his mirror and saw the Chief grieving for his daughter who had just died. The third brother said, "I have the power to bring her back to life. If we return quickly, I can save her."

The second brother said, "I have the power to take us home. Climb into my hammock."

Instantly, the hammock carried the three brothers back to the village. They went to the Chief's house and, using his magic power, the third brother brought the Chief's daughter back to life.

Then the grateful Chief said: "Though you did not find the Little People, you returned and brought my daughter back to life. You all con-tributed to saving her. But I have only one daughter. Only one of you can be my son-in-law. To the one who did the most, to him I will give my daughter."

Which one deserved the reward?

THREE SONS OF A CHIEF

The admiration for great feats of horsemanship among the Hausa people in
Nigeria is celebrated in this tall tale.

There was a Chief who had three sons. Each of them was greatly talented in the art of fighting and of riding.

One day the Chief called his people together. He announced he was going to test his sons to see who had the greatest skill.

"Here at this baobab tree that stands by our house," said the Chief, "we will see which of my sons is the most talented."

The sons quickly mounted their horses, galloped off a distance and stopped.

Then the eldest son raced his horse toward the baobab tree, thrust his spear through the great tree, and rode through the hole that he made.

The second son came next. He galloped his horse forward, and when he came to the tree, he and his horse leaped over it.

The youngest son was next. He rode forward, seized the baobab tree in his hand, and pulled it from the earth, roots and all. He rode on, waving the great tree high over his head.

Now, who was the greatest of them all?

ROOSTER IN A HUFF

Rooster's rude behavior costs him a delicious dinner and a very good time.

All the animals—the ducks, hens, turkeys, geese, pigs—
were invited to a big supper and dance at the next farmyard. They were all looking forward to the party, and
when it was time to go, they lined up to walk over. The
big farmyard rooster led the way, strutting and crowing
as he marched. Never have you heard such merry-mak-
ing noise with all that quacking, clucking, gobbling,
and oinking.

After some square dancing to sharpen their appetites, they were invited
into the supper room. In the center was a huge table filled with plates piled
high with food. But when they got closer, all the plates seemed to be
heaped with nothing but cornbread.

Well, now, the rooster got upset when he saw this. "I can get all the
cornbread I want at home," he sniffed. So he went off in a huff. But the

others were having too good a time to care about what was being served, and besides, they were hungry and ready to eat anything. No sooner had they eaten the outside of the cornbread than they discovered that underneath was a huge pile of bacon and greens. And at the bottom of that were pies and cakes and other good things.

Rooster was upset when he realized what he had walked away from. But word of what he had said was out, and no one ever knew Rooster to admit he was wrong.

Now, whenever Rooster sees some food in front of him, he always scratches around the place with his feet, and he never stops scratching until he gets to the bottom of it.

How the Skunk Became Feared

Grey Wolf spares Skunk's life but lives to regret it.

Skunk, the younger brother of the wolf, Catamount, was a disgrace to the family from the day he was born. He was sneaking, he was cowardly. He was thievish, too, for that matter. He thought more of getting at a bird's nest and stealing a few half rotten eggs than of seeking and overpowering worthy prey.

He gave his strength to catching field mice and even grasshoppers and locusts. Even gophers and moles despised him more than they feared him. Added to this, he was the most impertinent and insulting little beast that could be imagined—providing he was in a safe place and at some distance before calling to those whom he wished to insult. But worst of all, Skunk even showed disrespect to Grey Wolf.

This was not to be tolerated, so Grey Wolf called all the animals together and demanded to know what should be done.

With one voice, the answer came—

"Destroy him. He is of no use whatsoever."

Catamount and Black Wolf said nothing. Catamount could not excuse his brother, but nor would he condemn him. And Black Wolf had plans of his own for Skunk to carry out.

Grey Wolf, thinking that all were agreed, was about to destroy the miserable creature when the contemptible Skunk flattened himself out at the feet of his master and begged that his life be spared, even if all that adorned and made it pleasant be taken away. So in contempt, rather than in kindness, Grey Wolf spared the life of Skunk, but at the same time he shrunk and shriveled the creature till he was scarcely larger than Gopher. He also pared his claws and shortened his teeth. This done, the other animals scornfully departed without a backward glance, Catamount following after Grey Wolf.

Black Wolf, however, had only gone a little way when he turned and went softly back.

"Be of good cheer, little brother," he said to the dismayed Skunk. "Brother Grey Wolf has seen fit to arrange matters so that you shall be in terror of all living things. However, do as I say and even Grey Wolf himself will be in awe of you."

This he promised, not because he loved Skunk, but because it delighted him to oppose Grey Wolf's decisions.

Skunk miserably lifted up his head. "Thank you, Black Wolf," he said, "but what can you possibly do? My strength is gone, my claws are as grass and my teeth as willow-twigs."

"Watch me," said Black Wolf.

So Skunk watched as Black Wolf took an egg from a deserted nest and put in it sweat from his own body, the breath of a buzzard, wind that had passed over a field where dead still lay, and a little water from a green pool. When he had stirred those things together, he gave the egg to Skunk and said, "Wear this and you shall be the great conqueror. Your strongest adversaries will turn sickly and feeble before you. Not horns, claws, teeth, or muscles will make any difference to you."

So Skunk took the gift with a joyful heart and tried its power on Black Wolf at once.

Black Wolf, sick and howling, fled as fast as he could from the presence of the ungrateful Skunk he had so terribly endowed.

Skunk then knew for certain that Black Wolf had told him the truth about the gift. He immediately set out to find his tormentors, and when he did, they fled, every one, from the least to greatest.

Then Skunk contentedly laid himself down under a tree and went to sleep.

HOW TORTOISE GREW A TAIL

In this Yoruba tale, the tortoise chooses just the right example to teach his friend the boa a lesson.

Ijapa the tortoise had been on a long journey under the hot sun. After walking for many hours he was tired, hot, and hungry. At this point, he was outside the house of his friend, Ojola, the boa. He went to the door and called to him, certain he would get something to eat. Ojola, seeing that Ijapa was hot and tired, invited him in.

"Come in, Ijapa, and rest awhile. You are hot and tired. Please sit down and make yourself comfortable."

So Ijapa came in and they sat down together to talk. Meanwhile, Ojola's wife was cooking, and the tortoise could smell the wonderful aroma coming from the pot. He began to groan with hunger.

"Does the smell of the cooking bother you?" asked the boa.

"No, it just reminds me of home, where I would be eating a lovely supper cooked by my wife," replied Ijapa.

"Well, tonight you will eat with us," said Ojola. "You go and wash and all will be ready."

So Ijapa went out back to wash in the stream. Feeling refreshed, he came back inside to find that a large bowl of hot steaming vegetables and corn was already set down in the middle of the floor.

"Mmm!" said Ijapa, licking his lips. "That smells good."

"Just come here and help yourself," said Ojola wrapping himself around the bowl, and eagerly beginning to eat.

The tortoise, seeing the boa's thick coils wrapped around the bowl, walked to the other side to find a way in. But on all sides Ojola's fat coils were piled up around the bowl while he slurped and supped.

For a moment, Ojola raised his head. "This is delicious, Ijapa," he said. "What are you waiting for? Do join me before it's all gone."

"Yes, I would like to join you, Ojola, but why do you wrap yourself around the food? I can't get near it."

"This is our custom," said the boa. "We always eat our food like this. Do come quickly and have some."

Poor Ijapa scuttled this way and that and couldn't find a way in. Finally, the boa swallowed the last mouthful.

"Well, it is so nice to eat with friends," said Ojola. "We must do this again."

The tortoise did not complain, but he left Ojola's house in a bad mood—and hungrier than ever. When he got home he thought about how he could teach the boa a lesson. He decided to invite him over to his own house for the next festival day to return his hospitality.

While Ijapa's wife prepared a special festival meal, he busied himself weaving a long fat tail out of grass. When it was finished he stuck it on himself with tree-gum.

When Ojola arrived the tortoise greeted him at the door and invited him in.

"Come in, Ojola, and make yourself comfortable."

So the boa came in and they sat down together to talk. Ojola could smell the wonderful aroma coming from the cooking pot and began to lick his lips.

"That cooking smells good, Ijapa. When are we going to eat?"

"Let's eat right away," said the tortoise. "You go and wash and all will be ready."

So Ojola went out to the spring to wash. Feeling refreshed, he came back inside to find that a big feast was laid out in the middle of the floor.

"Mmm!" said Ojola, licking his lips. "That smells good."

"Just come here and help yourself," said Ijapa as he circled round and round the food until his fat tail surrounded it on all sides. Then the tortoise began to eat.

Ojola, seeing the tortoise's strange new tail wrapped around the food, slithered around to the other side to find a way in. But Ijapa's tail was piled up around the food while he slurped and supped.

"This is delicious," said Ijapa. "What are you waiting for, Ojola? Do join me before it's all gone."

"Yes, I would like to join you, Ijapa, but where did you get this big new tail? Before you were short, but now you're very long, and your tail is in my way."

"One learns about such things from one's friends," replied the tortoise.

Then Ojola remembered how when Ijapa was his guest he had wrapped his tail around the food and prevented the tortoise from eating. Ojola was ashamed. Without saying another word he went home.

From that occurrence comes the proverb:

We learn from our friends to be short
And we also learn to be tall.

WHY WORMS LIVE UNDERGROUND

Better to ignore a braggart's insult than to be forced into a losing battle.

When Eyo was ruling over all men and animals, from time to time he invited his subjects to his house for a huge feast. After everyone had eaten, it was the custom to make speeches.

After one such feast, the head driver ant got up and said he and his people were stronger than anyone, and that not even an elephant could stand before them— which, though boastful, was quite true. Then the driver ant made fun of the worms (whom he disliked very much), calling them poor wiggling things.

The worms were highly insulted and complained to the king. "The best way to settle this question about who is stronger," said the king, "is for both sides to meet on the road and fight the matter out." The king chose the third day after the feast for the contest, and all the people turned out to witness the battle.

The driver ants left their nest in the early morning in thousands and millions, and, marching in a line about one inch wide and densely packed, they looked like a never-ending dark-brown band moving over the country. In front of the moving column they had out their scouts, advance guards, and flankers. The main body followed in their millions close behind.

When they came to the battlefield the moving band spread out, and as the thousands upon thousands of ants rolled up, the whole piece of ground was a moving mass of ants and bunches of struggling worms.

The fight was over in a very few minutes, as the worms were bitten in pieces by the sharp pincer-like mouths of the driver ants. The few worms who survived squirmed away and buried themselves out of sight.

King Eyo declared the driver ants the undisputed winners, and ever since the worms have lived underground; and if they happen to come to the surface after the rain, they hide themselves under the ground whenever anything approaches.

WILEY AND THE HAIRY MAN

*After tricking the Hairy Man three times, brave little Wiley and his momma
know they won't be bothered anymore.*

Before Wiley headed off into the swamp, his momma
called to him.

"Wiley," she said, "the Hairy Man's done got your
papa, so when you're in the swamp, watch out that he
don't get you."

"Yes'm," he said. "I'll look out. I'll take my hound
dogs everywhere I go. The Hairy Man can't stand no
hound dog."

Wiley knew that because his momma had told him, and she knew
because she knew conjure.

So Wiley took his ax and went down to the swamp to cut some poles for
a hen roost and his hounds went with him. But they took off after a wild
pig and chased it so far that Wiley couldn't even hear them yelp.

"Well," he said, "I hope the Hairy Man ain't anywhere around here now."

He picked up his ax to start cutting the poles but before he could take the first swing, there came the Hairy Man with a big grin on his ugly face. He was hairy all over, his eyes burned like fire, and spit drooled all over his big teeth.

Wiley threw down his ax and climbed up a big bay tree. He noticed that the Hairy Man had feet like a cow, and so was pretty sure the Hairy Man couldn't climb a tree.

"Why'd you climb up there?" the Hairy Man asked Wiley from the bottom of the tree.

Wiley looked down from the very top of the tree. "My momma told me to stay away from you. What you got in that big croaker-sack?"

"Nothing," said the Hairy Man.

"Go on, get away from here," said Wiley.

The Hairy Man picked up Wiley's ax and started swinging. Chips were flying from the trunk of the big bay tree. Wiley grabbed the tree close, rubbed his belly against it and hollered, "Fly, chips, fly back in your same place."

The chips flew back in place, making the Hairy Man stomp and fume. Then he picked up the ax and started swinging faster than before. They both went to it—Wiley hollering and the Hairy Man chopping. Wiley hollered till he was hoarse, and he saw the Hairy Man was gaining on him.

"I'll come down part way," said Wiley, "if you'll make this bay tree twice as big around."

"I ain't studyin' you," said the Hairy Man, still swinging the ax.

"I bet you can't."

"I ain't gonna try."

Then they went to it again—Wiley hollering and the Hairy Man chopping. Wiley had about yelled himself out when he heard his hound dogs yelping way off.

"Hyeaaah, dog. Hyeaaah," he hollered.

"You ain't got no dogs. I sent that pig to draw them off."

"Hyeaaah, dog. Hyeaaah," hollered Wiley, and they both heard the hound dogs yelping and coming closer. The Hairy Man looked worried.

"Come on down and I'll teach you conjure," he said.

"I can learn all the conjure I want from my momma," said Wiley.

The Hairy Man grit his teeth. He threw the ax down and took off through the swamp.

When Wiley got home he told his momma that the Hairy Man had almost got him, but that the dogs ran him off.

"Did he have his sack?"

"Yes'm."

"Next time he comes after you, don't climb any trees. Just stay on the ground and say, "Hello, Hairy Man." Okay, Wiley?"

"No'm."

"He ain't gonna hurt you, child. You just do like I say. You say, "Hello, Hairy Man." He says, "Hello, Wiley." You say, "Hairy Man, I hear you're about the best conjure man around here." "I reckon I am." You say, "I bet you can't turn yourself into no giraffe." You keep telling him he can't and he will. Then you say, "I bet you can't turn yourself into no alligator." And he will. Then you say, "Anyone can turn into something as big as a man, but I bet you can't turn yourself into no possum." When he does, you grab him and throw him in the sack."

"It don't sound right," said Wiley, "but I'll do it." He tied up his dogs so they wouldn't scare the Hairy Man away, and went down to the swamp again. He hadn't been there long when he saw the Hairy Man grinning through the trees. The Hairy Man knew Wiley had gone off without his hound dogs. Wiley nearly climbed a tree when he saw the croaker sack.

"Hello, Hairy Man," he said.

"Hello, Wiley." He took the sack off his shoulder and started to open it.

"Hairy Man, I hear you're the best conjure man around here."

"I reckon that's true."

"I bet you can't turn yourself into no giraffe."

"Shucks, that's easy."

"I bet you can't do it."

The Hairy Man twisted around and turned himself into a giraffe.

"I bet you can't turn yourself into an alligator."

The giraffe twisted around and turned into an alligator, all the time watching Wiley to see he didn't try to run off.

"Anybody can turn into something as big as a man," said Wiley "but I bet you can't turn yourself into a possum."

The alligator twisted around and turned into a possum. Wiley grabbed the possum and threw it into the sack. He tied the sack up tight and then threw it into the river. But on his way home through the swamp, here come the Hairy Man again, grinning through the trees.

"I turned myself into the wind and blew out," he said. "Now I'm gonna sit right here until you get hungry and have to come down out of that bay tree."

Wiley thought for a while. He thought about the Hairy Man and about his hound dogs tied up almost a mile away.

"Well," he said, "you done some pretty smart tricks. But I bet you can't make things disappear and go where nobody knows."

"Yes, I can. Look at that old bird nest over there. Now look. It's gone."

"I didn't see any bird nest there. I bet you can't make something I know is there disappear."

"Ha!" said the Hairy Man. "Look at your shirt."

Wiley looked down and his shirt was gone.

"That was just a plain old shirt," he said. "but this rope I got tied round my britches has been conjured. I bet you can't make it disappear."

"Huh, I can make all the rope in this county disappear."

"Ha, ha, ha," laughed Wiley. "Bet you can't."

The Hairy Man looked mad. He opened his mouth wide and yelled out, "From now on all the rope in this county has disappeared."

Wiley held his britches with one hand and the tree limb with the other, and called out, "Hyeaaah, dog." He hollered loud enough to be heard in the next county.

When Wiley and the dogs got home he told his momma what had happened.

"Well, you fooled him twice. If you fool him again he has to leave you alone forever. He'll be mighty hard to fool the third time, though."

"We gotta find a way to fool him, Momma."

Wiley's momma sat down by the fire and held her chin between her hands and studied real hard. After a while, she said, "Wiley, go down to the pen and get that little suckin' pig away from the sow."

Wiley went and snatched the little pig through the rails and brought it back to his momma. She put it in his bed. "Now Wiley, you go on up to the loft and hide."

Before long he heard the wind howling and the trees shaking, and then the dogs started growling. He looked out through a knot-hole and saw the dog at the front door looking toward the swamp with his lips drawn back in a snarl.

Then a big animal with horns on its head ran out of the swamp toward the house. The dogs broke loose and took off after it.

"Oh, Lord," said Wiley, "the Hairy Man is coming here for sure."

Soon he heard something with feet like a cow scrambling around on the roof. He knew it was the Hairy Man because he heard him holler when he touched the hot chimney. The Hairy Man jumped off the roof and came up and knocked on the front door as big as you please.

"Wiley's momma! I done come after your baby!"

"You ain't gonna get him," momma hollered back.

"Give him here or I'll set your house on fire."

"I got plenty of water to put it out with."

"Give him here or I'll dry up your spring, make your cow go dry, and send a million boll weevils to eat up your cotton."

"Hairy Man, that's mighty mean."

"I'm a mighty mean man."

"If I give you my baby, will you go away from here and leave everything else alone?"

"I swear I will," said the Hairy Man. So momma opened the door and let him in.

"My baby's over there in that bed," she said.

The Hairy Man came in grinning. He stomped over to the bed and snatched the covers back.

"Hey," he hollered, "there ain't nothin' in this bed but a little suckin' pig."

"I ain't said what kind of baby I was givin' you."

The Hairy Man stomped, and raged, and gnashed his big teeth. Then he grabbed the pig and took off through the swamp, knocking down trees left and right. When the Hairy Man was gone, Wiley came down from the loft.

"Is he gone, Momma?"

"Yes, child. That old Hairy Man can never be back because we done fooled him three times."

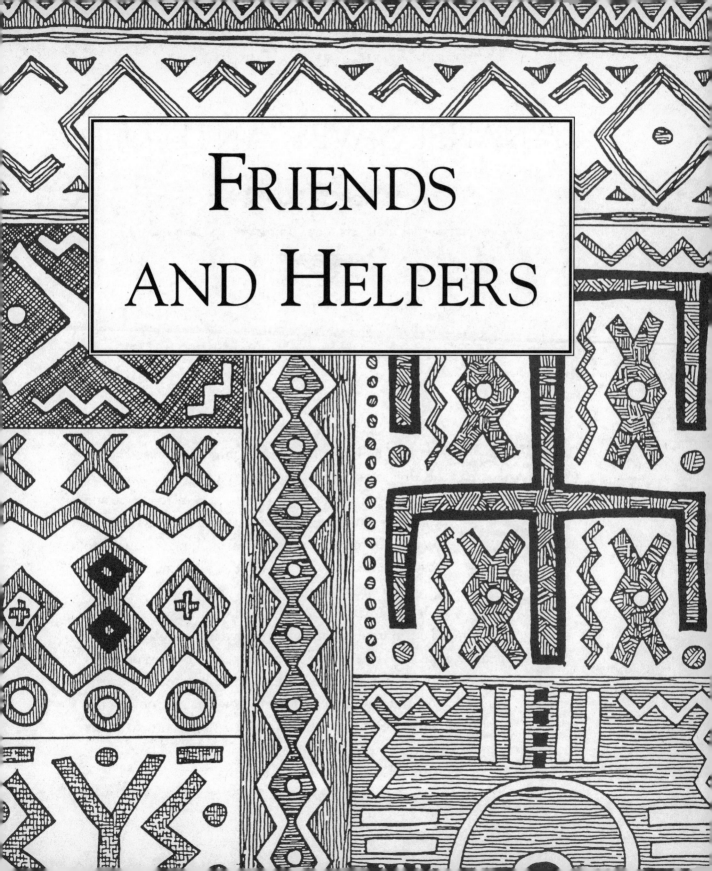

FRIENDS AND HELPERS

ANANSI SAVES ANTELOPE

Doing a favor for a tiny creature eventually pays a big reward.

A bolt of lightning had started a fire. As it raged across the dry savanna, the animals panicked. Some were already surrounded by flames with no way to escape and others were running around frantically looking for a way to safety. While an antelope was looking for a way to escape she heard a tiny voice: "Please let me sit in your ear so you can carry me out of here."

It was Anansi the Spider, and without waiting for an invitation, he jumped down from a branch and settled in the antelope's ear. There seemed to be fire everywhere, and the antelope had no idea of which way to go to avoid it. But the spider knew the way out, and he directed the antelope calmly and confidently: "Go to the left, now straight, now to the right . . . until the antelope's swift legs had carried them both to safety across streams and brooks.

When the fire was far behind them, the spider ran down to the ground along the antelope's leg. "Thank you very much," he said. "I am sure we will meet again."

Sometime later, the antelope gave birth to a little baby. Like all baby antelopes, it was defenseless and spent most of its first few weeks hidden in the shrubs. Later, it could be seen grazing beside its mother. One day, two hunters spotted the mother antelope. While the little one crouched down under the shrubs, the mother leaped up to catch the hunters' attention, and then ran off, staying just out of range of their arrows. After an hour the hunters gave up the chase, and went back to look for the baby antelope. Though they were sure they were searching in the right place, they eventually left the forest empty handed.

Much later, the mother came back. She, too, searched for the baby but could not find it. Then she heard a familiar voice calling her. It was the spider. Anansi led her to a thicket surrounded by a dense spider web. While the hunters had been chasing the mother, Anansi had been very busy weaving webs that had kept the baby invisible—and safe—from the hunters.

THE ANT AND THE PIGEON

An ant is saved by a pigeon, and almost immediately returns the favor.

One day an ant found a grain of corn and decided to take it home. He held it very tight, and hurried as fast as he could, so that nothing would take the grain of corn from him. There was a pond on the way home, but the ant, in its haste, had forgotten about it, and he fell in, corn and all.

The corn slipped from his mouth and went to the bottom of the pond. The ant stayed on top of the water and worked hard to find a place to get out. But after a while, the ant began to be afraid that his strength was about exhausted.

A pigeon came to the pond to drink, and she saw the ant struggling desperately. She decided that she would help the little fellow. She took a long, dry piece of grass and dripped it so that it fell near the ant. He climbed on to the grass and soon got out. The ant caught his breath, and then thanked the pigeon for saving him.

There was a boy near the pond with a bow and arrow. The ant saw him creeping up nearer and nearer to the pigeon. Hurrying as fast as he could, the ant climbed up the boy's leg and gave him a hard bite. The boy dropped his bow and arrow and cried out, and the pigeon saw him and flew to safety.

Each had saved the other. When the pigeon saved the ant she did not know that the ant would ever be able to do anything for her in return. Each was happier because of what each did for the other.

The Bura people say, "Every person is another's butter." Even a small person can do something for a great person.

BADGER AND OTTER ARE FRIENDS

Otter and Badger's friendship is tested when they let anger and hurt feelings keep them apart.

Badger and Otter became friends. "Let's exchange gifts as a mark of our friendship," suggested Badger. "I will bring you fresh honey every day."

"How nice," said Otter. "And I will catch a fish for you every day."

They soon were dear friends and visited each other all the time.

One day while Badger was collecting some honey, he met Tsuro, the hare.

"Where are you going?" asked the nosy hare.

"I am going to visit my good friend, Otter," answered Badger.

The next day Tsuro saw Otter on the path and asked where he was going.

"I am going to visit my dear friend, Badger," he answered.

Now, Tsuro was very annoyed because no one came to visit him. To himself he said, "I will break up this friendship."

The next day Tsuro saw Badger on his way to Otter's house with some honey. The hare ran ahead, hid near Otter's house, and watched. When Badger got closer, he called out, "You, Badger, do you hear me?"

"Who is that?" asked Badger.

"It is I, Otter," said the deceitful hare. "Do you know that my wife and children are ill from eating your wretched honey every day?"

Badger came nearer, intending to enter the house, but Tsuro shouted, "Go back. Don't come here again with your honey."

Badger asked, "My friend, why do you speak to me this way?"

"I told you. Your honey has made us sick. I do not want you to bring honey here any more."

So Badger went away and he was very angry.

The hare ran home quickly, and when he saw Badger coming, he asked, "Have you come back already? Was your friend not at home?"

"I do not wish to speak about him," Badger said. "He does not want my honey. He has insulted me. The friendship is over."

Then Tsuro said, "I would love to have your honey. Please give it to me and let us be friends."

Badger gave it to him, saying, "It is too heavy for me to carry home," and went on his way. When he got home, he told his wife and children what had happened.

The next day Otter caught a beautiful fish and started on his way with it to Badger's house. He said to himself, "I wonder why my friend did not come to see me yesterday? Maybe there is someone sick at his house. I had better go and see." He passed Tsuro's home, but the hare had run ahead and sat, hidden, waiting, near Badger's house.

"Where are you going, Otter?" asked the hare.

"I am going to your house," answered Otter, thinking he was talking to Badger.

"You had better not enter my house with your fish," shouted the hare. "One of my children has been much hurt by a bone from eating your fish. I do not want your old fish." Now Otter was angry, and he headed back home.

When Otter passed Tsuro's house, the hare called out, "What, back so soon? Did you not find your friend at home?"

"He insulted me greatly and that is why I am going home," replied Otter. Then the hare said, "Give me the fish and let us be friends." So Otter gave him the fish and went home.

Thereafter, Badger and Otter stayed at home and did not visit each other any more. But one day as Badger went to get honey, he met Otter on the road and said to him, "You are a bad fellow, Otter. You insulted me greatly the day I came to your house bringing you honey."

"I did not insult you," said Otter.

"Who was it then?" asked Badger.

"I do not know, but I was insulted at your house," said Otter.

"I am certain I never insulted you," said Badger.

"Well, then, let us renew our friendship and visit each other again," they both cried. Thus they became friends again.

When Tsuro saw Otter on his way to Badger's house, he said to him, "Why do you go to visit someone who insulted you?"

"I want to hear more about that matter," replied Otter, and continued on his way. Hearing that, Tsuro ran ahead and sat hidden, awaiting him.

"Do you dare to come here again," cried the hare to Otter. "My children have hardly recovered from the injuries they received from the fish bones. Why do you come again?"

Otter replied, "Stand there, my friend. I am coming to you."

The hare called out, "If you come here, I shall certainly beat you."

"Very well, but I am coming."

When Tsuro saw Otter coming towards him, he ran away.

As Otter could not find anyone, he called out, "Who was talking here?"

When Badger heard this, he came out of his house. "To whom are you talking?" he asked.

"Someone was here, insulting me," Otter replied, "but I do not know where he has gone."

"Let us search for his tracks and see who it was," said Badger.

They found Tsuro's footprints, and followed them to his house. When they reached the hare's house, Tsuro's wife told them her husband was very ill.

"How can he be ill?" said Otter. "I just passed him a little while ago and he was quite well. I want to see him and find out why he insulted me."

"Oh, please, come tomorrow," pleaded Tsuro's wife. "He is really so ill."

Thereupon, the two went away. During the night, Tsuro removed his home, and the next morning, when the two friends returned, everything was gone. "He is the one who tried to break up our friendship," said Otter. "He better never show his face around her again," said Badger. And he never did.

HELP FROM LIGHTNING

The Alur people, who live on the shore of Lake Albert, believe that nature comes to the aid of some people.

Two boys lived in the same village. They were the same age and liked to hunt and explore together. One day they went into the bush and set snares to catch birds. The first boy was lucky—he caught a pigeon. The second boy was unlucky—he only caught a spider. Feeling sorry for the tiny spider, he let it go.

The next day they went into the bush again to set snares. Once more the first boy was lucky—he caught a fat guinea fowl which is delicious to eat. But the second boy was unlucky—he caught only a stray bolt of lightning which he also released.

The following day, both boys were called before the king. He wanted some new grinding stones—large flat stones that are used to grind grain. Cutting a grinding stone is a difficult job, and is usually done by professional stone-cutters who have to chop the stone directly out of the rock.

Wondering what they were going to do, the two boys went out to a quarry near the village. They tried their best to cut some stones, but all they succeeded in doing was blunting the blades on their axes. The boys were becoming frightened. They knew the king would be angry if they failed to do what he had asked.

In desperation, the unlucky boy remembered the lightning he had released—maybe it would help. "Lightning!" he called. "I freed you from my snare, and now I need your help. Please come and cut some grinding stones for me."

Suddenly the sky flashed. Bolts of lightning struck the rock face. Sparks of fire and pieces of rock continued to fly in all directions until a pile of perfectly shaped grinding stones lay on the ground before the boys.

All the people in the village heard the thunder and saw the flashes of lightning. They came hurrying to see what had happened. They were amazed to see the pile of grinding stones, and helped the boys carry them to the king.

The king was very pleased with the two boys, but now he had an even more difficult task for them.

"Bring me a star from the sky," he commanded. No one had ever done such a thing before, and the boys had no idea how to go about this task. Then the unlucky boy remembered the spider he had released from his snare—maybe he would help.

"Spider! I freed you from my snare. Now I need your help. Please bring me a star from the sky."

The spider heard the boy's call for help. It spun an enormous web which reached from earth to sky. Then it climbed up into the sky and plucked a star which it then dragged back down to earth. The boys brought the star to the king.

Needless to say, the king was delighted. He was especially pleased with the second boy who had seemed so unlucky, but who had managed to achieve such wonderful success.

The boy was rewarded with many cows and baskets of food. He became wealthy and respected, and his advice was often sought by the other villagers.

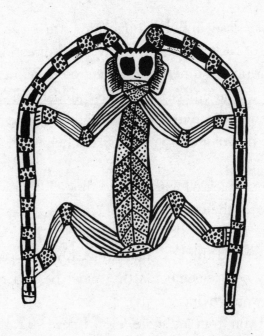

LION, HARE, AND HYENA

*For just a moment, a hyena's lies threaten the trust and friendship between
Simba the lion and his little friend, Sunguru the hare.*

Simba, a bachelor lion lived alone in a cave. In his
younger days the solitude had not bothered him, but
recently he had injured his leg so badly that he had not
been able to hunt, and had begun to realize that companionship had its advantages.

Things would have gone very badly for him if Sunguru
the hare had not looked into his cave one day. Realizing
that Simba was starving, Sunguru at once set about caring for the sick lion.

Under the hare's careful nursing, Simba regained his strength until finally
he was well enough to catch small game for the two of them to eat. Soon,
quite a pile of bones had accumulated outside the entrance to the lion's cave.

One day old Nyangau the hyena, while sniffing around in the hopes of
scrounging something for his supper, caught the scent of the bones. His nose

led him to Simba's cave, but as the bones were too visible from the inside for him to safely steal, he decided that the only means of gaining possession of such tasty morsels for his dinner, would be to make friends with Simba. Therefore, he crept up to the entrance of the cave and cleared his throat.

"Who makes the evening hideous with such dreadful noise?" demanded the lion, rising to his feet.

"It . . . it is I, your friend, Nyangau," stammered the hyena, feeling what little courage he had begin to fade. "I have come to tell you how much you have been missed by the people of the forest, and how greatly we are looking forward to your early return to good health."

"Well, get out!" growled the lion, "for it seems to me that a real friend would have inquired about my health long before this, instead of waiting until I can be of use to him once more. Get out, I say!"

The hyena darted off, his scruffy tail tucked between his bandy legs, and the insulting giggles of the hare ringing in his ears. But he could not forget the pile of tempting bones outside the lion's cave.

"I will try again," said the hyena to himself a few days later. This time he made a point of visiting while the hare was away fetching water to cook the evening meal.

"My friend," said Nyangau, "I am led to believe that the wound on your leg is not healing properly, thanks to the inferior treatment that you are receiving from your so-called friend, Sunguru."

"How dare you say such a thing!" snarled the lion. "It is thanks to Sunguru that I did not starve to death during the worst of my illness, while you never even showed your face!"

"Nevertheless, what I say is true," insisted the hyena. "It is well known throughout the countryside that Sunguru is purposely giving you the wrong treatment to delay your recovery. Don't you realize that when you are well, he will lose his position as your housekeeper? And a very comfortable position for him it is, to be sure! I warn you, my friend, Sunguru is up to no good!"

At that moment the hare returned from the river with his gourd full of water. "Well," he said to the hyena as he put down his load, "I did not expect to see you here again. Tell me, what do you want this time?"

Simba turned to the hare. "I have been listening," he said, "to Nyangau's tales about you. He tells me that you are renowned throughout the country-side for your skill as a healer. He also tells me that the medicines you prescribe are without rival, but he insists that you could have cured the wound upon my leg a long time ago, had it been in your best interests to do so. Is this true?"

Sunguru thought for a moment. He must handle this situation with care, for he knew that Nyangau was trying to trick him. "Well," he answered with hesitation, "yes, and no. You see, I am only a very small person, and some-times the medicines that I require are very big, and I am unable to procure them—as, for instance, in your case, dear Simba."

"What do you mean?" spluttered the lion, sitting up and leaning forward.

"Just this," replied the hare. "I need the skin off the back of a full-grown hyena to place upon your wound before it can be completely healed."

The lion sprang upon Nyangau before the surprised creature had time to get away and, tearing a strip of skin off the foolish fellow's back from his head to his tail, clapped it at once upon the wound on his leg. As the skin came away from the hyena's back, the hairs that remained firmly embedded in his flesh not only stretched, but stood on end as well.

Thus it is, that to this day, Nyangau and his kind have long, coarse hairs sticking up upon the crest of their misshapen bodies.

Sunguru's fame as a doctor spread far and wide after this episode, for the wound upon Simba's leg healed without further trouble, although it was many weeks before the hyena had the courage to show himself in public again.

THE MAN AND THE BIRD

A poor man's wishes will forever be granted, if he can only keep the cause of his good fortune a secret.

Long ago, there lived a poor man and his wife. Having no possessions, the husband was obliged to search the forest for the food they ate. Often, it would mean a meal of roots and berries, but sometimes he was fortunate enough to catch a bird or animal in one of the traps and snares he set along the trails.

There was, however, a very large and beautiful bird which, although he saw it everyday, had proved too clever to be enticed into even his most carefully hidden traps. Besides this, it seemed to mock him as it remained just out of range of his bow and arrow, so that eventually he determined that, come what may, he would capture it.

He was just about to return home empty-handed and hungry late one afternoon when he remembered a trap he had forgotten to check. He retraced his steps and, upon reaching it, gave a shout of joy for there,

securely caught by a leg, was the lovely creature that had fooled him so
often.

He rushed forward, and seizing the bird by the neck said, "Today I have
got you, my friend!" whereupon he took out his knife and prepared to kill
it, thankful that he would have at least something, if only a bird, to take
back to his wife that evening.

"Mercy, human, mercy!" cried the poor creature, as the grip upon its
throat tightened. "Spare my life, and you have my word that you will not
regret your kindness."

The man loosened his grasp and stepped back in surprise, the better to
view the rare, golden-plumaged creature that addressed him, while it continued to speak. "Although my only earthly possessions are these golden
feathers that cover me," said the bird, "yet in them lies a magic that will
provide you with both food and drink for ever more. Release me, good
human, for the thongs that hold me have eaten most painfully into my
flesh."

Now, this was a difficult situation for the man. What if the bird was
tricking him? He would lose the only food that he and his wife might have
for several days. And yet, the bird itself might also have a wife—and maybe
even babies—waiting anxiously for its return, also hungry, and hoping for
food.

Then again, what if the bird spoke the truth? Why, he would be able to
sit back in idleness for ever more! Such would be riches beyond counting.
Besides, who had ever heard of a bird that spoke? He decided that he would
risk it, and he untied the thong that had bitten so deeply into the poor
creature's leg.

Thankfully the lovely bird stretched its aching limbs then, carefully
pulling a golden-colored feather from each wing, gave them to the man.
"With this gift, human," it said, "I also give you words of warning: if you

wish to retain the magic properties of these feathers, you must neither speak nor boast to others of your good fortune. Should you do so, the power of my gift will vanish, and you will be left as poor as you are today. Therefore, do not treat my warning lightly. Wish as you hold these feathers in you hands, and they will fulfill your every desire."

The man thanked the bird for its gift and hastened home, wishing as he hurried along the path that he would find food in plenty waiting for him when he arrived. Which would he find, he wondered—starvation, or plenty?

The golden bird was as good as its word, for inside his hut the food vessels were overflowing, and the dried-up spring nearby gushed forth its sparkling waters once more, sparing his wife her daily walk to a water hole many miles away. Life smiled upon the couple at last. The husband was able to idle the days away, wishing for all the things that made life sweet, which came to him in abundance.

On many occasions the wife questioned her husband as to how it came about that though he no longer hunted in the forest, yet she always found food in her cooking pots, and luxuries besides? But each time she questioned him, the man avoided an explanation.

At last, as so often happens when life becomes too easy, the man grew careless of what he said, boasting to all around of his wealth, so that the woman grew increasingly suspicious of their good fortune. "Husband," she said, "you show no signs of astonishment at our wealth. You must be hiding something from me. Maybe at night while I sleep, you steal the good things that I find cooking upon the fire. Or perhaps you have secret dealings with 'the evil one' to bring sparkling water bubbling from the parched earth, when all else is dry! I must ask the witch-doctor to satisfy my mind upon these two matters."

Now, the very mention of witch-doctor struck terror into the heart of her simple husband, who had no wish for dealings with things he did not understand. "Wife," he begged, "do not call such a one, for by his arts he will surely find the magic feathers that provide us with all the good things that I bring."

Too late the man remembered the parting warning of the bird, as he realized that not only had he now shared his secret with his wife, but that he had boasted to others of his riches. It was with a deep foreboding that he held the feathers and wished his daily wishes on the following day, and his worst fears were confirmed—all his wishes remained unfulfilled and, on hastening to his bubbling spring, he found only drying mud.

Once more the couple felt the pangs of hunger, and the husband was obliged to reset his traps along the paths of the forest as of old. Life was harder, even than before, for the prolonged drought made food even harder to find. However, one day while visiting his traps as usual, he met a neighbor with his dog. "Let us hunt together," said Wanjobi, pleased to have company as he continued upon his rounds. To his great surprise they found the same golden bird, caught in one of the particularly well-hidden snares.

The husband rushed towards it exclaiming, "Once more you are in my power, oh golden bird, for I have caught you again! Give me two more of your magic feathers, and I will release you."

"Spare my life yet a second time, good human!" begged the bird, as he at once untied the noose that held it. But no sooner had he loosened the poor creature, than the neighbor's dog pounced upon it. Dragging the animal away with difficulty, the husband hastily picked up the bird and, running to the edge of the forest he released it, not waiting for his payment of the precious golden feathers.

"Once more, human, I thank you," said the bird gratefully. "But for your timely help, the dog would have killed me. In the past I made you a gift of my magic feathers because you spared my life when you and your wife were hungry, but there was a condition with my giving. You have suffered for not listening to my warning, and maybe you have learned your lesson.

"This time I will give you all that is within my power to give, and I make no condition with my gift. The magic in these feathers will last forever, for you have not only spared my life again—you have *saved* it. Also, you have trusted my word on two occasions."

Then, plucking two more feathers, one from each wing, the bird gave them to the man. Then, spreading its golden wings, the bird rose up into the heavens, and was gone.

It was a very happy man who returned to his wife that day. But he also never forgot that his failure to listen to his benefactor's warning had brought about his earlier downfall.

THE FOUR FRIENDS

Considered useless by their ungrateful owners, four elderly animals band together and live out their years together happily.

Lebende was a decrepit old donkey, but he had known better times—times when he was his master's most cherished possession, lovingly tended and fed. Life was good in those days, and he willingly toiled for the hand that fed him, obeying his master's every wish.

He carried heavy loads to and fro at reaping time, and patiently submitted to the children's demands as they rode him to herd his master's cows. Even his master's heavy weight was sometimes transported without complaint upon his sturdy back.

How different were things now, when old age had caused the strength to forsake his strong legs, leaving them shaky and insecure, so that they could no longer bear even the children's weight upon his sagging back.

Life would not be too bad, even now, if only they would allow him to drowse away in peace these last few years that were left to him. But no longer was he permitted to graze the lush pastures reserved for those who worked. He had to rely instead upon the tasteless, dry grass, and try to keep his scraggy body and tired soul together as best he could.

Matters were made even worse by the fact on that very morning he had heard his master grumble, "Wife, I can no longer stand the stubborn laziness of Lebende. It is time that I put an end to his uselessness, for all day long he hangs mournfully around our hut, eating the grass that would benefit our cows. Tomorrow, I will have him killed."

There were tears in the old donkey's eyes as he thought of his beloved master's plan. "I must leave this place at once," he decided, "before it is too late! There is greater safety for me among the wild creatures of the forest, than there is among those whom I have learned to trust."

Therefore, after darkness had fallen, Lebende sadly stole away into the wilds, wondering what the future had in store for him.

Caring little where he went, so long as it was away from human habitation, he walked for several miles until, weary and worn, he lay down to rest. The sun rose clear and smiling the following morning, and he felt more cheerful as he set off along the path upon which he found himself.

After traveling for about a mile, he came upon a dog lying disconsolately under a bush. "At least here is a familiar face," he thought, and so addressed him, "My friend, why do you appear so sorrowful upon such a bright and pleasant morning?" he asked.

The dog sighed mournfully. "I have good cause to be sad," he said, "for this very morning I overheard my master tell his wife that as I am now too old to assist in the chase, and to raise the alarm when thieves prowl around his hut at night, he intends to kill me. Do you wonder that I have left my home?"

"Well," said the donkey, "you and I are companions in distress. Let us throw in our lot together, and seek refuge in a far distant country, where we will be safe from the humans whom we have served so faithfully."

The dog gladly accepted the donkey's invitation to join him, and the two proceeded upon their journey.

Before they had traveled far they heard a pitiful meowing close by. "Listen!" said the dog. "Surely that cry of sorrow comes from one who has fallen upon worse misfortune than either you or me!" and they turned aside to find a pathetically thin and mangy cat.

"Hello!" said the dog and donkey together, "what are you doing so far from the haunts of the humans whom you serve?"

"Huh!" said the cat, "I have barely escaped with my life. Last night while I was sleeping peacefully by the fire in my mistress's hut, I was awakened by her telling her grandson to catch and put me into a bag, and throw me in the river. She said that I am too old and feeble to earn my keep by catching the rats that eat her grain. How easily these humans forget the years of service that we have rendered them in the past!"

"Then join us, friend," invited Lebende, "for we are in the same plight. Come, we will seek peace in a new country." And the three old animals set off together.

Their path led under a large, spreading tree, and they were about to pass beneath it when they saw a rooster sitting upon one of the overhanging branches. "What!" exclaimed the dog, "you, too, so far from mankind! Tell us, friend why are you sitting up there?"

The rooster gave a frightened look around. "Had I not still had some power left in these old wings, my master would have knocked me over," he sighed with relief. "It was fortunate that I happened to overhear him discussing the fact that, because I am too old to father any more of my kind,

I would provide the family with their next meal. A great pot of water was steaming upon the fire, ready to put me in . . . oh, it was dreadful!" and the poor bird shuddered at the memory of it.

A murmur of sympathy passed among the three travelers. "You are fortunate to have fallen in with us," said the donkey, "for we also have been forced to leave the security of our masters' homes. Join us, friend, and together we will seek the old age happiness that our masters would deny us."

The animals, each now happy in the companionship of the other three, continued along the path in search of a place in which to end their lives in peace. But as the night closed down upon them, they realized that they had been traveling since the early day and were tired, so they decided to rest until morning.

Finding a suitable resting place beneath a tree, the donkey and dog chose to sleep under its sheltering boughs, while the cat and rooster preferred the safety of the higher branches. The rooster scrambled to the very top of the tree, where he prepared to settle for the night. "Well, well!" he exclaimed, after first craning his neck to get a better view of the surroundings, "we are near a human habitation after all. We must be careful, for I see a light in the distance."

The cat and dog were relieved to hear this, because of the four of them, only the donkey was accustomed to sleep without a shelter over his head, and the night was cold. Therefore, the cat and dog suggested that someone should be sent to the hut to investigate.

"The night air has already set me shivering," said the dog, "and besides, we might find something to ease our hunger. It has been a long day without food."

The cat crept up to the hut from which the light came, and peeped inside. "*Ssss-kat!*" he spat when he returned to his friends, "it is a wicked place, for they eat their own kind! There can be no safety for us among such as these." And, sure enough, it was the abode of cannibals, for the floor was littered with human bones.

The rooster cleared his throat. "I have a plan," he said. "Such people should not be left to live in peace. Let us drive them from their home, and we will take possession of it. You, Lebende, must stand upon your hind legs with your front feet upon the wall beside the door; and you," turning to the dog, "must climb onto Lebende's back, with the cat mounted on top of you, and I will perch on top of the cat's head. Then, each and all together, we must raise our voices as loudly as we can. We will soon have the owners of the hut running for their lives!"

The rooster was right. The cannibals took one terrified look at the strange, ghostly apparition which they thought was about to attack them, and rushed out of the hut into the night.

"Splendid!" the donkey congratulated the rooster, "but what will happen when they return, as they are bound to do?"

"I have already thought of that," replied the rooster. "We must all four attack them with force from *inside* the hut. They will be far too frightened to return after a second shock." So when each had satisfied his hunger at the cannibals' expense, the donkey settled down behind the door; the dog stretched out beside him; the cat curled up in front of the fire, and the rooster perched on top of the half-closed door.

Some little time elapsed before the dog heard the approach of the owners of the hut, and warned his companions to be ready for them. Quietly, the leading cannibal crept in at the half-closed door and, seeing the cat's eyes glinting where the fire had been, he thought that some sparks still lingered.

He bent down to blow them back to life—but what a shock greeted him! The cat sprang into his face, scratching him with ten sharp claws, while at the same time the dog attacked his legs. He turned to escape the unseen danger only to be kicked by the donkey's hard hoofs and, as he reached the door, the rooster alighted upon his head and nearly pecked his eyes out.

With screams of fear and pain, the cannibal rushed from the hut and, joined by his companions, the three fled until they had put many miles between themselves and the fearful danger—never to return.

Thus the four friends lived united in happiness and security in their own little home until, one by one, they were separated by death—each being called to his rest naturally by the voice of Time, as they had wished—and not by the hand of man.

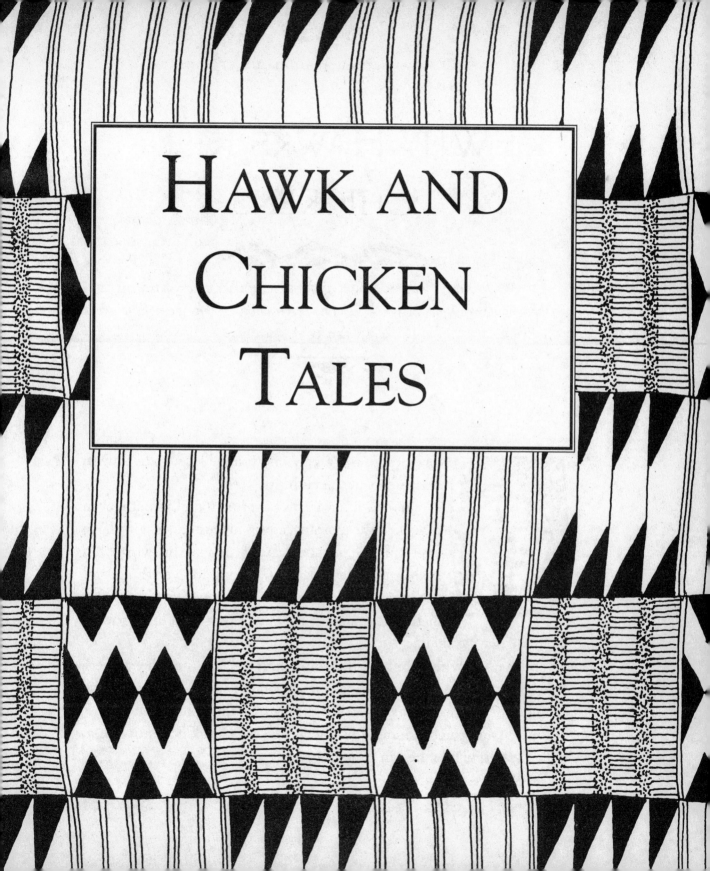

HAWK AND CHICKEN TALES

WHY HAWKS KILL CHICKENS

*When a hen's parents cannot afford to return her dowry payment,
the king decrees that the hawk, who has been wronged, has the right to eat
chickens whenever he pleases.*

Once there was a very fine young hen who lived with her parents in the bush.

One day a hawk was hovering round, about eleven o'clock in the morning, as was his custom, making large circles in the air and scarcely moving his wings. His keen eyes were wide open, taking in everything—for nothing moving ever escapes the eyes of a hawk, no matter how small it may be or how high up in the air the hawk may be circling.

This hawk saw the pretty hen picking up some corn near her father's house. He therefore closed his wings slightly, and in a flash was close to the ground. Then, spreading his wings out to check his flight, he alighted close to the hen and perched himself on the fence—as a hawk does not like to walk on the ground if he can help it.

He then greeted the young hen with his most enticing whistle, and offered to marry her. She agreed, so the hawk spoke to her parents, and paid the agreed amount of dowry, which consisted mostly of corn. The next day he returned, and took the young hen off to his home.

Shortly after this, a young cock who lived near the young hen's former home found out where she was living, and having been in love with her for some time—in fact, ever since his spurs had grown—determined to try and make her return to her own country. Therefore, at dawn, first having flapped his wings once or twice, he crowed in his best voice to the young hen. When she heard the sweet sound of the cock, she could not resist his invitation. She quickly went out to him, and together they walked off to her parent's house, the young cock strutting in front, crowing proudly at intervals.

The hawk, who was hovering high up in the sky, quite out of sight of any ordinary eye, saw what had happened, and was furious. He made up his mind at once that he would obtain justice from the king, and flew off to Calabar, where he told the whole story, and asked for immediate redress.

The king sent for the parents of the hen, and told them they must repay to the hawk the dowry they had received from him on the marriage of their daughter, which was according to the custom. But the hen's parents said that they were so poor that they could not possibly afford to pay. So the king told the hawk that he could eat any of the cock's children whenever and wherever he found them as payment of his dowry, and, if the cock made any complaint, the king would not listen to him.

HAWK'S GIFT FROM THE KING

Hawks have a good reason for choosing chickens as their favorite food.

During the reign of the king of Calabar, it was customary for rulers to give big feasts, to which all the subjects—the birds of the air and animals of the forest, and the things that lived in the water—were invited. The king always used the hawk—his favorite messenger—to deliver the invitations.

The hawk had served the king faithfully for many years, and finally was ready to retire. In gratitude for his long service, the king told the hawk to bring any living creature, bird or animal, to him, and after seeing it, he would allow the hawk to live on that particular species in the future.

The hawk then flew over the forests until he found a young owl which had tumbled out of its nest. This the hawk brought to the king, who agreed that the hawk had his permission to eat owls. The hawk then carried the owlet away, and told his friends what the king had said.

One of the wisest of the hawk's friends said, "Tell me, when you seized the young owlet, what did the parents say?" The hawk replied that the father and mother owls kept quiet, and never said anything. The hawk's friend then advised him to return the owlet to his parents, as he could never tell what the owls would do to him in the nighttime, and as they had made no noise, they surely must be plotting some dreadful reprisal.

The next day the hawk carried the owlet back to his parents and left him near the nest. He then flew about, trying to find some other bird which would do as his food; but as all the birds had heard that the hawk had seized the owlet, they hid themselves, and would not come out when he was near.

As he was flying home, he saw some fowls near a house, basking in the sun and scratching in the dust. There were also several small chickens running about and chasing insects, and an old hen clucking and calling to them from time to time.

The hawk decided that he would take a chicken, so he swooped down and caught the smallest one in his strong claws. Immediately, the cocks began to make a great noise, and the hen ran after him, with her feathers fluffed out, calling loudly for him to drop her child. But he carried it off, and all the fowls and chickens at once ran screaming around the yard, some taking shelter under bushes and others trying to hide themselves in the tall grass. He then carried the chicken to the king, telling him that he had returned the owlet to its parents, as he did not want him for food. The king told the hawk that for the future he could always feed on chickens.

The hawk then took the chicken home, and his friend who dropped in to see him, asked him what the parents of the chicken had done when they saw their child taken away.

"They all made a lot of noise," said the hawk, "and the old hen chased me, but nothing really happened."

His friend then said that it would now be quite safe to eat chickens, as the people who made plenty of noise in the daytime would go to sleep at night and not do him any injury. The only people to be afraid of were those who when they were injured, kept quite silent. You might be certain that they were plotting mischief, and would get revenge the first chance they got.

THE MISSING RING

A ring is necessary for a wedding ceremony, but the one the hawk had made for his bride is missing.

The hawk was ready to get married. He traveled about from one village to another until at last he found the right girl. He spoke to the girl's father, and all of the arrangements were made. After setting the date for the wedding, the hawk returned home.

He gathered all the gold dust he had saved and took it to a goldsmith to have a ring made. Because the hawk was so handsome, some creatures envied him and said unkind things behind his back. Not everyone wished him well.

When the day of the wedding was near, the hawk went to the goldsmith to get the ring for his bride. Then he called for his friends to accompany him to her village. His friend the lizard came. His friend the guinea fowl came. And so did his friends mantis and snake. Many others from his village also joined the wedding party.

They went to the house of the girl the hawk had chosen. The hawk introduced his friend's to the girl's family, and the celebration began. After much drumming and singing, the hawk put his hand in his pocket for the ring. But the ring was not there. He searched through his clothes, but the ring could not be found.

At last he cried out, "The ring has been stolen!"

The headman of the village said, "Let everyone be searched."

So everyone in the village was searched, but the ring was not found.

The hawk approached the girl's father. "I took all the gold dust I had been saving," he said, "and I had a most beautiful ring made. I brought it with me, but someone who does not wish me well has stolen it from my pocket."

The father of the girl said, "Everyone has been searched but the ring has not been found. Though you have an explanation, the fact remains—there is no ring. Therefore, the wedding cannot take place. When you return with the ring, we will talk of the matter again."

The hawk was overcome with shame. His friends, too, were ashamed. The lizard was speechless—he could only move his head from side to side as if to say, "Oh, what a terrible thing!"

The guinea fowl clapped his hands violently against his head, saying, "Disgrace, disgrace!"

The mantis kept hitting his sides with his fists, saying "Oh, no, it cannot be true!"

And the snake opened his mouth, and put out his tongue, turning this way and that to show everyone that he did not have the ring there.

The hawk and his friends went away. "I will search for the person who stole the ring," the hawk said. He flew into the air and soared over the countryside, looking for the thief.

As for the lizard, he has never spoken a word since that day. He simply moves his head from side to side as if to say, "Oh, what a terrible thing!" Because the guinea fowl repeatedly clapped his hands so hard against his head, his head became bald, and so it remained. Because the mantis struck his sides so hard with his fists, he became very thin. And whenever the snake meets someone, he opens his mouth and puts his tongue out to show that he does not have the ring hidden there.

The hawk has never given up the search. He forever soars and hovers in the sky, diving down now and then upon some moving creature to see if it is wearing the missing ring.

WHY THE HAWK CATCHES CHICKENS

Joel Chandler Harris

Uncle Remus always has an engaging story to explain why animals behave the way they do—as well as a lesson to be learned.

One day, Uncle Remus sat in the sun making a fish basket. The little boy watched him weave the white oak splits together a long time, waiting for a story. Finally a bantam rooster, wandering near, crowed shrilly three or four times. The noise broke the silence so unexpectedly that Uncle Remus jumped, and then hurled the unfinished basket at the rooster, which ran away screaming and cackling. The rooster belonged to the little boy, and was a favorite pet, but the youngster laughed heartily at Uncle Remus's irritation, which was partly real and partly affected.

"Nummine!" exclaimed the old man, recovering his basket. "What fattens de chickens fattens de hawk."

"Now, Uncle Remus," the child protested, not catching the meaning of the proverb, "you know hawks don't eat corn and worms and bugs."

"No, dey don't," responded the old man emphatically. "Ef de did, dat der bantin chicken might live ter git gray. Mos' eve'y mornin' der's a big hawk sailin' roun' here, en he'll sholy git dat der uppity little rooster. You better have 'im put in de pot now. I been noticin' dat hawks is got a spite at roosters, speshually when dey ain't too big fer um ter tote off. Dey wuz a time when de hawks ain't had no taste fer chicken, but dat time done gone by."

"Didn't hawks always catch chickens, Uncle Remus?" asked the little boy.

"Sholy I done tell you 'bout dat," the old man remarked, looking at the child with a great affectation of astonishment. "Now den, rack yo' brain, en tell me ef I ain't done tol' you how come de hawk be ter constant a-huntin' chickens en flyin' off wid um."

The little boy thought the matter over, and then shook his head.

"Well!" exclaimed Uncle Remus, "hit's in about de fus' tale I hear my grandaddy tel."

The little boy said nothing, but sat in an expectant attitude. The old man gathered together a dozen or more splits, placed them where they would be in reach, and then began:

" 'Tain't no use, ter tell you nothin' 'tall 'bout how hawks does now. Dey er done broke in ter ketchin' chickens, but way back yonder dey ain't know nothin' 'tall 'bout no chicken, kaze de ain't had de tas'e of um. I dunner know what they did eat, but I hear tell dat times got so hard wid ole Brer Hawk dat he had ter scuffle 'roun' right hard. Yit it seem like scufflin' ain't do no good. He fly dis away, en he fly dat, yet he ain't fin' nothin' ter eat. Whiles he wuz flyin' roun' he seed de Sun shinin' up dar in de elements, so he bowed his head en say, 'Howdy.' " En de Sun he howdied back, he did, en dey struck up a kinder speakin' 'quaintance.

"Bimeby, Brer Hawk made so bol' ez ter tell de Sun 'bout de trouble w'at he got, en so de Sun, he up'n 'low, he did, dat ef Brer Hawk kin ketch 'im in bed, he'll git 'im all de vittles he kin eat en show 'im whar ter git mo'."

"Catch the Sun in bed, Uncle Remus?" asked the little boy.

"Dat what I said, honey. Dis make mo' trouble fer Brer Hawk. He got up sooner en sooner eve'y mornin', but eve'y time he lay eyes on de Sun, he wuz up en a-shinin'. Den he sot up all night, but dat ain't make no diffunce. He can't ketch de Sun in bed. Hit went on dis away till Brer Hawk git so weak he kin skacely ruffle a fedder.

"He 'uz hoppin 'bout in de top uv a great big pine when he hear Brer Rooster callin' 'im. He tuck a notion dat Brer Rooster wuz des makin' game un 'im, so he holler back, sezee:

" 'Don't bodder 'long er me, Brer Rooster. Scratch up yo' little grub worms en cackle over um, en eat um, but don't pester 'long er me."

" 'Brer Rooster holler back, sezee:

" 'What de matter wid you? How come you look so pale?"

"Well," the old man continued, "atter while Brer Hawk drapped down en sot on de fence, whar he kin talk ter Brer Rooster, kaze he so hongry it make his tongue weak. He sot dar on de fence, he did, en up'n tol' Brer Rooster 'bout how he been tryin' ter ketch de Sun in bed. Dis make Brer Rooster laugh till you might er heerd 'im squall all over de place. He 'low, sezee:

" 'Massy, massy! Whyn't you tell me? Whyn't you tell me long ago?"

"Wid dat, Brer Rooster up'n say, sezee, dat dey ain't no mornin' but what he kin ketch de Sun in bed, en he tell Brer Hawk dat ef he'll des come en roos' some'rs close by, he kin ketch de Sun de ve'y nex' mornin'. Brer Rooster say, sezee, dat when he clap his wing en crow, den de time done come fer Brer Hawk ter start off ter ketch de Sun in bed.

"Well, den, ole Brer Hawk look like he mighty thankful. He bowed his head, he did, en say he gwine stay ez close ter Brer Rooster ez he kin. Dey sot dar on de roos', dey did, des like two bluebirds on a fence post. Bimeby, bout er nour 'fo' day, Brer Rooster woke up, en clap his wings en holler:

"'Now yo' time ter go!'"

"Wid dat, Brer Hawk riz en flew, en he flewd so fas' en he flewd so fur dat he come ter de place whar de Sun live at, en he cotch de Sun in bed."

"The Sun in bed, Uncle Remus?" exclaimed the little boy.

"In bed!" responded the old man, with unusual emphasis, "right dar in bed. En 'twant no trundle bed needer. It wuz one er deze yer big beds wid high posties. Yasser! De sun wuz in dar, en he had de bed kivver all drawd up 'roun' his head, en he 'uz snorin'. Brer Hawk rapped on de headboard, en holler out, sezee:

" 'Mos' time fer day ter break! Git up fum dar! Brekfus 'll be mighty late ef you lay dar all day!'"

"Sun 'low, 'Who dat?'"

"Brer Hawk say, ' 'Tain't nobody but me.'"

"Sun 'low' 'What you wanter come wakiní me up fer? I boun' I'll have de headache de whole blessid day.'"

"Den Brer Hawk put de Sun in min' er de promise what he made. Den de Sun got mad. He 'low, sezee:

" 'How you speck I gwine fin' you in vittles? Who show you de way ter my bed?'"

"Brer Hawk say it 'uz Brer Rooster. Den de Sun raise up in bed, he did, en wink one eye, en 'low, sezee:

" 'Go back dar en tell yo' Brer Rooster dat he got to fn' you in vittles.'"

"Brer Hawk ain't like dis much, en he sorter hung 'roun', like he waitin' fer sumpin. Dis make de Sun mad, en he jump out er bed en run Brer Hawk out'n de house. Brer Hawk ain't know what to do. He flewd back ter whar Brer Rooster wuz scratchin' in de trash pile, en tole 'im what de Sun say. Dis make Brer Rooster laugh. He 'low, sezee:

" 'How I gwine ter fin' you in vittles? I got a might big fambly ter look atter, en I be bless ef dey don't git hongrier en hongrier eve'y day dat comes.'"

"Brer Hawk 'low, sezee: 'I'm s'posed ter eat, Brer Rooster, en I'm lots hongrier dan what yo' fambly is."

"Brer Rooster 'low, sezee: "Well, Brer Hawk, you 'er mo' dan welcome ter drap down here en scratch in de trash. I speck yo' claws des ez good ez what min' is. 'Sides dat, you ain't s'posed ter holler en cackle eve'y time you fine a worm."

"But Brer Hawk shake his head. Dat kinder doin's don't nigh suit 'im. Hit look too much like work. So he sail up in de treetop, en sot dar, en bimeby here come ole Miss Hen wid 'er chickens, which dey let in ter scratchin' 'longside Brer Rooster. Brer Hawk look at um, en he ax hisse'f, sezee: 'What make my mouf water?" Den he 'membered 'bout how de sun wunk at 'im, en it come 'cross his min' dat chicken meat might tas'e good. Wid dat he drapped down on one er Brer Rooster's chilluns, en kyard it off, en it fit his appetite so mighty well dat he been eatiní Brer Rooster's fambly eve'y chance he git."

Uncle Remus paused to trim and smooth the end of a split. Then he said, "Brer Hawk hongry yit. You better watch out fer yo' bantam'."

RABBIT STORIES

Because Southern blacks drew much of their story material from the barnyard, fields and woods which made up their environment, forest creatures had a significant role in their stories. Brer (a contraction of "Brother") Rabbit, the popular trickster character who appears throughout so much of the African-American folklore, is the rascal who never tires of concocting deceptions and hoaxes. But just why the rabbit and the fox were so often featured in the stories, instead of the more familiar coon and possum, remains a mystery.

WHO ATE THE BUTTER?

Not only does Rabbit get out of doing any work, but he eats all the food out of Fox's icebox and then blames the theft on Bear.

The Fox had a big plantation and the rest of the animals were all working for him. Fox had them all chopping weeds out of the cornfield. Soon, Rabbit gets tired and wants to fool around so he starts thinking of an excuse to get away. But Fox had Bear overseeing for him, and Bear was pretty tough on Rabbit because he knew Rabbit was shiftless—just lollygagging around and doing nothing all day.

Well, pretty soon Rabbit calls Bear over and tells him he's going to have to take about an hour off. Bear wants to know what for, and Rabbit says his wife is about to have a baby and needs his help.

Bear says okay, and Rabbit skeddadles real fast. Then he looks around for some mischief to get into, and finally has an idea. He's all tired and hungry, and he knows that Fox has gone into the city, so Rabbit decides to go over to Fox's house. He looks in the icebox, finds some fried chicken and fruit, and eats it up. Then he skips out into the shrubs and rests until he notices the hour is about up.

When Rabbit gets back to the field everyone wants to know what he named the baby. The first thing that comes into Rabbit's mind is all the food in the icebox, which he wants to get back to, so he said, "Number One Gone."

Rabbit begins to work again, but the more he works the more he's thinking about that food still in the icebox, and how he can get back to it. Well, rabbits have more than one baby at time, so he calls Bear back and tells him, "It's about time, Mr. Bear."

"Time for what?" asks Bear.

"Time for my wife to have another baby," says Rabbit.

Bear let him go again, and Rabbit made a beeline for the icebox. He started on some ham, and didn't stop till it was all gone.

When Rabbit gets back to the field the others want to know what he named the second baby. Rabbit tells them, "Number Two Gone." Then Rabbit starts working again, while everyone else is wondering why he gave his babies such odd names.

After about an hour, Rabbit calls Bear over again with the same excuse, and then makes another beeline for Fox's icebox. This time he eats up all the beef—he can only eat so much at one time, you know. When he gets back he tells everyone that this baby's name is "Half Gone."

After working maybe a half hour, Rabbit says he has to take another leave of absence. He hurries over to Fox's icebox, drinks up all the juice and milk he can hold, and goes back to the field.

"What's this one's name?" they want to know.

"Three Fourths Gone," says Rabbit.

Rabbit works a little bit longer and then says he has to go again. This time he drinks up all the cream, and eats all the cheese and butter. When he gets back to the field he tells everyone, "Well, that's the last baby and I named him 'All Gone.' "

Late in the afternoon, Fox comes back from town, driving in his big

Cadillac out to the field. "What's been goin' on while I was gone?" he says. "Someone ate up all my food."

"Well, everyone's been here all day except for Brother Rabbit," said Bear, "and I really don't think he had time to do it because he's been helping his wife have her babies."

"Well, when everyone gets in camp tonight, I'll find out who done it," said Fox.

That night Fox arranged for a big barbecue. After working hard all day, and then eating so much barbecue, everyone is just exhausted and they go right to sleep. While they're sleeping, Fox builds a great big fire. He knows that the heat from the fire will make the butter run out of whoever ate it. But Fox was drowsy, too, and while he was sitting up waiting to see who the butter was coming out of, he fell asleep.

For some reason, Rabbit woke up and saw a pool of butter all around him—and he knew what Fox was up to. He rubbed the butter all over Bear and then tiptoed down to the pond and washed himself off—not a speck of butter was left on him. When he got back to camp, everybody was sound asleep and the fire was still going. Soon, Rabbit's fur was all fluffy and dry. Rabbit picked up a little pebble, threw it at Fox to wake him up, and then laid down and pretended he was asleep.

Fox wakes up and decides it's time to examine everyone while they're still asleep. Since Rabbit was the only one that left the field that day, he thought he should check him first. But Rabbit was all dry.

"Bear's the biggest and best able to eat two pounds of butter," thought Fox, "so I'll check him next." Sure enough, Bear was covered in butter.

Rabbit, who was watching everything, knew Fox was headed to the house to get his shotgun. He lay real quiet, just watching. When Fox was almost within shooting distance of Bear, Rabbit wakes Bear up and tells him Fox is going to shoot him for eating up all his food. Bear is all surprised and confused and wants to argue about it, but Rabbit tells him, "You better run."

"I don't have anything to run for," says Bear.

"You just wait a minute more and you'll have something to run for," says Rabbit.

Just then, Fox sees Bear standing up and figures he's trying to get away, and lets both barrels loose.

"Well, Brother Bear, I guess you got something to run for now," says Brother Rabbit.

Bear cut out through the thicket while Fox was reloading, and the two of them went running—Bear with Fox shooting at him.

Rabbit tells Fox he'll help catch Bear, but instead he runs off and hides. After a while, Fox loses sight of Bear and gives up the chase.

Pretty soon, Rabbit catches up with Bear and says, "I told you so, I told you Fox was going to kill you for eating up all his food."

"But, Brother Rabbit, I swear I didn't do it," says Bear.

"It don't make no difference," says Rabbit. "He's going to kill you anyway because you know you'll never change his mind."

Bear was so upset. "What should I do?" he asked Rabbit.

"Well if I were you, I'd go to some other part of the woods," advised Rabbit, "because you definitely can't live around here anymore."

And that's what Bear did.

Rabbit couldn't have been more pleased with himself. He skipped back to Fox's house. Fox was sitting on his front porch with his shotgun across his lap—just in case Bear came back and tried to soft-talk him. But Rabbit told Fox he didn't have anything to worry about any more.

"How come?" said Fox.

"Because I chased Bear into some quicksand," said Rabbit.

Fox was so grateful he made Rabbit his new foreman, and no one ever heard from Bear again.

WHY THE RABBIT HAS A SHORT TAIL AND LONG EARS

Though there are many stories about how clever Brother Rabbit is, in this one he is finally outsmarted.

Once upon a time, Brother Rabbit had a beautiful, long bushy tail. He thought he was very handsome, and was mighty proud of that tail. And every time he'd see Brother Fox, he'd shake his tail and wave it all around. This made Brother Fox pretty angry, and he studied how to get even with that boastful Rabbit.

Well, one day, Brother Fox went fishing and he had mighty good luck. As he was coming home with a whole mess of fish slung over his shoulder, he bumped into Brother Rabbit. "Say, Brother Fox," he asked, "how did you catch so many fish?" Brother Rabbit just *loved* fish.

Brother Fox said to himself, "I think I know just how to get even with Brother Rabbit for always showing off his bushy tail." But out loud he said, "It's easy, Brother Rabbit. Any cold night, all you got to do is go down to the creek and hang your tail in the water. But you have to let it hang there from sundown to sunup the next morning, and you'll have more fish than you can pull out."

"All right," said Brother Rabbit, "I believe that I'll go fishing tonight." So he took a blanket, and bait, and sat on a log with his tail in the water in the middle of the creek. It got so cold that he shivered all over, and his teeth chattered. His fingers and toes were red, and he thought his ears and nose would freeze. But he sat there all night, with his tail in the creek, thinking about the fried fish he was going to have for breakfast. When the sun began to rise, Brother Rabbit was ready to pull in his fish, but his tail was frozen in the ice. He pulled and he pulled, but his tail was stuck fast. Now that it was daylight, and he was right out in the open, Brother Rabbit was afraid that Man would come along and see him. So he began to holler, "Help! Help! Help!"

Brother Owl was the first to hear him. He flew over the creek, and there he saw Brother Rabbit sitting on a log. Brother Owl took a hold of Brother Rabbit's right ear and began to pull. The ear grew longer and longer. Brother Rabbit said, "Try pulling my left ear." So Brother Owl caught hold of Brother Rabbit's left ear and he pulled and pulled. The more he pulled, the longer that ear got.

"Brother Owl," shouted Brother Rabbit, "look what you did! You pulled my ears until they're so long my best friend wouldn't recognize me. Try pulling my tail instead."

So Brother Owl grabbed Brother Rabbit's tail. He pulled and pulled until—off came Rabbit's tail. And ever since that day to this, Brother Rabbit has had long ears and a short tail.

THE HARE, THE HIPPO, AND THE ELEPHANT

The hippo and elephant may be big and strong, but that doesn't mean any-thing when it comes to dealing with a very smart hare.

The hare was splashing around in the river when he met the hippo. "My, my, you surely look strong," said the hare to the hippo. "Do you think if I tied myself to you and went into the bush, you could pull me into the river?"

"Certainly I could pull you into the river," snorted the hippo. "That would be very easy, for you are but a little thing."

"Well, we will see about that," the hare said to himself.

To the hippo he said, "Very well, then. When you feel a tug on the rope, start pulling."

The hare tied one end of the rope to the hippo. Holding the other end of the rope, he ran into the bush where he met the elephant.

"Hello, elephant," said the hare. "You surely look strong. Do you think if I tied this rope to you, you could pull me out of the river?"

"Well, of course, I could!" said the elephant. "That would be easy, for you are but a very small thing." And so the hare tied the other end of the rope around the elephant.

"When I get to the water, I will tug on the rope, and you can start pulling," the hare said to the elephant.

The hare hurried out of sight, tugged on the rope, and ran off. The elephant began to pull at one end, and the hippo at the other. The hippo said, "How can that little hare be so strong?"

Likewise, the elephant said, "How can I be pulling for so long against such a tiny creature?"

When the two had been tugging at each other for a long time, the hippo left the river to find the hare, and the elephant headed to the river to do the same. The two were very surprised when they met.

"Is it you, my friend, who has been pulling?" the hippo said to the elephant.

The other replied, "Is it you who has been pulling at the other end?" Thereupon they became friends.

After that the hippo always came on land to eat grass, and the elephant went to the river to drink water.

GRANNY, CUTTA THE CORD

Brer Wolf should know not to trust Brer Rabbit, but somehow he never learns his lesson.

One time food got very scarce. The rice crop was poor. Fish were swimming too low to catch and birds were flying too high to shoot. It was really very hard times and all the animals were mighty hungry. Brer Rabbit and Brer Wolf put their heads together to figure out what to do.

After a while, Brer Rabbit, weeping bitter tears, said the only thing left to do was to eat their grandmothers. Brer Wolf just wailed. Brer Rabbit said, "If you're going to take it so hard, Brer Wolf, it would be better for you to kill your grandmother first and get it over with. That way you'll be done with your grieving faster."

So Brer Wolf dried his eyes and killed his grandmother. Then he and Brer Rabbit went off and they ate and ate day and night until the food was all gone. Soon after, Brer Wolf went visiting Brer Rabbit and said, "Brer Rabbit, I am hungry through and through. It's time to kill your grandmother now so we can have something to eat."

Brer Rabbit threw back his head and burst out laughing. "You think I'm going to kill my own grandmother?" he said. "Oh no, Brer Wolf, I could never do that."

This made Brer Wolf so mad he tore at his hair with his claws and howled. He said he was going to make Brer Rabbit kill his grandmother somehow.

That night, Brer Rabbit took his grandmother by the hand and led her way off into the woods. He hid her at the top of a huge coconut tree and told her to stay there quietly. Then he gave her a little basket with a cord tied to it so that he could send food up to her.

The next morning, Brer Rabbit went to the foot of the tree, and hollered in a fine voice:

Granny, granny, o granny! Cutta the cord.

When the grandmother heard this, she let down the basket with the cord, and Brer Rabbit filled it with things to eat. Every day he came back and did the same thing, and every day she let down the basket.

Brer Wolf watched and listened. He crept up close and bye and bye he heard what Brer Rabbit was saying, and he saw the basket swing down on the cord and go back up again. When Brer Rabbit left, Brer Wolf sneaked up to the foot of the tree and said:

Granny, granny, o granny! Shoota the cord.

Old Granny Rabbit listened closely. She said, "What's happening here? My grandson doesn't talk like that." When Brer Rabbit came back to see his grandmother, she told him about how someone was hollering "shoota the cord." Brer Rabbit just laughed until he couldn't laugh anymore.

When Brer Rabbit went away, Brer Wolf came back to the tree and hollered:

Granny, granny, o granny! Cutta the cord.

Granny Rabbit held her head to one side and listened hard. "I'm sorry, my son, that you have such a bad cold. Your voice is sounding very hoarse." Then she peeked through the branches and saw Brer Wolf. "You can't fool me," she said. "Go away, now, you hear?"

Brer Wolf snorted and gnashed his teeth, and stomped off into the swamp to think about his problem. Bye and bye, he went to the blacksmith and asked him how he could make his voice less hoarse-sounding, so that it could sound fine like Brer Rabbit's.

The blacksmith said, "I can run this hot poker down your throat and then you'll be able to talk nice and easy like Brer Rabbit." Well, it hurt real bad and it was a long time before Brer Wolf could talk at all, but he finally walked back to that coconut tree. When he got there he hollered:

Granny, granny, o granny! Cutta the cord.

The voice sounded so nice and fine to Granny Rabbit that she was sure it was Brer Rabbit. She let down the basket and Brer Wolf climbed in. Then Granny Rabbit started to pull on the cord.

"Lord, this load is heavy," she said. "My grandson must be sending me an awful lot of food this time."

Brer Wolf couldn't help grinning when he heard her say this, but he kept real still. Granny Rabbit pulled hard. She pulled until she got so tired she had to rest, leaving Brer Wolf dangling way up high in the air. Brer

Wolf was up so high that when he looked down he got dizzy. When he looked up, though, his mouth started to water. Then he looked down again and he saw Brer Rabbit. That scared Brer Wolf and he jerked on the rope a little.

Brer Rabbit got to the bottom of the coconut tree and hollered:
Granny, granny, o granny! Cutta the cord.

Granny Rabbit cut the cord on the basket and Brer Wolf fell to the ground and never bothered anyone else again.

MEETING TROUBLE

Brer Rabbit knows that anyone foolish enough to ask for
Trouble is sure to find it.

Brer Alligator's back used to be as smooth and white as
a catfish skin. When he sunned himself on the mud-
bank, he shined like a piece of silver. He was mighty
proud of that hide. Truth be told, he was mighty pleased
with himself in every way.

He and his family lived at the edge of a rice field.
They had plenty of fish to eat and never had to bother
with any of the animals on the land—unless they fell
into the water. They were very satisfied with themselves, and thought that
there wasn't anybody else quite as good as they were.

Well, one hot day, Brer Gator was resting on the bank when along came
Brer Rabbit. Now Brer Rabbit had no love for Brer Gator, but he stopped
all the same to pass the time of day with him because Brer Rabbit loved to

talk. He'd talk to anyone, even one of those ridiculous animals who don't know any better than to live in the water.

"Howdy, Brer Alligator," he said. "How's Sister Alligator, and all the young alligators?" At first Brer Gator didn't even reply. It just seemed like he didn't care what any other animal thought about him, or how they were getting along themselves.

But after a while he fixed his eye on Brer Rabbit and said, "They're getting on just fine. But it's no wonder that those children are smart and pretty and raised right, because they live right here in the river. I swear to God, I can't see how you others get by living up on top of that dry, drafty land. And you and all the other animals that aren't fit to live in the water just seem to spend all your time fighting with each other until you must be worn out before the day is half-finished."

Brer Rabbit got real angry with Brer Gator for being so superior in his manners, so he decided to tell him what he thought about that kind of talk. But you know how Brer Rabbit can hide it when he's angry. He just stayed calm and then sighed and shook his head and said, real mournful like, "Maybe so. We sure have been seeing a lot of trouble up here lately."

"Who's that you're talking about, Brer Rabbit—Trouble?"

Brer Rabbit thought Brer Gator must be joking.

"What's that, Brer Gator! You never heard of—Trouble?"

Brer Gator shook his head. "No. I never heard of him and I've never seen him. What does he look like?"

Brer Rabbit couldn't believe his ears. "Oh, for crying out loud, Brer Alligator! Old as you are and you've never seen Trouble?"

"I tell you, Brer Rabbit, I've never heard anything about this here Trouble. What does Trouble look like?"

Brer Rabbit scratched his head. He figured that if Brer Gator is so stupid, and so satisfied with himself, and so ridiculous and unmannerly about everything that lives on land, that this will be his chance to teach Brer Gator a lesson.

"I don't know that I can tell you exactly what Trouble looks like. But maybe you'd like to see him?" he asked. "I can show him to you, Brer Gator, but I don't know that I want to. Maybe you won't like him."

"What are you talking about? I just want to see him. If I don't like him, that won't matter at all to me."

"Well, I'm pretty busy right now," said Brer Rabbit.

"Oh, come on, Brer Rabbit! After all, it is me, Brer Alligator, requesting this from you, don't forget that!"

"But I have to fix my house up, and Sister Rabbit is not feeling well, and the children have to be watched, and—"

"All of that can wait!" said Brer Gator. And he coaxed and begged and pleaded until at last Brer Rabbit agreed to show him Trouble.

"Meet me here as soon as the dew is dry on the grass next Saturday," said Brer Rabbit. "Trouble may have some time off on Sunday."

On Saturday Brer Gator got up before dawn and started to make himself presentable. But Sister Alligator wanted to know where he was going. She wouldn't stop asking until he said he was going out with Brer Rabbit to meet Trouble.

"Well, I'd like to meet Trouble, too," said Sister Alligator.

Brer Gator said no but Sister Alligator kept asking and asking until Brer Gator finally said okay.

Now Sister Alligator got busy fixing herself up and then all the little alligators woke up. They saw their mammy and pappy fixing themselves up to go out, and they started begging to go, too.

Now Brer Gator was fed up with so much fuss, so he said, "Well, all right, but fix yourselves up nice and pretty. And be sure you mind your manners. You have to show Brer Rabbit how much better water children are than woods children."

They ran to fix themselves up nice and soon they were all dressed up for going out. They had on their best, with mud on their heads, and marsh on their backs, and didn't they think they looked fine! And they all came out, crowding each other, going down the rice field bank to wait for Brer Rabbit.

They hadn't been there long before Brer Rabbit came along. He was surprised to see the whole family there, and laughed to himself, but all he said was, "Howdy!" And then he told them how nice the children looked, but all the time he was saying to himself, "Oh, Lord! This is an ugly gang of people!"

Brer Gator didn't even apologize for bringing such a big crowd with him. All he said was, "They all begged me so I had to give in and let them come."

Brer Rabbit said, "There's plenty of room for everybody. I hope you will all enjoy yourselves."

The children were so glad that Brer Rabbit didn't send them home that they danced around with joy. They all looked so funny that Brer Rabbit almost laughed in their faces, but instead he knit his eyebrows and looked at his watch, and said, "Time to get going, I guess."

Brer Rabbit led them up through a patch of woods until he got to a field overgrown with broomgrass and briar. In the middle of the field, Brer Rabbit stopped. He cupped his ear and pretended he was listening for something. "*Sh! Sh!*" he told the children.

After Brer Rabbit listened some more, he shouted out, "Who is that calling Brer Rabbit?" Then he pretended he heard something more, and he yelled back, "Yes. It's me. What do you want with me?"

He cupped his hand to his ear again and then he said, "I'm coming right now." He turned to Brer Gator and said, "I beg your pardon, but someone is calling me away a minute on business. Please wait right here and I'll be right back."

Brer Rabbit ran along the path out of sight. At the edge of the woods he stopped to chuckle, and then he got down to business.

He smelled the wind and looked which way it was blowing. Then he pulled a handful of that long, dry broomgrass, and he set it afire. Then he ran along the edge of the field with the fire, and set the field ablaze all around. When he finished, he got up on a high stump where he could see real good, and sat down and waited.

All this time the alligators were down in the middle of the field. They were tired because they had walked so far, and were happy to rest awhile.

But Sister Alligator couldn't stop pestering Brer Gator with which-and-why talk: "Which way will Trouble be coming? Why didn't you make Brer Rabbit tell you more? How long do we have to wait?" Brer Gator didn't answer. He just sat still and grunted once in a while.

The fire burned and burned. At last the wind caught it and it flared up high, and the sparks and flames flew up in the sky. One of the little alligators saw that and he hollered out, "Look there!" And the rest of the little alligators looked toward where their brother had pointed and they sang out "Look there!" And one got a notion and he yelled out, "That must be Trouble." And Sister Alligator turned and looked and said, "Look Pa! Do you think that's Trouble?"

Brer Gator was so ignorant he didn't even know. He lived in the water and mud, and had never seen fire, but he didn't feel easy in his mind. "I guess maybe Brer Rabbit got lost or something," he said.

Then one of the children called out, "Trouble is pretty!" And all of them began to sing, "Trouble is pretty! Trouble is pretty!"

And Brer Gator said, "If that is Trouble, he sure is pretty! The child speaks the truth!" And he and his wife sat staring at the fire, watching it come closer. And the children stared and kept quiet as if they were afraid that they might scare Trouble away.

At last a hot spark landed right on one of the little alligator's back, and he screamed, "Trouble hurts!" And then a spark landed on Sister Alligator and she started to jump around and holler, "It's true! Trouble hurts!"

"Brer Rabbit, Brer Rabbit!" they all called. "We don't want to see Trouble anymore!" The sparks kept falling, and all the alligators were so confused they didn't know what to do. And they hollered out again, "Brer Rabbit, where are you? Tell Trouble to go away!"

But Brer Rabbit didn't come and he didn't answer. The gators stopped calling him and got ready to get through the fire the best they could.

Sister Alligator hollered, "Children, follow your pa."

And right through the scorching fire they ran. They went past Brer Rabbit on the stump, but they didn't even see him, they were running so fast. And they looked so funny that Brer Rabbit almost fell off the stump, he was laughing so hard.

"Brer Alligator!" he shouted, "I guess you have seen Trouble now! Get back in the water where you belong. And don't ever hunt Trouble anymore."

The gators didn't stop running until they got to the rice field bank and jumped in the river. And they were still so hot from the fire when they went over the bank that when the water hit them, steam rose up like a cloud.

They didn't come out again the whole day or that night, but when they got a chance to look at each other, they found that the fire had burned them so bad that their white skin was just as black and crinkly as a burned log of wood, and as rough as the bark on a live oak.

And ever since then, alligators have had a horny hide.

RABBIT'S HORSE

The most outrageous scheme is okay with Rabbit if it will get
him what he wants.

A very long time ago, Rabbit and Tiger were best
friends. But when they discovered that they both were
courting the same young lady, they became very jealous
of each other.

Well, you know Rabbit—always looking to get the
advantage. One day, he goes over to the young lady's
house and, as usual, starts bragging on himself, and
telling her that Tiger wasn't anything but his father's old
riding horse. A little later, Tiger stopped by to call on this girl he thought was
his sweetheart. But she said, "Go on now! How can you just come along
courting when I just heard you are nothing but an old riding horse?"

"What?" said Tiger. "Whoever told you such a thing is making up stories
about me and filling your head with big lies. Tell you what I'll do. I'll go

straight to my friend Rabbit, and he'll tell you that all of this is just nonsense. I never have been his fathers old riding horse."

So Tiger took up his walking stick, and walking just as respectfully as he can, he goes straight to Rabbit's house. He found Rabbit lying there on his bed moaning with fever. So he lifted the latch and called out, "Brer Rabbit! Brer Rabbit!"

Rabbit heard him just fine, but he answered real soft and sicklike, "Brer Tiger, is that you calling me?" He knew that Tiger was going to be mad at him, you know.

Tiger said, "Yes, it's me. I came right over to your house because someone has been telling lies about me, and I wanted to find out if it was you. I want to hear it from your own mouth. If you said those things, I'm going to make you prove it."

"Oooh," Rabbit groaned. "Can't you see I have a fever? My stomach is hurting me bad, and I have just been to the doctor and taken some medi- cine."

"Is that so?" said Tiger. "I don't believe you."

"I just swallowed two pills, Brer Tiger, so how do you think I could ever get up and go to any lady's yard and prove anything tonight?"

"I don't want to have an argument," said Brer Tiger, "but I think you bet- ter come with me anyhow and tell that lady tonight that I am not your father's old riding horse."

"Oh, Lord!" cried Rabbit. "This pain in my chest just won't let me. But if you insist, I'll try to go with you even though I'm feeling so sick."

Then Tiger said, "Well, since you're so sick, maybe I could help you get there. How can I help?"

"Well, just lift me up a little and I'll see how I feel," said Rabbit.

So Tiger lifted him up and Rabbit said, "Oh, Lord! I'm feeling dizzy."

"Don't worry," said Tiger "Just grab my neck and I'll carry you on my back."

But Rabbit insisted he couldn't get up at all. And every time that Tiger lifted him, he just fell back into bed. Finally, Rabbit looked up and said, "Why don't you get that saddle up there in the rafters and put it on, and I could maybe grab hold of that and you could carry me." So Tiger took down Brer Rabbit's saddle.

"Now, just put that on your back, brother," said Brer Rabbit, "and I can sit down soft."

Rabbit got in the saddle and then got his bridle and reins. "Hey!" said Tiger, "what are you going to do with that?"

Brer Rabbit said, "If you just put that through your mouth, brother, then I can tell you if you're going too fast so I won't fall off."

"All right, then, put it on," said Tiger.

Next Rabbit took out his whip. "Hey!" said Tiger, "what are you going to do with that?"

"If a fly comes on your ear or back, brother, I'll be able to take this whip and lick it off."

Tiger said, "Well, okay."

Then Rabbit put on his spurs. "Hey!" said Tiger. "Now what are you going to do with those?"

"If a flies comes on your side, brother, I can brush them away with my spurs."

"Okay, then. Put them on."

Then Rabbit moaned, "Well, Brer Tiger, if you stoop down, I can get on."

Rabbit mounted Tiger's back, and he started off. After about a mile or so, Rabbit took his whip and gave Tiger a lick on the ear. "Hey! What's that for?"

"Well, there was a fly on your ear. Shoo fly! Shoo!"

"All right, brother, but next time don't hit me so hard."

Tiger went on for another mile or so and Rabbit stuck his spurs in his side. Tiger jumped and cried out, "Now wait a minute! What do you think you're doing?"

"Those bothersome flies were biting your sides."

Tiger went on until he came to the lady's yard. The lady's house had two doors, a front one and a back one. Just as he came to the entrance to the yard, Rabbit rose up in his saddle just like a jockey on a race horse, and he took out his whip and he lashed Tiger hard!

"Hey!" cried Tiger. But Rabbit lashed him some more until he started to run. Then Rabbit took his spurs and stuck them into Tiger's side, and made him run right up to the lady's front door.

At the door, Rabbit took off his hat and waved it above his head. "Good morning, miss," he said. "Didn't I tell you that Tiger was nothing but my father's old riding horse?"

Rabbit hopped off Tiger and went into the lady's house. And poor Tiger was so embarrassed that he galloped off, and was never heard of again.

WANTING A LONG TAIL

Brer Rabbit has never been satisfied with his little stump of a tail, and doesn't see why he can't have a beautiful, long tail like some of the other creatures.

One hot summer day, the mosquitoes were biting hard and the flies were buzzing thick. The little pests were bothering Brer Rabbit so much that he went to scheming to see what he could do to get rid of them all.

He noticed that Brother Bull Cow, standing quietly under a tree chewing his cud, just switched his tail whenever a bug landed on him. And when a big fly buzzed around Brother Horse, one flip of his tail killed it dead.

Brother Rabbit was mad that he didn't have a long tail. How come when things like that were handed out, he didn't get one? All he got was a stumpy little bit of cottontail—not much good for anything.

He went home and he thought and thought until he hatched a plan. It was a bold plan, but then Brer Rabbit is a real bold creature. There isn't anything he won't try at least once.

Brer Rabbit put on his good blue pants and his fine yellow shoes. He cocked his straw hat on his head, and took the path that went to Heaven. He would just ask God if he wouldn't be so kind as to please give him a long tail like some of the other creatures have. Brer Rabbit kept traveling along that rambling path until at last he was right at the front gate of Heaven. He pushed right in, walked along a grand drive, and at last he was right in front of the Big House.

That house sure is big! thought Brer Rabbit. He had to walk about a mile just to get to the back porch. When he got there, he took off his hat, wiped his face, and then reached over and knocked softly. *Tap! Tap! Tap!*

There was no answer. He waited a bit and then knocked again—a little louder. This time God hollered out in a great big voice, "Who's there?" Brer Rabbit was scared. "It's me, sir," he almost whispered.

"Who is me?"

"Just me, Brer Rabbit, sir."

"Well, what do you want, Brer Rabbit?"

"Just a little thing. Won't take you but a minute to do it."

"Humph! Well, I guess I better see what sort of mischief you are up to now," God said. "Sit down. I'll be right out." When God came out on the porch, Brer Rabbit was so scared that he almost ran off, but then he remembered how much he wanted that tail.

"Now, Brer Rabbit," said God, sounding kind of irritated, "what little thing do you want so badly that you've gotten bold enough to come up here like this?"

"Master," said Brer Rabbit, "this weather is so hard on us poor creatures, I don't see how we survive. We have to contend with all kinds of biting, stinging, troubling things. The gnats and green-head flies, and sandflies, and redbugs, and ticks, and chiggers bother us all day. And when darkness comes, the mosquitoes take over, sucking our blood and tormenting us until daybreak. Even so, Master, some creatures make out better than the rest because they have a real tail—not some leftover stump like mine—to shoo away the bugs.

When a fly bothers Brother Bull Cow or Brother Horse, all they have to do is wave their tales in the air, and the mosquitoes and flies are almost scared to death. Now, Master, what I've come here to ask is for you to be so kind as to please give me a long tail so I can brush away those pesky critters, too."

God just stared down at Brer Rabbit with his mouth all pinched together. "Humph! Even with all the blessings you have, you still want a tail like all the best creatures have. You are made like you are made. You're lucky to have any tail at all," said God. "Besides, you are mighty little to have a long tail. Why don't you just jump around in the grass to keep those flies off?"

"That's exactly what I have been doing, sir, and it just wears me out."

God kind of smiled then. "Well, you are smart enough to get here and that counts for something. I'll set you a task to see just how smart you are, and if you do it, I might give you a long tail."

After saying that, God went back into the house, and came right back out with something in his hand.

God gave Brer Rabbit a crocus bag and said, "Knock out Brother Alligator's eye teeth with this hammer and give them to me." Last, God handed Brer Rabbit a calabash. "Fill this with Brother Deer's eye water. Now, get away from here and don't come back bothering me until you've done everything I told you."

Brer Rabbit could hardly pick up his head. His heart was heavy and his feet dragged along the ground. How could he catch blackbirds by the sack? He wasn't a hawk! And why would anyone with any sense even go *near* Brother Alligator's mouth?

And tears from Brother Deer! Why everyone knows that Brother Deer is so skittery that if you even *ask* him something, he runs off. God sure did fix it so it would be mighty hard to get a long tail.

Now, you know, that Brer Rabbit is little, but he is smart. And he figured out a scheme to get those blackbirds. During the fall, the white folks burn off the grass that grows along the rice-field bank. The fire goes along, and the smoke rolls ahead of it, and the birds living in the grass get all scared by the smoke and fly around like crazy.

So when they started that year, Brer Rabbit got behind a big clump of grass a little way in front of where they were starting to burn. When the fire came that way, and the smoke reached them, the blackbirds started flying around, landing on one bush and then another. At last they came down right in front of Brer Rabbit's clump of grass. He jumped out and caught a bird and put it in the sack, and he just kept jumping out until the whole sack was filled with blackbirds.

Next, he got his fiddle and went down by the river. Now, when Brer Rabbit played the fiddle there aren't any feet around that can keep from tapping. Brer Rabbit sat down on a stump and started to play and sing and tap his foot. He knew no animal could resist that music, especially Brer Alligator. Brer Alligator came to the top of the water, poked his head out, and looked around to see who was playing. The music started to pull Brer Alligator out of the water, and he swam over to the bank. Brer Rabbit didn't pay any attention. He just went on playing and singing like no one was around. Brer Alligator crawled right up on the bank, and sat down by Brer Rabbit.

Brer Rabbit stopped at last. Brer Alligator praised him to the sky for his playing and singing and fiddling. Then he asked Brer Rabbit, "Can you teach me to play like that?"

Brer Rabbit pretended he was thinking and then said, "Can't say about the singing because it depends on how a man's mouth is made if he can lern to sing or not."

"Look in my mouth, Brer Rabbit, and tell me if it's made right." Brer Rabbit pretended that he didn't want to look. "It's hard to teach anyone to sing," he said and started to hum a tune.

"Please, Brer Rabbit," begged Brer Alligator, "look and see if I have the kind of mouth that you can teach how to sing."

Brer Rabbit just yawned and stretched and looked down at Brer Alligator.

"All right, maybe I can, but you have to do what I say."

"Sure! Sure! Brer Rabbit. Anything you say."

"Then shut your eyes tight until I tell you to open them."

Brer Alligator shut his eyes. "Open your mouth real wide," said Brer Rabbit. Brer Alligator did just as he was told.

Brer Rabbit grabbed a stick and jammed it into Brer Alligator's jaws to keep them wide open and said, "Bite on that a minute and keep still." Then he took out his hammer, knocked out both of Brer Alligator's eye teeth, and ran off with them. Brer Alligator yelled and thrashed around, but Brer Rabbit didn't pay any attention. He just scampered home, feeling mighty satisfied with himself.

The last thing Brer Rabbit had to do was get the calabash full of Brother Deer's eye water. He knew getting the eye water would be the hardest thing to do. He couldn't think of anything except to ask Brer Deer straight out to help him. But that wouldn't work because Brer Deer knew Brer Rabbit too well and would figure out that he was going to play some kind of trick on him.

The problem was so hard that Brer Rabbit almost gave up, but then he saw Brother Bull Cow and Brother Horse with their nice long tails just switching and swinging, and it reminded him of how fine he would look if he had one of those long tails. And finally, he got an idea.

Brer Deer lived way down in the woods. A long time ago, he used to live in the village and was good friends with Brer Dog. But they had a falling out, and finally Brer Dog and his family chased Brer Deer and his family away. Poor Brer Deer was scared of almost all the animals because of that experience. In fact, he was the most frightened creature in the woods.

Brer Rabbit went deep into the woods till he came to the little clearing where Brer Deer had his house. He found Brer Deer lying down in the sun, and they chatted for a while. Finally, Brer Rabbit said, "Brer Deer, you know I am your friend, right?"

"Yes, Brer Rabbit, I know that."

"You know I always stick up for you, right?"

"Yes, I know that."

"Well, I had to come tell you that in the village they're all saying that you are no good at jumping any more. They say that Sister Nanny Goat takes the prize for jumping nowadays."

"Who could say such a thing! Why, I can jump three times higher than that no-count little thing!"

"Brer Dog said you couldn't and I told him that wasn't so. And I came up here to give you the chance to show me how you can still jump higher than anyone. But I have to tell you that I did see Sister Nanny Goat jump a bush almost as high as that one over there, and she could jump it good. Can you jump that high?"

Brer Deer just smiled. "Man! I could jump bushes like that before I could even walk!" he said.

"Well then, why don't you show me? Then I could pass the word along to Brer Dog."

Brer Deer jumped over the bush just as graceful as could be. Brer Rabbit looked astonished. He praised Brer Deer for how high he could jump.

"That isn't anything," said Brer Deer, and he jumped over a higher bush, just to show what he could do.

"Brer Dog is sure going to have to shut his lying mouth now," said Brer Rabbit. "You sure are some jumper. I reckon you could even jump that big bush yonder?"

Brer Deer jumped that one as well. Brer Rabbit pointed to higher and higher bushes, till at last he fixed on one that wasn't a bush—it was a young tree with a heavy fork at the top, and was all tangled up with jasmine and cat briar and other kinds of vines.

This time, Brother Deer sort of hesitated. But Brother Rabbit praised his jumping ability so much that he reared back and jumped it. He leaped very high, but he landed right in the middle of the big fork!

Brer Rabbit made sure he was caught fast and then said, "Hold on, Brother Deer. I'll go to the village and get help."

Instead, Brer Rabbit ran down the path until he was out of sight, and rolled on the ground laughing at how he had tricked Brer Deer. After a bit, he ran back wailing and sobbing. "Hurry, Brother Deer, and get out of that tree. Brother Dog and his whole family are on their way to get you."

Hearing that, Brother Deer burst into tears. Brer Rabbit held the little calabash under Brother Deer's eyes and caught every drop of his eye water. Then he just walked away, leaving Brother Deer high up in the tree fork.

Now that Brer Rabbit was all done with the tasks God had given him, he didn't waste any time. He went home and put on his good clothes, picked up the three things that God had asked for, and swaggered all the way up the path to God's house. This time, he walked straight up to the front door, and knocked real loud. *BAM! BAM! BAM!*

God hollered out, "Who's there?"

"It's me, sir, Brer Rabbit."

"What? Back already? Have you done all the tasks I set you to?"

"Yes, sir."

After a while, God came to the door. Brer Rabbit puffed himself up. He was so pleased that he was grinning from ear to ear. Then he noticed that God looked annoyed so he put on a serious face. He put down the sack full of blackbirds, unwrapped Brer Alligator's two eye teeth, and handed God the calabash full of Brother Deer's tears.

God tasted it, smelled it, and then he said, "You are smart, aren't you, Brother Rabbit?" He pointed to a pine tree out in the yard. "Go seat yourself under that tree till I can fix you up." And he turned around and went into the house and slammed the door.

Brer Rabbit went and did as he was told and sat down under the tree. But he didn't like the way God had slammed the door and all. And he didn't like the way God had talked to him. And he noticed that God's eyes showed red like fire when he looked at the pine tree. Something wasn't right, and Brer Rabbit was getting more and more scared. Little by little, he moved away from the tree till he got way over in a corner of the yard where he could hide himself under a heavy sucklebush.

Well, sir! He was hardly under that sucklebush before *BAM!* Out of the clear blue sky, that didn't have so much as a cloud in it, came the biggest lightning bolt that you ever did see. It just crashed down on the pine tree where Brer Rabbit was supposed to be waiting. And the next minute, where that pine tree had stood, there wasn't anything at all except a pile of kindling, and that was afire.

Brer Rabbit took off like a shot, running lickety-split for the Big Gate. About that time, God in the Big House looked out the window and saw him, and he hollered out, "Since you are so smart, get a long tail yourself!"

THE FAVORITE UNCLE REMUS

Joel Chandler Harris

No child could ever be better entertained than the little boy fortunate enough to be told stories by the man he called Uncle Remus.

THE WONDERFUL TAR BABY

"Didn't the fox ever catch the rabbit, Uncle Remus?" asked the little boy the next morning.

He come mighty nigh it, honey, sho's you bawn—Brer Fox did. One day Brer went ter wuk en got 'im some tar, and mix it wid some turkentime, en fix up a contraption w'at he call a Tar-Baby en he set 'er in de big road, en den he lay off in de bushes fer to see w'at de news was gwineter be. En he didn't hatter wait long, needer, kaze bimeby yer come Brer Rabbit pacin' down de road—*lippity-clippity, clippity, lippity*—des ez sassy ez a jay-bird.

Brer Fox, he lay low. Brer Rabbit come prancin' long till he spy de Tar-Baby, en den he fotch up on his behime legs like he wuz 'stonished. De Tar-Baby, she sot dar, she did, en Brer Fox, he lay low.

"Mawnin!" sez Brer Rabbit, sezee—"nice wedder dis mawnin", sezee.

Tar-Baby ain't sayin' nothin', en Brer Fox, he lay low.

"How does yo' sym'toms seem ter segashuate?" sez Brer Rabbit, sezee.

Brer Fox, he wink his eye slow, en lay low, en de Tar-Baby, she ain't sayin' nothin'.

"How you come on, den? Is you deaf?" sez Brer Rabbit, sezee. "Kaze if you is, I kin holler louder," sezee.

Tar-Baby stay still, en Brer Fox, he lay low.

"Youer stuck up, dat's w'at you is," sez Brer Rabbit, sezee, "en I'm gwineter cure you, dat's w'at I'm a-gwineter do," sezee.

Brer Fox, he sorter chuckle in his stomach, he did, but Tar-Baby ain't sayin' nothin'.

"I'm gwineter larn you how ter talk ter 'spectable folks ef hit's de las' ack," sez Brer Rabbit, sezee. "Ef you don't take off dat hat en tell me howdy, I'm gwineter bus' you wide open," sezee.

Tar-Baby stay still, en Brer Fox, he lay low.

Brer Rabbit keep on axin' 'im, en de Tar-Baby, she keep on sayin' nothin', til present'y Brer Rabbit draw back wid his fis', he did, en *blip* he tuck 'er side er de head. Right dar's whar he broke his merlasses jug. His fis' stuck, en he can't pull loose. De tar holt 'im. But Tar-Baby, she stay still, en Brer Fox, he lay low.

"Ef you don't lemme loose, I'll knock you agin," sez Brer Rabbit, sezee, en wid dat he fotch 'er a wipe wid de udder han', en dat stuck. Tar-Baby, she ain't sayin' nothin', en Brer Fox, he lay low.

"Tu'n me loose, fo' I kick de natal stuffin' outen you," sez Brer Rabbit, sezee, but de Tar-Baby, she ain't sayin' nothin'. She des hilt on, en den Brer

Rabbit lose de use er his foots in de same way. Brer Fox, he lay low. Den Brer Rabbit squall out dat ef de Tar-Baby don't tu'n 'im loose he butt 'er cranksided. En den he butter, en his head got stuck. Den Brer Fox, he sa'ntered fort', lookin' des ez innercent ez one er yo' mammy's mockin'-birds.

"Howdy, Brer Rabbit," sez Brer Fox, sezee. "You look sorter stuck up dis mawnin'," sezee, en den he rolled on de groun', en laffed en laffed till he couldn't laff no mo'.

THE BRIAR PATCH

Uncle Remus, asked the little boy the next evening, did the fox kill and eat the rabbit when he caught him with the Tar-Baby?

"Law honey, w'at I tell you w'en I fus' begin? I tole you Brer Rabbit wuz a monstus soon creetur—leas'ways dat's w'at I laid out fer ter tell you. Well den, honey, don't you go en make no calkalations, kaze in dem days Brer Rabbit en his fambly wuz at de head er de gang w'en any racket wuz on han', en dar dey stayed. 'Fo' you begins fer ter wipe yo' eyes 'bout Brer Barrit, you wait en see whar'bouts Brer Rabbit gwineter fetch up at.

Wíen Brer Fox fine Brer Rabbit mixed up wid de Tar-Baby, he feel mighty good, en he roll on de groun' en laff. Bimeby he got up'n say, sezee:

"Well, I speck I got you dis time, Brer Rabbit, sezee; 'maybe I ain't, but I speck I is. You bin runnin' roun' here sassin' atter me a mighty long time, but I speck you done come ter de eén' er de row. You bin cuttin' up yo' capers en bouncin' roun' in dis neighborhood till you come ter b'lieve yo'se'f de boss er de whole gang. En den youer allers some'rs whar you got no business," sez Brer Fox, sezee. "Who ax you fer ter come en strike up a'quain'tance wid dish yer Tar-Baby? En who stuck you up dar whar you is? Nobody in de roun' worril. You des tuck en jam yo'se'f on dat Tar-Baby widout waitin' fer any invite," sez Brer Fox, sezee, "en dar you is, en dar you'll stay till I fixes up a bresh-pile en fires her up, kaze I'm gwineter bobbycue you dis day, sho," sez Brer Fox, sezee.

Den Brer Rabbit talk mighty 'umble.

"I don't keer w'at you do wid me, Brer Fox," sezee, "so you don't fling me in dat briar-patch. Roas' me" Brer Fox, sezee, "but don't fling me in dat briar-patch," sezee.

"Hit's so much trouble fer ter kin'le a fire," sez Brer Fox, sezee, "dat I speck I'll hatter hang you," sezee.

"Hang me des ez high ez you please, Brer Fox," sez Brer Rabbit, sezee, "but do fer de Lord's sake don't fling me in dat briar-patch," sezee.

"I ain't got no string," sez Brer Fox, sezee, "en now I speck I'll hatter drown you," sezee.

"Drown me des ez deep ez you please, Brer Fox," sez Brer Rabbit, sezee, "but do don't fling me in dat briar-patch," sezee.

"Dey ain't no water nigh," sez Brer Fox, sezee, "en now I speck I'll hatter skin you," sezee.

"Skin me, Brer Fox," sez Brer Rabbit, sezee, "snatch out my eyeballs, t'ar out my years by de roots, en cut off my legs," sezee, "but please, Brer Fox, don't fling me in dat briar-patch," sezee.

Co'se Brer Fox wanter hu't Brer Rabbit bad ez he kin, so he kotch 'im by de behime legs en slung 'im right in de middle er de briar-patch. Dar wuz a consider'ble flutter whar Brer Rabbit struck de bushes, en Brer Fox sorter hang roun' fer ter see w'at wuz gwineter happen. Bimeby he year somebody call 'im, en way up de hill he see Brer Rabbit settin' cross-legged on a chinkapin log combin' de pitch outen his ha'r wid a chip. Den Brer Fox know dat he bin swop off mighty bad. Brer Rabbit wuz bleedz fer ter fling back some er his sass, en he holler out:

"Bred en bawn in a briar-patch, Brer Fox—bred en bawn in a briar-patch!" en wid dat he skip out des ez lively ez a cricket in de embers.

THE MONEY MINT

Brer Rabbit makes up an outrageous story about where he got a pocketful of money, but he has little trouble convincing Brer Fox that it's true.

One day the little boy was telling Uncle Remus about how much money one of his mother's brothers was going to make. Oh, it was ever so much—fifty, a hundred, maybe a thousand bales of cotton in one season. Uncle Remus groaned a little during this recital.

"Wharbouts he gwine ter make it?" the old man inquired with some asperity.

"Oh, in Mississippi," said the little boy. Uncle James told papa that the cotton out there grows so high that a man sitting on his horse could hide in it.

"Did Marse Jeems see dat cotton hisse'f?" asked Uncle Remus.

"Yes, he did. He's been out there, and he saw it with his own eyes. He says he can make ever so many hundred dollars in Mississippi where he makes one here."

"Eve'y time I year folks talk 'bout makin' mo' money off dar dan dey kin anywhars nigher home," said Uncle Remus, "it put me in mine er de time w'en Brer Fox went huntin' de place whar dey make money."

Brer Fox meet up wid Brer Rabbit in de big road, en dey pass de time er day, en ax wunner nudder how der fambly connection is. Brer Fox say he sorter middlin' peart, en Brer Rabbit say he sorter 'twix *"My gracious!"* en *"Thank gracious!"* W'iles dey er runnin' on en confabbinn', Brer Fox year sumpin' rattlin' in Brer Rabbit's pocket.

He 'low, "Ef I aint mighty much mistaken, Brer Rabbit, I year money rattlin'."

Brer Rabbit sorter grin slow en hole is head keerless.

He say, " 'Taint nothin' much—des some small change w'at I bleedz ter take wid me in de case er needcessity."

Wid dat he drawed out a big han'ful er speeshy dollars, en quarter, en sev'mpunces, en thrips, en all right spang-bang new. Hit shined in de sun twel it fair bline yo' eyes.

Brer Fox 'low, "Laws a massy, Brer Rabbit! I aint seed so much money sence I sole my watermillions las' year. Ain't you skeered some un 'll fling you down en take it 'way fum you?"

Brer Rabbit say, "Dem w'at man 'nuff ter take it kin have it'; en he des strut 'long de road dar mo' samer dan one er dese yer milliumterry mens w'at got yaller stripes on der britches.

Brer Fox 'low, "Whar de name er goodness you git so much new speeshy, Brer Rabbit?"

Brer Rabbit say, "I git it whar dey make it at; dat whar I git it."

Brer Fox stop by de side er de road, en look 'stonish. He 'low, "Wharabouts does dey make dish yer speeshy at?"

Brer Rabbit say, "Fus' in one place en den in nudder. You got ter do like me, Brer Fox; you got ter keep yo' eye wide open."

Brer Fox 'low, "Fer massy sake, Brer Rabbit, tell me how I gwine ter fine de place."

He beg en he beg, Brer Fox did, en Brer Rabbit look at 'im hard, like he got some doubts on his mine. Den Brer Rabbit sot down by de side er de road en mark in de san' wid his walkin' cane.

Bimeby he say, "Well, s'posin' I tell you, you'll go blabbin' it roun' de whole neighborhoods, en den dey'll git it all, en we won't git none't all."

But Brer Fox des vow en 'clar' ter gracious dat he won't ell a livin' soul, en den ole Brer Rabbit sorter bent hisse'f back en cle'r up his th'oat.

He say, " 'Taint much atter you fine it out, Brer Fox; all you got ter do is ter watch de road twel you see a waggin come 'long. Ef you'll look right close, you'll see dat de waggin, ef hit's de right kind er waggin, is got two front wheels en two behime wheels; en you'll see fuddermo' dat de front wheels is lots littler dan de behime wheels. Now, w'en you see dat, w'at is you bleedz ter bílieve?"

Brer Fox study little w'ile, en den shuck his head. He 'low, "You too much fer me, Brer Rabbit."

Brer Rabbit look like he feel sorry kaze Brer Fox sech a numbskull. He say, "W'en you see dat, you bleedzter b'lieve dat atter so long a time de big wheel gwine ter ketch de little one. Yo' common sense ought ter tell you dat."

Brer Fox 'low, "Hit sholy look so."

Brer Rabbit say, "Ef you know dat de big wheel gwine ter ketch de little wheel, en dat bran new money gwinte ter drop fum'twix um w'en dey grind up agin wunner nudder, w'at you gwine do den?"

Still Brer Fox study, en shuck his head. Brer Rabbit look like he gittin' sick.

He say, "You kin set down en let de waggin go on by, ef you don't want no bran new money. Den agin, ef you want de money, you kin foller 'long en keep watch, en see w'en de behime wheels overtake de front uns en be on han' w'en de money starts ter droppin'."

Brer Fox look like he sorter got de idee. He sorter laff.

Brer Rabbit say, "Nex' time you see a waggin gwine by, Brer Fox, des holler fer me ef you don't want ter take no chances. Des bawl out! I aint got 'nuff speeshy, en I aint gwine ter have 'nuff."

Brer Fox, he broke off a broom straw en 'gun ter chaw on it, en des 'bout dat time, dey year a waggin comin' 'crost de hill.

Brer Rabbit 'low, "Des say de word, Brer Fox, en ef you aint gwine 'long atter de waggin, I'll go myse'f!"

Brer Fox say, "Maybe de wheels done grinded tergedder back yonder a piece."

Brer Rabbit 'low, "I aint got time ter 'spute, Brer Fox. Ef you aint gwine, des say de word!"

Brer Fox sorter laff like he shame. He say, "I b'lieve I'll go a little piece er de way en see how de wheels run."

Wid dat, Brer Rabbit wish Brer Fox good luck, en went on 'bout his business. Yit he aint go so fur dat he can't watch Brer Fox's motions. At de rise er de nex' hill he look back, en dar he see Brer Fox trottin' 'long atter de waggin. W'en he see dat, Brer Rabbit des lay down in de grass en kick up his heels en holler.

"Well, honey," said Uncle Remus, 'he des foller 'long, trottin' en gallopin', waitin' fer de wheels ter ketch up wid wunner nudder. Ef he aint in Massasip by dis time, I'm mighty much mistaken."

THE FATE OF MR. JACK SPARROW

*Uncle Remus gives his devoted little listener a lesson about what
happens to tattle tales.*

"You'll tromple on dat bark till hit won't be fitten fer ter fling 'way, let 'lone make hoss-collars out'n," said Uncle Remus, as the little boy came running into his cabin out of the rain. All over the floor long strips of "wahoo" bark were spread, and these the old man was weaving into horse-collars.

"I'll sit down, Uncle Remus," said the little boy.

"Well, den, you better, honey," responded the old man, "kaze I 'spizes fer ter have my wahoo trompled on. Ef 'twuz shucks, now, hit mout be diffunt, but I'm a gittin' too old fer ter be projickin' longer shuck collars."

For a few minutes the old man went on with his work, but with a solemn air altogether unusual. Once or twice he sighed deeply, and the sighs ended in a prolonged groan, that seemed to the little boy to be the result of the most unspeakable mental agony. He knew by experience that he had done something which failed to meet the approval of Uncle Remus, and he tried to remember what it was, so as to frame an excuse; but his memory failed him. He could think of nothing he had done calculated to stir Uncle Remus's grief. He was not exactly seized with remorse, but he was very uneasy. Presently Uncle Remus looked at him in a sad and hopeless way, and asked:

"W'at dat long rigmarole you bin tellin' Miss Sally 'bout yo' little brer dis mawnin?"

"Which, Uncle Remus?" asked the little boy, blushing guiltily.

"Dat des w'at I'm a axin' un you now. I hear Miss Sally say she's a gwineter stripe his jacket, en den I knowed you bin tellin' on 'im."

"Well, Uncle Remus, he was pulling up your onions, and then he went and flung a rock at me," said the child, plaintively.

"Lemme tell you dis," said the old man, laying down the section of horse-collar he had been plaiting, and looking hard at the little boy— "lemme tell you dis—der ain't no way fer ter make tattlers en tail-b'arers turn out good. No, dey ain't. I been mixin' up wid folks now gwine on eighty year, en I ain't seed no tattler come ter no good een'. Dat I ain't. En ef ole man M'thoozlum wuz livin' clean till yit, he'd up'n tell you de same. Sho ez youer settin' dar. You 'member w'at come ere de bird w'at went tat-tlin' 'roun' 'bout Brer Rabbit?"

The little boy didn't remember, but he was very anxious to know, and he also wanted to know what kind of a bird it was that so disgraced itself.

"Hit wuz wunner dese yer uppity little Jack Sparrers, I speck," said the old man; "dey wuz allers bodder'n' longer udder fokes's bizness, en dey keeps at it down ter dis day—peckin' yer, en pickin' dar, en scratchin' out yander. One day, atter he been fool by ole Brer Tarrypin, Brer Rabbit wuz settin' down in de wooods studdyin' how he wuz gwineter git even. He feel mighty lonesome, en he feel mighty mad, Brer Rabbit did. Tain't put down in de tale, but I speck he cusst en roar'd 'roun' considerbul. Leas'ways, he wuz set-tin' out dar by hisse'f, en dar he sot, en study en study, till bimeby he jump up en holler out:

" 'Well, dog-gone my cats ef I can't gallop 'roun' ole Brer Fox, en I'm gwineter do it. I'll show Miss Meadows en de gals dat I'm de boss er Brer Fox," sezee.

"Jack Sparrer, up in de tree, he hear Brer Rabbit, he did, en he sing out:

" 'I'm gwine tell Brer Fox! I'm gwine tell Brer Fox! Chick-a-biddy-win'-a-blowin'-acuns-fallin'! I'm gwine tell Brer Fox!'"

Uncle Remus accompanied the speech of the bird with a peculiar whistling sound in his throat that was a marvelous imitation of a sparrow's chirp, and the little boy clapped his hands with delight, and insisted on a repetition.

"Dis kinder tarrify Brer Rabbbit, en he skasely know w'at he gwine do; but bimeby he study ter hisse'f dat de man w'at see Brer Fox fus wuz boun'ter have de inturn, en den he go hoppin' off toward home. He didn't git fur w'en who should he meet but Brer Fox, en den Brer Rabbit, he open up:

" 'W'at dis twix' you en me, Brer Fox?' sez Brer Rabbit, sezee. "I hear tell you gwine ter sen' me ter 'struckshun, en nab my fambly, en 'stroy my shanty," sezee.

Den Brer Fox he git mighty mad.

"Who bin tellin' you all dis?" sezee.

"Brer Rabbit make like he didn't want ter tell, but Brer Fox he 'sist en 'sist, till at las' Brer Rabbit he up en tell Brer Fox dat he hear Jack Sparrer say all dis.

" 'Co'se,' sez Brer Rabbit, sezee, 'w'en Brer Jack Sparrer tell me dat I flew up, I did, en I use some langwidge w'ich I'm mighty glad dey weren't no ladies 'round' nowhars so dey could hear me go on,' sezee.

"Brer Fox he sorter gap, he did, en say he speck he better be sa'nter'n on. But, bless yo' soul, honey, Brer Fox ain't sa'nter fur, 'fo' Jack Sparrer flip down on a 'simmon-bush by de side er de road, en holler out:

" 'Brer Fox! Oh, Brer Fox!—Brer Fox!'

"Brer Fox he des sorter canter 'long, he did, en make like he don't hear 'im. Den Jack Sparrer upín sing out agin:

"'Brer Fox! Oh, Brer Fox! Hole on, Brer Fox! I got some news fer you. Wait, Brer Fox! Hit'll 'stonish you."

" 'Brer Fox he make like he don't see Jack Sparrer, ner needer do he hear 'im, but bimeby he lay down by de road, en sorter stretch hisse'f like he fixin' fer ter nap. De tattlin' Jack Sparrer he flew'd 'long, en keep on calliní:

" 'I got sump'n fer ter tell you, Brer Fox."

"Git on my tail, little Jack Sparrer," sez Brer Fox, sezee, " 'kaze I'm de'f in one year, en I can't hear out'n de udder. Git on my tail," sezee.

"Den de little bird he up'n hop on Brer Fox's tail.

" 'Git on my back, little Jack Sparrer, 'kaze I'm de'f in one year, en I can't hear out'n de udder.

"Den de little bird hop on his back.

" 'Hop on my head, little Jack Sparrer, 'kaze I'm de'f in bofe years."

" 'Up hop de little bird.

" 'Hop on my toof, little Jack Sparrer, 'kaze I'm de'f in one year, en I can't hear out'n de udder."

"De tattlin' little bird hop on Brer Fox's toof, en den—"

Here Uncle Remus paused, opened wide his mouth and closed it again in a way that told the whole story.

"Did the Fox eat the bird all—all—up?" asked the little boy.

"Jedge Bar come 'long nex' day," replied Uncle Remus, "en he fine some fedders, en fum dat word went roun' dat ole man Squinch Owl done kotch nudder watizname."

How Sandy Got His Meat

Thanks to Brer Rabbit, Brer Coon was able to catch enough frogs to feed his family for quite some time

Brer Rabbit and Brer Coon were fishermen. Brer Rabbit fished for fish and Brer Coon fished for frogs.

After a while the frogs all got so smart Brer Coon couldn't catch them anymore. He hadn't brought any meat home for weeks. His children were hungry, and his wife was upset.

Brer Coon felt mighty bad and he was walking along the road with his head down wondering what he was going to do. Just then Brer Rabbit was skipping down the road. He could tell Brer Coon was worried, so he threw up his ears and said:

"Mornin', Brer Coon."

"Mornin', Brer Rabbit."

"How you doin', Brer Coon?"

"Poorly, Brer Rabbit, poorly. The frogs has all got so wiley I can't catch 'em, and I got no meat to my house and my wife is mad and the children is hungry. Brer Rabbit, I need help."

Old Brer Rabbit looked away cross the river a long time. Then he scratched his ear with his hind foot and said:

"I'll tell you what we do, Brer Coon. We'll get every one of them frogs. You go down on the sand bar and lie down and play like you're dead. Don't move. No matter what, just stay still."

Old Brer Coon moseyed down to the river. The frogs heard him coming and the big frog said, "You better look round. You better look round."

Another frog said, "Knee deep, knee deep."

And *kerchung!* All the frogs went in the water.

But Brer Coon just laid down on the sand and stretched out just like he was dead. The flies got all over him, but he didn't move. The sun shone hot, but he didn't move.

Directly Brer Rabbit came running through the woods and out on the sand bar, and put his ears up high and hollered out:

"I don't bleve it. I don't bleve it!"

And all the little frogs around the edge said:

"I don't bleve it. I don't bleve it!"

But the old coon played like he was dead, and all the frogs came up out of the river and sat around where the old coon lay.

Just then Brer Rabbit winked his eye and said:

"I'll tell you what I'd do, Brer Frogs. I'd bury ole Sandy, bury him so deep he never could scratch out."

Then all the frogs started to dig out the sand from under the old coon. When they had dug a great, deep hole with the old coon in the middle of it, the frogs all got tired and the big frog said:

"Deep enough. Deep enough. Deep enough."

Brer Rabbit was taking a nap in the sun, and he woke up and said:

"Can you jump out?"

The big frog looked up to the top of the hole and said:

"Yes I can. Yes I can. Yes I can."

And the little frogs said:

"Yes I can. Yes I can. Yes I can."

Brer Rabbit said:

"Dig it deeper."

Then all the frogs went to work and dug a great, deep hole way down inside the sand bar with Brer Coon right in the middle just like he was dead. The frogs were getting pretty tired and the big frog sang out:

"Deep enough. Deep enough. Deep enough."

And Brer Rabbit woke up again and asked:

"Can you jump out?"

"I bleve I can. I bleve I can. I bleve I can."

Brer Rabbit looked down in the hole and said:

"Dig that hole deeper."

Then all the frogs went to work throwing out sand, throwing out sand, clear till almost sundown, and they had a great deep hole way down in the sand, with the old coon laying right in the middle. The frogs were plum tuckered out and the big frog said:

"Deep enough. Deep enough. Deep enough."

And all the little frogs said:

"Deep enough. Deep enough. Deep enough."

Brer Rabbit peeped down in the hole and said:

"Can you jump out?"

And the big frog said:

"No I can't. No I can't. No I can't."
And all the little frogs said:
"No I can't. No I can't. No I can't."
Then Brer Rabbit jumped up quick and hollered:
"RISE UP SANDY AND GET YOUR MEAT."
And all Brer Coon's family had meat for supper that night.

LIAR, FOOL, AND TALL TALES

THE CHAMPION LIAR

*Really outrageous stories were called gallyfloppers, long bows, windies,
or tall tales—and the art was to be able to tell them with a straight
face and solemn expression.*

 There once was a man who could tell more lies than
anyone else. One day, he went out with his cow to tell
lies. He said that if anyone could tell more lies than he
could, he would give him his cow.

Well, he went from neighbor to neighbor, but
nobody could beat him lying. Late that night, he came
to a little hut, and inside he found a small boy.

"Could I have a light for my pipe?" he asked the boy.
The boy began to shake the fire up and down, up and down, until the man
got tired of waiting.

"Little boy, what are you doing with that fire?" he asked.

"I'm dividing today's fire from yesterday's, and yesterday's from the day
before yesterday's, to give you."

"Never mind," said the man. "Could I have some water?"

"All right," said the boy. He began to shake the water up and down, up and down, until the man got tired of waiting.

"Little boy, what are you doing with that water?" he asked.

"I'm dividing today's water from yesterday's, and yesterday's from the day before yesterday's, so as to give you fresh water."

"Little boy," said the man, "have you a mother?"

"Yes, sir," said the boy.

"Where is she?"

"She has gone to the king's palace to sew it up with her needle and thread where it got torn last night."

"What!" exclaimed the man. "And where is your father?"

"He has gone to the river to get some water to throw on the land with a flower pot with a hole in it, to make a garden."

"Is that so?" said the man.

"Little boy, did you hear that a child was born last night with seven arms, seven legs, and seven necks?"

"Sir, I can't be sure, but this morning, when I went to the spring for water, I found a dress with seven sleeves and seven collars, and I think it must have belonged to that baby."

"Is that so?" said the man.

"Little boy, did you hear that a donkey took a journey into the sky last week?"

"Sir, I can't be sure, but when I went to the spring last week, I heard a clap of thunder, and when I looked up, I saw a pack saddle falling down from the sky, and I think it must have belonged to that donkey."

"Little boy, did you hear that last week the river caught fire?"

"Sir, I can't be sure, but last week when we went fishing, we caught a lot of fish burnt on one side and raw on the other. I think they must have been cooked when the river caught fire."

"My dear, child, take my cow. You are the smartest little fellow I ever saw."

On his way home, the man met Mr. Wolf. "Why do you look so sad?" Mr. Wolf asked him.

"I thought I was the biggest liar in the world, so I said I would give my cow to anyone who could beat me lying. Then I met an innocent little child who told bigger lies than me, so I had to give him the cow. I don't know what to do to get the cow back from him."

"I'll go back with you," said Mr. Wolf. "I have seven bags here full of lies. If I open but one of my bags, the whole town will be covered with lies."

"All right," said the man. "Let's go."

When the little boy saw them coming towards his house, he knew they were going to try to take his cow. Before they got any closer, he called out, "How come you're only bringing one of the wolves you promised my father? Well, I guess he'll have to do. Bring him in and we'll cook him up."

"What?" cried Mr. Wolf. "Is that why you brought me?" And Mr. Wolf ran for home as fast as his legs would carry him.

"Sir, why are you still standing there?" asked the little boy. "If you wait, Mr. Wolf will steal the road and put it in his pocket, and then how will you get home?"

"What?" said the man, and he started running after Mr. Wolf to catch him before he stole the road and put it in his pocket.

The little boy never saw either one of them again. He went inside happy because he had his cow, and because he was the smartest little boy in the world.

Fertile Land Pumpkins, Potatoes, and Corn

Southern blacks are gifted storytellers, especially of tall tales about astonishing vegetables, fertile farmland, and amazing marksmen.

Pumpkins and Potatoes

When it was time to drop the pumpkin seed, Jack rode the fastest horse in the lot out to the field. He made a hole with a stick, dropped the seed, and galloped back to the house. But the pumpkin vine still got back to the house before him. Jack thought he'd be better off growing potatoes. But when a storekeeper asked to buy a hundred pounds of spuds, Jack said, "Sorry, I never cut a potato in half."

The night Jack planted his special variety of corn, it broke out of the ground. By morning, it was about six feet high. One of the neighbors tied his team to it and stopped to talk. Pretty soon, the sun came out and the corn began to grow and took the team, wagon and all, right up into the sky with it. Jack called for one of the lumberjacks from his timber land. The corn grew so fast that the lumberjack couldn't hit twice in the same place. Jack finally coiled one of his railroad lines around the stalk and let it pinch itself to death. Then they got to looking for the farmer and his team. They found him in another ear making a crop. Jack had such fertile land that when he left the walnut staff he always carried sticking in the cornfield and forgot about it, he later found a bushel of walnuts and ten ears of corn all growing from the same stalk.

SALT THE PUDDIN'

Too many cooks spoil the broth—as well as the puddin'.

Mrs. Simpson was having company, and thought she'd show off some by making her special puddin' for the crowd.

Well, that day everything was a-hustle and a-bustle over at the Simpsons and soon it was almost night and no puddin' cooked. Mrs. Simpson had already made her brags all around and she just had to have that puddin'. Her five girls were as busy as bees washing and ironing, and primping and cleaning up the house. So their ma tore out to the kitchen and started making her puddin'.

Now, she was known to be the best puddin' maker in the whole settlement. But she was so frazzled that evening she plumb forgot to add the salt.

Now puddin' just needs a teensy pinch of salt, but if it doesn't have that pinch, it's just not puddin'.

Mrs. Simpson got the fire going just right in the stove and slammed the puddin' in there. Then she rushed around dusting the chairs and the organ in the sitting room.

About that time it hit her about the salt. Her hands were dirty and she knew she couldn't salt the puddin' without stopping to wash first. So she just kept a-dusting figuring she'd have one of the girls tend to it for her.

"Fanny," she says, "will you go salt the puddin'? My hands are dirty."

"Can't, Ma. I'm polishing my shoes."

"Sara, how about you?"

"Can't, Ma. I'm ironing my dress."

"Bertha, can you salt the puddin'?"

"No, Ma, I'm curling my hair."

"Jenny, go salt the puddin'."

"Ask Lily, Ma. I'm braiding my hair."

"All right. Lily, run salt the puddin' please, honey."

"Can't. I'm looking high and low for my hair ribbon."

So Mrs. Simpson threw her dust rag across a chair back, washed her hands, and salted the puddin'.

Just about the time she got back to her dusting, Lily got to thinking how she should help her ma. So she hurried into the kitchen and salted the puddin'.

Lily had no more than got back to searching for her hair ribbon when Jenny got to feeling bad about being so sassy. So she ran down to the kitchen and salted the puddin'.

Bertha always was the queen of the family. She never did much more than lay around reading a romance novel, but if there was a thing she liked more than reading it was eating her ma's puddin'. So she went and salted it. She got to the kitchen just after Sara left.

Well, that puddin' sure baked pretty and when Mrs. Simpson carried it out that night you could just hear everybody sort of smack their lips.

The preacher was there, so naturally he got the first helping. His eyes were shining and he said something about nothing being better than Mrs. Simpson's puddin'. Then he took a whopping big mouthful.

When he bit down to kind of let the flavor soak in, his eyes squinched up and his mouth turned down. Then he asked for some water.

Well, everybody just sat there with their mouths open wide and their eyes bugged out. Mrs. Simpson sort of caught on that something was wrong, so she took a taste herself. Then she knew.

"Which one of you girls salted the puddin'?"

"I did, Ma," all five of them said together.

"And so did I," said their ma. "It sure looks like too many cooks spoiled this puddin'."

And nobody could deny it.

THE SPLENDID LIAR

One father would not settle for anyone but an accomplished
liar for his son-in-law.

There was a man who had a pretty daughter, and for some strange reason, he wanted her to marry a clever liar.

Many young men came who wished to marry the daughter, but whatever lies they told, her father easily could top, and so they were turned away.

One day a young man came to the man's courtyard and called out, "All the hares of this country have horns. I saw a hare today with horns as long as my arm." But the girl's father quickly answered, "Is that all? Have you only seen that today?" The father then pointed to a man nearby wearing a hat with the horn of an antelope. "Look at that man," he said, "he is wearing the horn of a hare I killed yesterday." All the men who were listening to this exchange laughed, and the young man went on his way.

The next day another suitor came. "It is a simple matter," he announced, "to catch fish with stone traps set in the veld." Thereupon the father went into his house and brought back a fish he had netted in the river the day before and said, "You speak of fish. Why, I always dig them out in the yard, where there are any number. Here is one I dug out yesterday."

And with that, the young man left while the men of the village enjoyed another good laugh.

On the next day, a young man dug a hole under a path, then got a long pole which he put into the hole, and went to the village. "Come, father," he shouted, "I want you to help me shift a path and put it at another place."

"That is quite simple," replied the father. "We shifted this path from over yonder and brought it here."

To this the young man replied, "Well, come, let us do likewise to the path over there."

Now the father thought to himself, "If I refuse to go the others will say, "He is beaten. He cannot top such a lie." So he went with the young man, saying, "Very well, let us go and move the path."

When they reached the spot where the hole had been dug, the young man said, "Hold onto the pole and pry up the path." The father took the pole and, using all his strength, attempted to lift up the path while the young man urged him on, saying "It is moving! It is moving!"

The father, becoming convinced that the path was moving, strained harder and harder. When he realized the path was not moving, he cried out, "Young man, you are a splendid liar! Today I give you my daughter."

The young man married the girl, and that is the end of the story.

LUCKY SHOT

*When you can shoot like the hunter in this tall tale,
one shell is all you need.*

One morning, a fellow went out hunting with just one shell. He happened to look up, and saw ten ducks sitting on a tree limb. Before taking a shot, he looked to his right and saw a mountain lion standing there. He looked to his left, and saw a big buck. He looked behind, and there was a flock of partridge. While he was deciding which one to shoot at, he looked straight ahead, and saw a big grizzly bear coming towards him.

Well, he knew he had to shoot the bear, because the bear was getting ready to attack him. So he cocked both muzzles of his double-barreled muzzle loader, and pulled both triggers at the same time. The single shell killed the bear. The ramrod shot out of the other muzzle, hit the tree limb, and caught all the ducks by their toes before they could fly away. The hammer on the left flew off and killed the deer. The right hammer flew off and killed the mountain lion. In a flash, the hunter whipped off his overcoat, and smothered the whole flock of partridges.

To get all this game back home he would have to build a sled. He pulled out his big knife, cut down two saplings and fitted them across with pussy willows. Then he skinned the deer, and cut strips from the hide about three inches wide. That was for a harness to pull the sled. He headed for home, pulling the loaded sled, but by the time he got there, the harness had stretched so much there was no sign of the sled.

"Well, I'm hungry," he said. "I'll eat first and then go back for the sled."

While he was having lunch, the sun came out. It was so hot, the harness dried and soon was back to its original length.

When the man finished eating and went to the door, his sled and all the game on it was just rolling into sight.

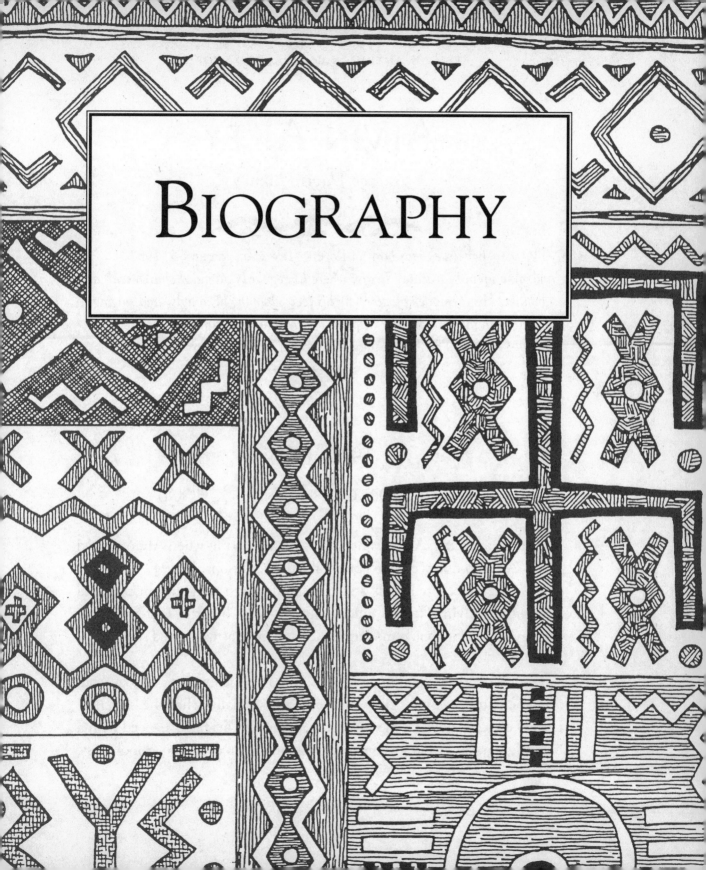

BIOGRAPHY

ALVIN AILEY

Andrea Davis Pinkney

*Alvin Ailey was born in Rogers, Texas, on January 5, 1931,
and grew up in Navasota, Texas, where he regularly attended church with his
mother. His memories of stomping his feet, clapping his hands, and singing
along with the church choir inspired the rhythms and dances he created for
The Alvin Ailey American Dance Theater.*

1949–1953

LESTER HORTON'S DANCE SCHOOL

More than anything, Alvin wanted to study dance. But when Alvin arrived
in Los Angeles not everyone could take dance lessons. In 1949 not many
dance schools accepted black students. And almost none taught the fluid
moves that Alvin liked so much—almost none but the Lester Horton
Dance Theater School, a modern dance school that welcomed students of
all races.

Lester's door was open to anyone serious about learning to dance. And,
at age eighteen, Alvin Ailey was serious, especially when he saw how
Lester's dancers moved. One student, Carmen de Lavallade, danced with a
butterfly's grace. Another, James Truitte, made modern dance look easy.

But Lester worked his students hard. Sometimes they danced all day.

After hours in the studio, droplets of sweat dotted Alvin's forehead. He tingled inside, ready to try Lester's steps once more. At first, Alvin kept time to Lester's beat and followed Lester's moves. Then Alvin's own rhythm took over, and he started creating his own steps. Alvin's tempo worked from his belly to his elbows, then oozed through his thighs and feet.

Alvin danced at Lester Horton's school almost every day. He taught the other students his special moves.

In 1950, Alvin joined Lester Horton's dance company. Soon Alvin performed his own choreography for small audiences who gathered at Lester's studio. Alvin's dances told stories. He flung his arms and shim-shammed his middle to express jubilation. His dips and slides could even show anger and pain. Modern dance let Alvin's imagination whirl.

All the while, Lester watched Alvin grow into a strong dancer and choreographer. Lester told Alvin to study and learn as much as he could about dance. He encouraged Alvin to use his memories and his African-American heritage to make dances that were unforgettable.

"What is Alvin *doing?*" one student asked.

"Whatever he's doing, he's sure doing it fine," two dancers agreed.

Some tried to follow Alvin's moves, but even Alvin didn't know which way his body would reel him next.

Alvin's steps flowed from one to another. His loops and spins just came to him, the way daydreams do.

1958–1960
BLUES SUITE—REVELATIONS

Alvin's satchel hung heavy on his shoulder. His shoes rapped a beat on the sidewalk while taxicabs honked their horns. He was glad to be in New York City, where he came to learn ballet from Karel Shook and modern dance techniques from Martha Graham, two of the best teachers in the world.

Alvin took dance classes all over town, and he met dancers who showed him moves he'd never seen before. So many dancers were black. Like Alvin, their dreams soared higher than New York's tallest skyscrapers.

Alvin gathered some of the dancers he'd seen in classes around the city. He chose the men and women who had just the right moves to dance his choreography. Alvin told them he wanted to start a modern dance company that would dance to blues and gospel music—the heritage of African-American people. Nine dancers believed in Alvin's idea. This was the beginning of the Alvin Ailey American Dance Theater.

On March 30, 1958, on an old wooden stage at the 92nd Street Y, Alvin and his friends premiered with *Blues Suite*, dances set in a honky-tonk dance hall. Stage lights cast moody shadows against the glimmer of each dancer's skin. The women flaunted red-hot dresses with shoes and stockings to match; the men wore black hats slouched low on their heads. They danced to the swanky-swank of a jazz rhapsody.

Alvin's choreography depicted the blues, that weepy sadness all folks feel now and then. *Blues Suite* stirred every soul in the room.

Alvin was on his way to making it big. Word spread quickly about him and his dancers. Newspapers hailed Alvin. Radio announced his debut.

An even bigger thrill came when the 92nd Street Y asked Alvin to perform again. He knew they hardly ever invited dance companies to come back. Alvin was eager to show off his next work.

On January 31, 1960, gospel harmonies filled the concert hall at the 92nd Street Y.

Rock-rock-rock
Rocka-my-soul
Ohhh, rocka-my-soul

Alvin clapped in time to the music, the same way he did when he was a boy. But now, Alvin rejoiced onstage in *Revelations*, a suite of dances he created to celebrate the traditions of True Vine Baptist Church in Navasota, Texas.

The audience swayed in their seats as Alvin and his company gloried in their dance. High-stepping ladies appeared onstage sweeping their skirts. They danced with grace and haughty attitudes. Alvin and the other men jumped lively to the rhythm, strutting and dipping in sassy revelry.

Revelations honored the heart and the dignity of black people while showing that hope and joy are for everyone. With his sleek moves, Alvin shared his experiences and his dreams in a way no dancer had ever done.

When *Revelations* ended, the audience went wild with applause. They stomped and shouted. "More!" they yelled. "More!"

Taking a bow, Alvin let out a breath. He raised his eyes toward heaven, satisfied and proud.

ARTHUR ASHE

David K. Wright

Arthur Ashe, the first male African American to play professional tennis, won thirty-three championship titles during his tennis career. In addition to his success on the court, he was also a teacher, author, and activist—always reaching out to those in need and providing inspiration to all who knew him.

GROWING UP

Arthur Ashe, Jr., was one of two children of Arthur Ashe, Sr., and Mattie Cordell Cunningham Ashe. He was born on July 10, 1943, in Richmond, Virginia, the capital of the Confederate States of America during the Civil War (1861–1865). Richmond is a handsome city halfway between the Atlantic Ocean and the Appalachian Mountains. Today it has a population of more than two hundred thousand. Much of the area was burned during the Civil War but recovered quickly because of the tobacco industry. Although it is just over one hundred miles south of Washington, D.C., the Richmond where Arthur grew up was a very segregated, very southern community.

African Americans in the 1940s were not allowed to sit in the front half of Richmond's public buses. They attended separate schools. There were separate drinking fountains and restrooms and houses of worship and public parks for blacks and for whites. The races played sports separately, sat in different parts of movie theaters, and ate in different sections of restaurants. Perhaps most important, they had very different views of history.

Longtime white residents of Richmond were proud of their battlefield memorials and their southern heritage. Many blacks knew little or nothing of their own history—their ancestors had been prevented from learning to read or write, taking the stories of their lives with them to the grave. Yet Arthur Ashe and his family were fortunate. Large, close, and inquisitive, they traced their roots back more than three hundred years to an African woman who survived the frightful voyage from the continent of her birth to Virginia on board an eighty-ton English ship known as *The Doddington*.

A West African, as were most slaves, the young woman was known only by a number until she was purchased by a man named Blackwell. She took the name of Blackwell and married a slave with that name. They had a daughter, Lucy, according to Virginia records. She was the first American-born member of Arthur Ashes's family tree. Several generations later, a person on the Blackwell side of the family married a South Carolina native who bore the name of Ashe, from an early governor of North Carolina. The Ashes had a son, Arthur, who married and became the tennis star's father.

How could the Ashe family know this? Fortunately, an aunt still keeps a huge family tree, painted on canvas, with the names of dozens of family members. Each is represented by a single leaf. The tree stands six by seven feet and was put together through years of careful research in old and musty courthouses along the East Coast. In the middle of the tree is a family crest showing a chain with a broken link. The broken chain symbolizes freedom for the slaves. Tennis star Arthur Ashe is the only person among fifteen hundred family members whose leaf is painted in gleaming gold.

Arthur certainly did not seem destined for stardom on July 10, 1943. He was a small, thin baby, and his lean appearance would stay with him all of his days. He remembered himself as a child with ears that stuck out and legs so skinny that friends and relatives believed he had some sort of disease.

Mattie Ashe, Arthur's mother, died shortly before his seventh birthday. Her death occurred at the pitifully young age of twenty-seven and was caused by a stroke brought on by a problem pregnancy and complicated by a weak heart. She had been ill for some time—Arthur later realized that he often envisioned her in a blue corduroy dressing gown. Arthur, Sr., broke the news of his wife's death tearfully to Arthur and his younger brother, Johnnie, as the three sat on the lower bunk in the boys' bedroom.

"Don't cry, Daddy," Arthur told his father. "As long as we have each other, we'll be all right."

The young boy's words were prophetic. His father kept a close eye on Arthur and Johnnie, and the two boys would do well in school and elsewhere. Young Arthur's father was not educated or wealthy, but one of the jobs he held in the city was an important one—he maintained the parks where African Americans were permitted to play. Part of his job was to keep tennis courts in these parks in good playing condition. Shortly after his mother's death, Arthur stood beside one of the courts one morning watching Ron Charity, Richmond's best African-American tennis player.

Charity was practicing his high, hard serves. He could feel the eyes of the thin, silent boy who lived in the only house in leafy, eighteen-acre Brook Field playground. Charity stopped practicing long enough to approach young Arthur and ask, "Would you like to learn to play?" Arthur said he would. "As casually as that, my life was transformed," Arthur would later remember.

Arthur, Sr., felt his son was too thin for football and other contact sports, and he made him take naps long after other children stayed up all day. He was relieved to see the boy learn the rules of tennis as he swatted madly at the bouncing balls. Young Arthur loved the game and showed real ability. A couple of years later, in 1953, the ten-year-old would pose for a newspaper photo amid a number of trophies. But these were trophies won mostly at Brook Field playground, not at the larger and better equipped whites-only private clubs. Except for an occasional white player who wandered onto his local court, Arthur was unable to compete against most of the good players in Richmond.

Many people, in and outside his family, helped young Arthur with his game. But none did more for him than a former college athlete who took up tennis to stay in shape. Robert Walter Johnson was a rugged man, a baseball player, and a college football player in the days when no helmets were worn. He attended several African-American colleges after World War I, eventually earning a medical degree. Johnson settled into his practice in Lynchburg, Virginia, where he spent some time looking for a sport he could play the rest of his life.

A thoughtful man, Johnson tried basketball and several other sports before picking up a tennis racket. He stuck with tennis because it was not an easy thing for him to master. But master it he did, playing at the local black YMCA and analyzing the games of white players at parks or at private clubs. Johnson thought enough of tennis to enter and win important African-American tournaments and pay for the construction of a court in his back yard.

Johnson decided to organize young African-American tennis players. He wanted to help local boys enter the United States Lawn Tennis Association's national high-school tournament, held nearby each year. The first two boys he entered were overwhelmed by more experienced white players. Was it true what some tennis publications said—that African Americans lacked the subtle touch required to be great players?

Johnson did not believe so. He spent a large sum of money to make his backyard facility an all-weather, enclosed court, and he invited more and more boys to stay at his home each summer to learn his favorite game. Living and practicing with Johnson was no picnic: He forced his players to control their emotions on the court. No one was allowed to raise his voice, throw his racket, or otherwise draw attention to himself.

Off the court, he set the children to work raking his yard, maintaining the court, cleaning the dog kennel, making their beds, and more. They were taught which foods were good for them, they learned table manners, and they were told how to act when a lady or an adult entered the room. Johnson's goal, he said, was for the players to be "accepted without being a center of attraction." He knew white people would more readily allow black players on tennis courts if they behaved.

Each year in the early 1950s, boys under Johnson's care would enter the big high-school tournament. Each year they would be beaten, though they were no longer humiliated by their lack of ability. Meanwhile, in 1953, Ron Charity called Dr. Johnson. A recent college graduate and a ranked player in a national African-American tennis association, Charity told the doctor that he had been teaching a boy for a couple of years who showed promise. Though small, ten-year-old Arthur Ashe seemed to care a great deal about the game, and Charity wanted someone else who was a good judge to see him play.

RAY CHARLES

David Ritz

Ray Charles's remarkable mother made sure that her son would be able to survive on his own despite losing his sight while still a small child. Indeed, Charles triumphed over blindness, poverty and racism to become one of the most highly acclaimed musicians in the world, shaping the gospel and blues of his youth into his own personal style.

THE DARK

In the small waiting room of Dr. McCloud's office, Ray sat next to his mother. It had been more than a year since his brother had died, and Ray's head was filled with troubling thoughts. For months now, after waking up in the morning, his eyes had been covered with thick crust. Aretha Robinson used a damp cloth to wipe Ray's matted eyelids; after about 10 minutes, he would begin blinking and adjusting to the morning light. But there was definitely something wrong with his eyes. Each week he saw less and less. The process was gradual, yet the signs were clear.

There were two doctors in Greensville, both white men, Dr. King and Dr. McCloud. King administered only to white people, whereas McCloud treated blacks as well as whites.

"Will Dr. McCloud be able to help me?" Ray asked his mother.

"I don't know," she replied.

Ray was uneasy during the examination. The doctor appeared before him as a large blob, and Ray could not make out the features on Dr. McCloud's face.

"Tell me what you can and cannot see," the physician told Ray.

"I used to be able to make out people and trees and cars, things like that," Ray explained. "Big things. Then everything got blurred but I could still make out the different colors, the blue in the sky and the green in the grass. Then even the colors got blurred, but I can still see if it's day or night. I know if it's light or dark."

While Ray was speaking, the doctor looked into his eyes with special lights. Ray felt the heat from the instruments; he imagined looking into the burning sun.

When the examination was over, Dr. McCloud prescribed some ointments and eye drops, hoping that these medications would be of some help. Weeks passed, however, and nothing seemed to aid Ray's condition. Eventually, Dr. McCloud recommended that Mrs. Robinson take her son to a clinic in Madison, not far from Greensville. Mother and son went to the doctor's office in Madison, where Ray was thoroughly examined. Mrs. Robinson turned to the doctor and said, "Tell me, is there hope?"

The doctor paused a long while before he replied. "I'm afraid not, Mrs. Robinson. Your boy is losing his sight."

"But what about cures?" asked Aretha Robinson. "There must be cures."

"I don't know of any," answered the physician, who believed that the blindness was being caused by a disease known as glaucoma.

"I understand," she replied.

Aretha Robinson took Ray by the hand and led him out of the clinic. When they reached Greensville, they walked down the main street of town—past the bank, the post office, the general store, and across the rail-road tracks, back into the woods and into their one-room shack. Aretha Robinson had said nothing to her son until they were in the privacy of their home.

"This is not the end of the world," she told Ray. "I'm not saying it's going to be easy, but it's not going to be impossible. You aren't dying. You're losing your sight, not your mind. The rest of your body works fine. Your mind is good, Ray. You can still do whatever you want to do. But I'm going to have to teach you, and you're going to have to pay special attention. I'm going to teach you to cook and clean and do all your chores like any other child. And the reason I'm going to teach you is 'cause I won't always be around to do for you."

"Don't say that," Ray protested. "You'll always be here."

"No, I won't. You got to know that. And when I'm gone, you're gonna have to do for yourself. Understand?"

Mrs. Robinson reached down and hugged her son with all the strength of her frail body. She kissed his forehead and said, "I love you and I'm going to help you. I'm going to help you do for yourself."

A week later, on a Saturday morning, a woman named Mary Jane came to visit. Mary Jane was Aretha Robinson's age and once had been married to Bailey, Ray's father. Over the years she had grown especially fond of Ray. In fact, the two were so close that, although he called Aretha "Mama," he referred to Mary Jane as "Mother."

Ray responded to Mary Jane's knock on the door. He had a scrub brush in his hand when she entered the shack and she saw how his eyes were squeezed together, closed tight. "What in the world are you doing?" she asked.

"Scrubbing the floor, like Mama showed me," answered Ray.

"Your mama shouldn't be making you do stuff like that," said Mary Jane, handing Ray several pieces of his favorite chocolate.

"Why not?" asked Mrs. Robinson, who had just arrived from town. The two women were friendly but differed greatly when it came to raising Ray. Aretha Robinson was a strict disciplinarian, whereas Mary Jane was extremely lenient. In different ways and for different reasons, Ray loved both women.

"Everyone's talkin' 'bout how you are treating this boy like he can see," said Mary Jane.

"Not seeing don't keep him from playing the piano, does it?" Aretha asked.

"I love playing the piano," Ray interjected.

"But he shouldn't be . . ." Mary Jane started to argue.

"He should be doing what most other kids are doing because he's as smart and strong as any of them," Aretha tersely replied.

"Look, 'Retha," Mary Jane tried to explain, "I know about strong. I'm working over at the sawmill right beside all those men, doing the same heavy hauling as them. But being blind is different."

"It's different," countered Aretha, "only in that the blind gotta go to different schools. That's what I been talkin' to the folks in town about. They say there's a school in St. Augustine, a state school for the deaf and the blind. They say that's where Ray should be going to school. That's where he gotta get his education."

"But St. Augustine is far away," said Ray.

"You'll go there to live," explained his mother. "All the kids live at school."

"But I wanna stay here. . ."

"It ain't right, 'Retha, to be sending a blind boy away from home," Mary Jane protested.

"What ain't right," Aretha replied, "is keeping Ray away from learning."

The days that followed were not easy for Ray. He knew there was no changing his mother's mind. He spent a lot of time with Mary Jane, who comforted him by cooking his favorite meals. At Mary Jane's house, there were no errands to run, no cleaning up to do, and no pressures. He wished he could live there or continue to live with his mother. It seemed as though anything would be better than having to go away to school.

Ray shuddered every time he thought about attending the Florida School for the Deaf and the Blind. He understood that he could not continue to go to a regular school; the teachers there did not know how to teach a blind person to read or write. But what about his friends? He did not want to leave them. And what about Mr. Pit, the man who always let him play the piano? What would he do without Mr. Pit and the Red Wing Cafe? Who else could show him music, the kind of boogie-woogie music Ray loved so much? Ray imagined that going away to school was worse than going blind.

Finally, in the fall of 1937, the day came. Ray's pleas did him no good. Aretha Robinson had done all she could to make him independent. This was the most difficult step for them both. Mrs. Robinson did not want to relinquish hold of her son, and yet she knew—to be responsible, to secure his survival—she had no choice but to let him go. She realized that Ray needed a decent education more than he needed her daily companionship. So far, he had responded well to the way in which she had pushed him out into the world. Ray was able to walk alone to his friends' homes; he traveled into town himself, taking little steps, cautiously making his way over a landscape that he had learned by feel—a tree here, a row of bushes there. Aretha Robinson had even seen her son ride a bicycle by himself.

The neighbors were amazed by, and some were even scornful of, Mrs. Robinson's attitude, but their opinions were beside the point. She was pleased that her son had displayed the confidence to ride the bicycle in an open field, his buddies giving him verbal instructions on how and where to direct the two-wheeler. Ray continued to show talent at the piano, and his interest in mechanics—taking apart engines of any kind—was keen. He lacked only sight.

By the fall of 1937, he was almost completely blind, able only to see bright lights. Mrs. Robinson knew he needed special instruction and there was no going back. The train was leaving for St. Augustine, located 160 miles east of Greensville, and Ray, only seven years old, was leaving home for the first time in his life.

DANIEL "CHAPPIE" JAMES

Glennette Tiley Turner

Realizing a dream is not easy, especially when there are many obstacles to overcome. But Daniel "Chappie" James achieved even more than he had thought possible.

When Daniel "Chappie" James was a little boy he used to see airplanes take off from the Naval Air Base in his hometown of Pensacola, Florida. This was in the 1920s, and airplanes weren't as commonplace as they are now. The public was fascinated by flight. Like many other children, Daniel James watched, and wished that he could fly a plane when he grew up. There were, however, many hurdles he would have to overcome in order to become a pilot.

He not only overcame the hurdles that it took to become a pilot, he went on to become a four-star general. He was the first black American to hold this rank. Most people who knew the times and circumstances in which Daniel James was born would not have predicted that he'd reach those heights.

James never doubted himself, though, and that was the secret to his success. He developed a knack for being in the right place at the right time, and creating an influential role for himself wherever he went. If he was in a situation where people were in disagreement, he was often able to say something to help solve—or smooth over—the problem.

He got his confidence and other important character traits from his parents. His father, Daniel James, Sr., was an ambitious, hardworking man who had come from Alabama to Florida as a migrant laborer. Once in Pensacola, he was able to improve his work situation. He found work as a lamplighter for the city of Pensacola. Later he took a job at the municipal gas plant. There he did skilled work and supervised other workers. He took his job and himself very seriously.

He set an example for his children as a person who didn't settle for second-best. He wasn't highly educated, but he wanted what he believed to be the best for his family. For example, he settled in a residential neighborhood rather than the Railroad Avenue area where migrant workers lived. He bought some other property, in addition to his home, and was a good provider for his family.

"Chappie" James's mother had grown up in Pensacola. She was a member of a family that had enjoyed opportunities and privileges that were not available to most black families. She had received a good education at St. Joseph's Catholic School. She firmly believed that the more education a black person had, the more opportunities he or she had. So she was determined that her children would have an excellent education. She was able to guarantee this, since she conducted her own private school in the family's backyard—even though she already had her hands full as the mother of seventeen children. Her standards were high, and being both mother and teacher, she was able to insist that her children strive for perfection. Her motto was what she called "the Eleventh Commandment": "Thou shalt never quit."

Daniel James took this advice to heart. Whenever he was faced with a problem, he figured out a way to get through it rather than quit. One of the first problems he had to solve was what to do about his name. Being the youngest in the family, he was called "Dan Baby." He liked the special place he held in the family, but when he'd finished his mother's grade school and was about to enter high school, he wanted more of a he-man nickname. He borrowed his new nickname from an older brother, Charles, who had been an outstanding college athlete. "Chappie" was Charles's nickname, so "Dan Baby" started calling himself "Little Chappie," which was later shortened to "Chappie," especially when he became a strapping six feet, four inches.

Another problem James had to deal with was what to do when he was in situations where he did not excel. His self-confidence and desire to be popular enabled him to stick with a difficult situation and make the best of it. He wanted to play high school football. He liked the glory and attention the players enjoyed. Even though he was not the greatest player, his enthusiasm and ability to encourage his teammates made him a well-liked member of the team. These personality traits helped him become "Big Man on Campus" when he entered college at Tuskegee Institute in Alabama. Most of the girls on campus admired him, but he married the one girl who was unimpressed with him. That was what made him pay attention to Dorothy Watkins. She was a shy girl who had grown up in the town of Tuskegee. It took "Chappie" four years to convince her he was as wonderful as everyone else thought he was.

Not only did James meet his bride at Tuskegee, it was there that "Chappie" first realized his childhood dream of learning to fly. In 1938—shortly before World War II—the Civil Aeronautics Administration responded to the urging of black newspapers and the NAACP that blacks have the same opportunity as other Americans to qualify for the U.S. Air

Corps. Flight training programs were set up at a number of black colleges to train civilian pilots. In March of 1941, Tuskegee Institute was chosen as the exclusive site for training black military pilots. "Chappie" James was in the right place at the right time. He excelled in the civilian Pilot Training Program and the military's advanced flying program. Although there was a handful of individual black men and women who held private pilot licenses, flight training had been generally inaccessible to black people. The "Tuskegee Experiment" provided the first real opportunity for black men to learn to fly. The cadets relished the challenge, and the success of the Tuskegee program was a great source of pride to black Americans.

As the Tuskegee pilots completed their training, they became commissioned officers in the United States Air Force. Many went into combat during World War II, serving in Europe and North Africa under the leadership of Colonel Benjamin O. Davis, Jr., a West Point graduate and son of the nation's only black general. Davis commanded the all-black 99th Pursuit Squadron which became a part of the 332nd Group. The 332nd won a Distinguished Unit Citation for its outstanding performance.

"Chappie" James was commissioned a second lieutenant in July of 1943. From then until the end of the war his main assignment was to train pilots for the 99th Pursuit Squadron. He had developed skill flying a variety of planes. His specialty was as a fighter pilot. It was in the Korean War that James first demonstrated his flying ability in combat. He flew 101 combat missions. He demonstrated his skill again in Vietnam when he flew 78 combat missions.

In the years between Korea and service in Vietnam, James had graduated from Air Command and Staff College at Maxwell Air Force Base in Alabama. He had been promoted and held important assignments in the United States and abroad. Upon his return from Vietnam, James was vice-commander of the 33rd Tactical Fighter Wing, Eglin Air Force Base in Florida. In 1969, he was promoted to the rank of brigadier general and named base commander of Wheelus Air Force Base in Libya.

The following year he became Deputy Assistant Secretary of Defense for Public Affairs, and was named major general while holding that post. In 1974, he became vice-commander of the Military Airlift Command at Scott Air Force Base in Illinois. One year later he became America's first black four-star general. (Benjamin O. Davis, Jr., was a lieutenant general when he retired.) At that time James became the commander of the North American Air Defense Command (NORAD), which meant that he was responsible for all aspects of the air defense of the United States and Canada. He remained in that command until health problems forced him to step down in December of 1977.

James played an important role throughout the 1960s and '70s when America was trying to resolve the discrepancies between the opportunities available to its black and white citizens. He was a living example of a black man who had made good. He was often asked to give talks on how he had overcome the hurdles he'd faced. He liked to tell young people—including his own children, Daniel, Claude, and Danice—the things he'd learned from his parents.

James's work had taken so much of his time and energy that he didn't get to spend a lot of time with his family. All through their marriage his wife had tried to get him to slow down. He had slowed down after he left NORAD, but he still had speaking engagements. One engagement was in Colorado the last week in February of 1978. Before leaving his wife, who was hospitalized with rheumatoid arthritis, they laughed and hugged and he told her he hoped she'd be feeling better by the time he got back.

After saying good-bye, "Chappie" James left for Colorado Springs. He had a heart attack and died there on February 25, 1978—just fourteen days after his fifty-eighth birthday. His body was flown back to Washington, D.C., where he was buried with the kind of honors usually reserved for presidents and other heads of state. More than 1,500 people attended his funeral. He was buried at Arlington National Cemetery.

In his relatively brief lifetime, "Chappie" James had dreamed what seemed to be an impossible dream—and he saw his dream come true.

MARTIN LUTHER KING, JR.

Robert Jakoubek

Martin Luther King, Jr., minister, Nobel laureate, and one of the best-known and most inspiring speakers and civil rights leaders in the country, believed in using nonviolent tactics to achieve equality. Those who share King's vision are still working to make his dream of a just society a reality.

YOU ARE SOMEBODY

The Reverend Martin Luther King, Sr., pastor of the Ebenezer Baptist Church, a leader of black Atlanta, demanded and claimed respect.

In his youth, he had been known as Mike, and he had come up the hard way. Born in 1899, he was from an unhappy family of poor sharecroppers in central Georgia. As a boy, Mike loved church, spent hours studying his Bible, and early on decided to become a minister. "I always felt extremely happy and completely at ease within the church setting," he recalled. "I never tired of going to the revivals, the baptisms, weddings, all the gatherings where people would be found bearing a particular witness."

When Mike reached the age of 15, the deacons of his church licensed him to minister, and he was soon traveling along back roads, preaching the gospel and singing hymns in black churches. Most of his days, however, were spent behind the plow, and he came to hate the tedium of farm work and rural life. After he turned 18, he left home for good, heading for Atlanta.

In the big city, Mike King took one job after another — vulcanizing tires, loading bales of cotton, driving a truck — and in a used Model T Ford that his mother had bought for him by selling a cow, he became something of a man about town. With such a fine car, he remembered, "Nothing, I now felt, could stop me. Nothing."

The ministry was still his goal, but country preachers were a dime a dozen in Atlanta. To get ahead, to become the preacher of a leading church, he needed a degree in theology. For an uneducated young man from backcountry Georgia, that was a lot to ask. But Mike's ambition pulled him along. He worked during the day, and at night he studied for a high school diploma. Finally, in 1926, he was admitted to Morehouse College, a respected black school, where he began divinity studies.

Shortly after arriving in Atlanta, Mike King met Alberta Williams, the shy, genteel daughter of one of the city's prominent Baptist ministers. Mike was captivated. Before long, he was the most regular caller at the Williamses' large house on Auburn Avenue. On nice days, the properly chaperoned couple took long rides in Mike's Model T.

During Mike's courtship of Alberta, he won the respect of her father, the Reverend Adam Daniel Williams, pastor of the Ebenezer Baptist Church. The Reverend Williams had risen about as high as a black person could in Atlanta. He ministered to a large congregation, took part in black civic organizations, and was a leading light and charter member of the local chapter of the National Association for the Advancement of Colored

People (NAACP), the nation's foremost antidiscrimination organization. Williams let his daughter know that Mike would make a fine husband, and, he added, a fine assistant minister at Ebenezer.

On Thanksgiving Day, 1926, Mike and Alberta were married. They moved in with Alberta's parents, there being plenty of space in the upstairs of the Williamses' 12-room house. Soon, King accepted his father-in-law's offer to become his assistant at Ebenezer, and when Williams died suddenly in 1931, Mike succeeded him in the pastorate.

When the Reverend King first settled in at Ebenezer, old friends still knew him as Mike. But as the years passed, more and more people were calling him "Daddy," and for the rest of his life that was how he would be best known — as Daddy King. The name fit. Not only was he the fatherly head of the church, but he and Alberta had a family of three splendid children: a daughter, Willie Christine, born in 1927, and two sons, Martin Luther and Alfred Daniel.

Martin Luther King, Jr., arrived in the world at noon on January 15, 1929, in a bedroom of his grandparents' house at 501 Auburn Avenue. Daddy King was so overjoyed at the birth of his first son that he leaped into the air and touched the ceiling. The family quickly took to calling the pudgy, healthy baby "M. L.," and a year and a half later, when a second boy was born, they nicknamed Alfred Daniel "A. D."

Daddy constantly prayed, "God grant my children will not have to come up the way I did." His prayers were answered; the family was well-off. "Not really wealthy," his son Martin would recall, "but Negro-wealthy. We never lived in a rental house and we never rode too long in a car on which payment was due, and I never had to leave school to work."

Quite naturally, life revolved around the Ebenezer church. Among M. L.'s earliest memories were the Sunday mornings when his father preached emotional, heartfelt sermons and his mother, the church's musical director, played lovely Christian hymns on the great pipe organ. The King children spent all day Sunday at church, and they were there several afternoons during the week as well. By the time M. L. was five, he was performing gospel songs at church affairs. Accompanied on the piano by his mother, he never tired of singing "I Want to Be More and More Like Jesus."

At home, M. L. was no saint. Once, he clobbered his brother, A. D., over the head with a telephone, knocking him out, and his sister Christine, could not help but notice how he always seemed to be in the bathroom when it was his turn to do the dishes.

The three children could put aside their squabbling though not always with a happy result. None of them cared for the piano lessons their mother insisted on, so they conspired against them. A. D. favored a direct approach and started assaulting the living-room piano with a hammer, but M. L. and Christine convinced him to try the more subtle tactic of loosening the legs of the piano stool. Their sabotage went off like clockwork: The music teacher arrived, sat on the stool, and crashed to the floor. Had anything, the children laughed, ever been so funny? Not in the least amused by the prank, their father gave each of them a thrashing.

Grandmother Williams, who lived with the Kings, was closest to M. L., and after a spanking, Christine remembered, she always had for him "a hug, kiss, or kind word to help the hurt go away."

M. L. lovingly called her "Mama," and he could not bear the thought of living without her. One day when he was roughhousing with A. D., his brother slid down the banister of the front stairway, missed his mark, and slammed into Mama, knocking her down. When she did not get up, M. L. was sure he and A. D. had killed her. Tears pouring from his eyes, he rushed into a bedroom and threw himself out of a window, landing hard on the ground 12 feet below. When his family hurried to him, shouting that Mama was fine, just a little bruised, M. L. picked himself up and strolled away.

Not long afterward, on a Sunday, M. L. sneaked away to watch a parade—something Daddy had strictly forbidden. When the youngster returned home, the house was filled with sobbing relatives. His grand-mother had suffered a heart attack and was dead. Shattered, sensing terri-ble guilt for having gone to the parade, he once more ran to a second-story window and jumped out. Unhurt beyond some bumps and scrapes, M. L. did not walk away this time. He cried and pounded the ground, a captive of grief.

M. L.'s leaps from upstairs windows naturally concerned his parents. What was he trying to do, they wondered—kill himself? But that seemed unlikely. He never again tried to do himself harm, and in every other was he was a normal, contented youngster. Like most boys, he did neighbor-hood jobs and delivered newspapers, once saving up $13 of his own. Although always a little small for his age, he enjoyed sports and competed fiercely, especially on the football field, where, said a friend, "he ran over anybody who got in his way." Sometimes, though, he left the playground, usually with a book. "Even before he could read he kept books around him, he just liked the idea of having them," Daddy recalled. In school, he was a teacher's dream—smart, disciplined, and well-mannered—and he breezed through with such good marks that he skipped grades in elementary school and high school.

By the time M. L was into his early teens, people commented on how mature he seemed. They took special notice when he spoke. Almost overnight, his voice had changed from a child's chirp into a beautiful , vibrant baritone. Girls his age loved the deep voice and liked the careful way he dressed. In those days, he favored a brown tweed suit, with trousers tight at the ankles and baggy in the legs. Boys, not nearly as impressed, for years called him "Tweed."

At Booker T. Washington High School, M. L. saw his studies suffer a bit because of the time he devoted to romance and dancing. A. D. said of his brother, "I decided I couldn't keep up with him. Especially since he was crazy about dances, and just about the best jitterbug in town."

When M. L put his mind to it, he could also be the best student in town. When he was 14 and in the 11th grade, he entered an oratorical contest sponsored by a fraternal group, the Negro Elks, and spoke on "The Negro and the Constitution." It was easily the best address, and M. L won first prize.

ROSA PARKS

Mary Hull

On a warm evening in December, Rosa Parks took a seat on a city bus in Montgomery, Alabama and when she later refused to give it up for a white passenger, the bus driver had her arrested. Her arrest led to a citywide bus boycott by black riders, ignited the civil rights movement, and ultimately brought an end to legal segregation in the South.

It was nearly 5:30 P.M. when Rosa Parks put away the piles of new suits she was working on and left her job at the Montgomery Fair department store to board a bus for home. The petite, bespectacled woman had been raising and lowering hemlines, altering waistbands, and adjusting sleeve lengths all day at her job as a tailor's assistant in the alterations department of the store. The holiday season was the busiest time of year for store workers, and this afternoon she was tired and her shoulder ached from bending over her sewing machine. As Rosa walked the half-block from the department store to the bus stop at Court Square, passing beneath the city's Christmas decorations, she was thinking of all the work she still had to do at home that night.

When the Cleveland Avenue bus pulled over to its stop at Court Square on that warm Thursday afternoon in 1955, Rosa Parks noticed that there were passengers standing inside, so she let the bus pass her by with the hope that the next one would be less crowded. While she waited for it to come along, she crossed the street and did some shopping. When she returned to the square with her shopping bag, a Cleveland Avenue bus stopped. Since no one appeared to be standing inside, she paid the ten-cent fare, boarded, and sat down in the first vacant seat she saw, in the eleventh seat back, on the aisle, immediately behind the whites-only section of the bus. A black man occupied the window seat to her right; two blacks sat in the seats across the aisle to her left.

The first 10 seats of every Montgomery city bus were reserved for white people only. Even if, as frequently happened, the bus was filled with only black passengers, to the extent that people were standing in the aisles, blacks were not to use these seats. (This differed from the practice in most other southern cities, where blacks would fill seats from the rear forward and whites from the front back; if no white passengers boarded on a particular route, blacks could occupy every seat on the bus.) Under the letter of the Montgomery city law, blacks could sit anywhere behind this whites-only section; they could be compelled to surrender their seat for a white passenger only if another was available. Alabama state law, however, gave bus drivers virtually unlimited discretion in enforcing segregation on their buses, and black passengers in Montgomery were frequently ordered to the rear of the bus to make way for white passengers once the whites-only section was filled to capacity. Often an entire row of black passengers was forced to stand or move rearward in order to free a single seat for a white rider, as segregation statutes prohibited a white and a black from sitting next to or even across the aisle from one another.

Many Montgomery bus drivers extended this kind of discrimination to their general treatment of black passengers. Although blacks paid the same bus fare as whites, many drivers did not extend them the same courtesies. For instance, drivers always picked up white passengers at every block, but they usually picked up black passengers at every other block. Some drivers forced blacks to enter their buses through the rear door; often, a black would pay his fare to the driver up front, only to have the driver take off before he or she was able to get back on.

Happy and relieved to have found a seat, Parks sat with her purse and shopping bag in her lap, thinking of the work still ahead of her at home, where she would prepare the letters she had to mail as part of her responsibilities as the volunteer secretary for the Montgomery branch of the NAACP (National Association for the Advancement of Colored People), the nation's oldest and most prominent civil rights organization. By now, she thought, her husband, Raymond, would already be home.

The bus pulled over to its stop at the Empire Theater, and six white passengers boarded. One white man did not find a seat. Although he did not raise any objection and stood quietly, the driver noticed that he was standing. Immediately, the driver, a portly man named J. F. Blake, ordered the four blacks in the sixth row to move so the white man could sit down.

"All right, you folks, I want those seats," he yelled back to them. (These words, quoted from David Garrow's Bearing the Cross, represent the politer of the many existing versions of what the bus driver said on that fateful day. According to the Reverend Ralph Abernathy, for example, in his autobiography And the Walls Came Tumbling Down, the driver referred to the four passengers he was addressing as "niggers," not "folks.") For a second, nobody moved. "Ya'll better make it light on yourselves and let me have those seats," the driver yelled. The man to Parks's right stood up to move. She shifted her legs to let him and then she herself moved — to the seat next to the window. Then the two women across the aisle got up. The driver repeated his order: "Look, woman, I told you I wanted the seat. Are you going to stand up?"

In a firm, steady voice, Parks questioned him. "Why should I have to get up and stand? Why should we have to be pushed around?" The driver slammed on the brakes and pulled the bus over to the curb. He walked back to her seat and stood over her. He asked her if she was going to move, and Parks said, "No." He told her he would call the police if she did not move. "Go ahead. You may do that," Parks answered. Blake left the bus angrily and went for the police. Several passengers—all of them black—followed, reluctant to become involved in an incident that invited trouble with whites. While everyone else aboard the bus waited to see what would happen next, Parks looked out the window at Montgomery.

Parks's mother and grandparents had always taught her not to regard herself as inferior to whites because she was black, but she admitted that until that fateful December day on the bus "every part of my life pointed to the white superiority and Negro inferiority." She was uncertain about what exactly had provoked her not to move on the bus driver's order, but her feet certainly hurt, her shoulders ached, and suddenly everything became too much. "I had had enough," Parks later said. She was tired of giving in. "I wanted to be treated like a human being. I knew someone had to take the first step, and I made up my mind not to move."

Two policemen returned with Blake to the bus. The driver pointed to Parks and said, "That one won't stand up."

"Why do you treat us so badly, always shoving us around?" Parks asked as the policemen approached. "I don't know," one of the officers said, "but the law is the law, and you're under arrest." One officer took Parks's purse, and the other took her shopping bag while she was led off the bus. As they left, an officer asked Blake if he wanted to press charges. "Yes," said the driver.

Parks rode in the back of the police car to Montgomery City Hall, where the police took her packages, asked her if there was anything in her pockets, and questioned her as to whether she was drunk, unable to believe that any respectable, sober woman would challenge white authority as Parks had done.

City police arrested Parks on charges of violating the segregation laws of Montgomery, but the city prosecutor, recognizing that technically Parks had not violated the city ordinance, decided that the arrest should be based on the segregation laws of the state of Alabama instead, a more serious offense. Parks was not allowed to call her husband until she was photographed and fingerprinted.

Meanwhile, unknown to Parks, someone who had seen her arrested had called Edgar Daniel Nixon, the former leader of the Montgomery NAACP and the city's most prominent black activist. Parks and R. D. Nixon, as his friends called him, had known each other since she joined the organization in 1943. As soon as Nixon learned of Parks's arrest, he telephoned the police station to ask what the charge was. "It's none of your goddamed business," the officer who answered his call told him. Nixon then called some white friends of Ray and Rosa Parks, Clifford and Virginia Durr. Clifford Durr, a lawyer with some influence in Montgomery, who had known the Parkses for several years, called the police station and found out that Parks had been arrested under the segregation laws. The Durrs drove Nixon to the police station and posted a $100 bond in exchange for Parks's release. . . .

After two hours in the cell, Parks was glad to see Nixon and the Durrs. Nixon had been looking for a chance to test the segregation laws of Montgomery and Alabama in court, and he regarded Parks's arrest as a prime opportunity. He explained later why Parks was such a perfect candidate for testing the law: "She was decent. And she was committed. . . nobody could point no dirt at her. You had to respect her as a lady."

What neither she nor anyone else could have foreseen was that the spontaneous individual action of this self-described "timid" woman would give rise to a collective movement that would force the entire United States, not just the city government of Montgomery, to confront its legacy of racial inequality and its professed belief in Thomas Jefferson's words, from the Declaration of Independence, that all men are created equal.

COLIN POWELL

Warren Brown

Colin Powell rose from the inner-city streets of New York to become a national hero. In 1989, President George Bush appointed him to America's top military post—chairman of the Joint Chiefs of Staff, making Powell the most powerful black military officer in American history.

MAKE SOMETHING OF YOUR LIFE

Colin Luther Powell was born on April 5, 1937, in New York City's Harlem district. Formerly an area of open farmland and country estates, Harlem became a residential neighborhood in the late 19th century, when a mixture of wealthy and working-class whites moved there to escape Manhattan's congested downtown area. To keep pace with the growing demand for housing, real estate developers constructed magnificent town houses and apartment buildings in this uptown section. By 1900, Harlem had emerged as one of the most desirable places to live in the city.

These developers overestimated the demand for housing, however, and by the early 1900s many apartments in Harlem were empty because not enough people could afford to live in such a high-rent district. Desperate to fill the vacant apartments, Harlem landlords drastically lowered their rents. The sudden availability of quality housing attracted large numbers of blacks seeking to escape the racial violence and poor living conditions on the city's congested West Side ghetto, and they moved to Harlem in droves. By the beginning of Word War I, 50,000 blacks resided in Harlem and formed a vibrant community with a middle-class standard of living.

Colin's parents, Luther Theopolis Powell and the former Maud Ariel McKoy, arrived in Harlem during the early 1920s, when the community was at its most prosperous. Both parents were from the island of Jamaica and had left their Caribbean homeland in the hope of finding their fortune in the United States. Like so many other immigrants drawn by the booming American economy during the 1920s, they settled in New York City, the thriving metropolis at the mouth of the Hudson River; with its bustling port and enormous wealth, the city seemed to offer limitless opportunity to anyone who sought a better life.

Neither Luther Powell nor Maud McKoy had finished high school, and so they had little choice but to join the large pool of working-class immigrants that served as the backbone of the city's labor force. Luther, a husky young man with a pleasant, round face, found work as a shipping clerk in a garment factory. At a picnic one day in the Bronx, New York City's only mainland borough, he met Maud McKoy. Shortly afterward, the pair married and made their home in Harlem.

Meanwhile, Harlem had begun to take on a special allure. As it became one of the few areas in the country where blacks could enjoy an unusually high quality of life, its writers, musicians, and actors celebrated their racial heritage and promoted their own culture. This awakening of black artistic and intellectual achievement came to be known as the Harlem Renaissance.

Yet underneath the surface of this growing, closely knit community lay the symptoms of decline. By 1930, 200,000 of New York City's 327,000 blacks lived in Harlem, and they were all crowded together in an area that had housed only a quarter of that number 15 years earlier. When the Great Depression began to ravage the nation in the 1930s, Harlem was especially hard hit. Long lines of unemployed people in search of food and clothing stretched in front of the local churches and charity organizations. Families evicted from their apartments because they could not pay the rent crowded into the homes of relatives or lived on the street. What had previously been one of New York City's most beautiful areas began to deteriorate rapidly.

It was into this black community, in desperate decline but still treasuring proud memories, that Colin Powell was born. He lived in Harlem until he was three years old, then his parents decided it was time to relocate. In 1940, Luther and Maud Powell packed their belongings, and with Colin and his sister, Marylin, who was five and a half years older than him, in tow, they followed the city's ever expanding elevated railway line northeast, across the Harlem River to the Bronx.

The Powells settled in Hunts Point, a working-class neighborhood in the southeastern section of the borough. The family made its home in a walk-up apartment building on Kelly Street. In time, the area would reach the extreme levels of urban decay and devastation that have come to characterize Harlem. But in the 1940s, residents called the borough "the beautiful Bronx," and Harlemites who moved into Hunts Point's blue-collar neighborhood felt that they had moved up in the world.

Although the local population was mainly Jewish, Hunts Point contained a mixture of New York City's various immigrant groups. Jews mixed freely with blacks, Irish, Italians, Poles, and Puerto Ricans, and their children mingled unself-consciously in play. As a result, young Colin never paid much attention to the color of his skin. "I grew up in a neighborhood where everybody was a minority," he recalled. "I never thought there was something wrong with me because I was black."

The fact that his parents came from Jamaica also contributed to Colin's lack of self-consciousness about his race. Even though blacks in Jamaica were British subjects, they rarely experienced the sort of racial oppression that many black Americans, particularly those in the southern states, endured. When Powell's parents arrived in the United States, they did not view themselves as second-class citizens, and they never allowed their children to think that way either.

Instead, Luther and Maud Powell instilled in their son and daughter a strong faith in the Anglican church and a healthy respect for formal education. They wanted Colin and Marylin to do well in life and insisted that getting ahead in America depended on learning as much as possible. As a result, the Powell children often received lectures from their parents to "strive for a good education. Make something of your life."

Luther and Maud Powell also told their children that only hard work and perseverance could lead to success. Colin recalled later, "There was something of a tradition of hard work being the way to succeed, and there was simply an expectation that existed in the family—you were supposed to do better. And it was a bloody disappointment to the family if you didn't."

Colin's parents certainly led by example. Each morning, Luther Powell left home at an early hour to catch the elevated train to his job in New York City's Garment District, and he remained there all day, never returning home form work until at least 7:00 or 8:00 in the evening. Maud Powell found a job as a seamstress, and she too spent many long hours doing her work. "It wasn't a matter of spending a great deal of time with my parents discussing things," Colin remembered. "We didn't sit down at night . . . and review the work of the day. It was just the way they lived their lives."

Even though both his parents worked, young Colin never went unsupervised during the day. Maud's mother, who was known to everyone as Miss Alice, and other relatives stayed with him and his sister to enforce discipline. In addition, nearby families made a habit of watching one another's children. Marylin recalled years later that "when you walked down the street, you had all these eyes watching you."

In spite of this upbringing, Colin showed few signs during his childhood of responding to his parents' desire that he apply himself in school. Early on in elementary school, when he was about eight years old, he attempted to play hooky. The young truant estimated the time wrong, however, and arrived home too early. A family friend caught him, and a family discussion ensued. In the days that followed, an adult was always present to take Colin by the hand and lead him to the classroom door.

Colin, however, did not change his ways. As a fifth grader at Public School 39, he was such a lackluster student that he landed in the slow class. At both Intermediate School 52 and Morris High School, he continued to apply himself indifferently. In his own words, he "horsed around a lot" and managed to keep his grades only barely above passing. His unspectacular marks kept him from realizing an ambition to attend the Bronx High School of Science, one of the nation's finest schools.

By this time, Colin had developed into a tall, strong teenager with a natural flair for leadership. At Morris High School, he was elected class representative, served as treasurer of the Service League, whose members helped out around the school, and lettered in track. Neighborhood youths learned not to push him around. He moved freely among Hunts Point's various racial groups and even managed to learn some Yiddish while working after school at Sickser's, a store that sold baby furniture. In his free time, Colin and his best friend, Gene Norman, raced bicycles along the sweeping curve of Kelly Street or played games of stickball.

When Colin graduated from Morris High School in early 1954, he said that he wanted to become an engineer; but in reality, he had very little idea of what he wanted to do with his life. His parents, insisting that he lift himself out of Hunts Point's "$40-a-week, lower blue-collar environment,"

made it clear that they expected him to go to college. Colin had no particular urge to get a higher education, but he had a deeply ingrained sense
of obedience to his mother and father. If they expected him to attend college, he would go.

Colin applied to New York University and to the City College of New
York. Despite his low grades, both institutions accepted him. Tuition costs
helped Colin narrow down his choice. New York University charged students $750 per year to attend. The City College of New York, situated on
138th Street in upper Manhattan, enrolled any graduate from a New York
City high school for only a token $10 fee. Accordingly, on a cold winter
day in February 1954, Colin took a bus to Manhattan and began his life as
a City College student.

Colin enrolled in City College's engineering program, and he did mod-
erately well at first, ending his initial semester with a B average. But during the summer of 1954, he took a mechanical drawing course, and it
proved to be the most miserable summer of his life. When, on a boiling hot
afternoon, his instructor asked him to imagine a cone intersecting a plane
in space, Colin decided that he had had enough of engineering and
dropped out of the program.

Colin decided to change his major to geology, not because of any strong
interest in the subject but because he thought it would be easy. He did not
push himself very hard and saw his average creep down to a C.

Nevertheless, Colin was about to display his first real enthusiasm for a
school-related activity. During his first spring at City College, he had
noticed uniformed members of the Army Reserve Officers' Training Corps
walking around the campus. The ROTC offered students military training
that could lead to a commission as an officer in the U.S. Army. Colin
decided that he liked the serious look of the members of the Pershing

Rifles, the ROTC drill team, who wore small whipped cords on their uniform shoulders.

Colin already possessed a mild interest in the military. In high school, he had closely followed the unfolding of the Korean War. His interest aroused, Colin signed up for the ROTC for the fall semester of 1954 and pledged himself to the Pershing Rifles.

At that point, Colin had no intention of making the army a career. He wanted only to find a way to escape from New York City for a while and, in his own words, "have some excitement." Besides, joining the ROTC would help him find work. He expected to serve no more than two years in the army after graduating from college "and then come home and get a real job." But as it turned out, he had stumbled onto his life's calling.

Arthur A. Schomburg

Glennette Tiley Turner

*In Arthur A. Schomburg's quest to find and document the
achievements of countless blacks whose contributions had gone unrecognized,
he also secured his own place in history.*

Do you like to solve mysteries? Arthur A. Schomburg sure did.

From the time he was a boy in Puerto Rico until his death in New York years later, he conducted a lifelong search for "missing persons." He believed that proper credit had not been given to many of the accomplishments of black people throughout history. The names and deeds of black kings and queens, explorers, mathematicians, inventors, philosophers, and artists were relatively unknown. Yet these persons had made great contributions.

Schomburg felt it was important for everyone to know about the achievements of these "missing persons." Learning about these achievers would have special meaning to people of African ancestry. They would have these people as role models. They would know that other black people had accomplished great things, and they could do the same if they tried.

Armed with only a few clues, Schomburg's search was especially difficult because when he began, even he did not know the names of many of the people he was trying to find.

Arthur Alfonso Schomburg was born in San Juan, Puerto Rico, on January 1874. Little is known about his early years, but it is known that his parents were Charles Schomburg and Mary Joseph. His father was a merchant whose father probably come to Puerto Rico from Hamburg, Germany, and married Maria Monserrate Bercedonis of Aguadilla, Puerto Rico. His mother was a washerwoman and a midwife. Her parents were from St. Croix in the Virgin Islands.

Information about Schomburg's education is sketchy. The accounts of his life do not agree about the amount of education he received. Most say that he was largely self-taught. He spent a lot of time around the cigar workers of Puerto Rico. According to one source, the cigar workers helped teach him his ABCs.

At some point in his growing up years, he went to the Virgin Islands to live with his mother's father, Nicholas Joseph. He probably attended the College of St. Thomas during this period.

He returned to San Juan on at least one occasion. While there he participated in an international history club. The members of the club were all social equals. Schomburg noted, however, that the white members knew and took pride in their history. The members of African ancestry were not as familiar with their history. Not knowing their history, they could not draw inspiration from it.

This prompted Schomburg to learn all he could so that he could speak knowledgeably. At first he read all he could about the history of black Puerto Ricans. He noted that "The works of José Julian Acosta and Salvador Brau have been my first inspiration to a further and intense study of the Negro." His study soon broadened and he began to try to unearth the history of Africans and their descendants in the Caribbean and elsewhere around the world.

Like every good detective, he followed every clue. He would write down every fact he could find. The more he looked for information, the more he was able to find. Schomburg believed it was important to have evidence — to be able to show proof—of things black people had accomplished. He was not only interested in history. He was interested in every kind of black self-expression. He collected documents, manuscripts, poems, plays, sermons, letters, music, and artwork.

Schomburg traveled far and wide in his effort to find evidence of the worldwide African presence. He conducted a tireless search of the book markets of the United States, Latin America, and Europe. Once when in Spain, he used his knowledge of black Spanish artists and slavery to do some superb detective work that probably no one else in the world was in a position to do. He located a long-lost picture by artist Juan de Pareja.

It was in April of 1891 when Arthur Schomburg moved to New York City. He lived in the community of Puerto Rican and Cuban cigar workers and artisans. At that time, both Puerto Rico and Cuba were Spanish colonies. Schomburg's neighbors belonged to political organizations that worked to free their homelands from Spanish rule.

Soon after Schomburg landed in New York he went to see Flor Baerga, a leader in the Caribbean independence movement and an amateur book collector. Schomburg shared Baerga's political philosophy and his interest in collecting.

By 1926, Schomburg had 11,000 books and other items he had collected. He had financed his purchases with his earnings. His first job in New York was in the law offices of Pryor, Mellis, and Harris. After five years he went to work for Bankers Trust Company on Wall Street and he remained there for twenty-three years.

Throughout these years Schomburg spoke and wrote about his abiding interest in books. One of the things he did was to compile a bibliography. His essay, "The Negro Digs Up His Past," appeared in Alain Locke's book, *The New Negro*. In 1911, Locke and John E. Bruce had founded the Negro Society for Historical Research. They published a paper in which Schomburg made a plea for more African and African-American history to be taught in schools and colleges.

Meanwhile, Schomburg's private collection had become so extensive and so highly respected that the National Urban League worked out an arrangement with the Carnegie Corporation to purchase the collection for the New York Public Library system. Carnegie paid $10,000. The collection was to remain intact and be housed at the 135th Street library.

This arrangement fulfilled two of Schomburg's wishes. He had wanted the collection to be accessible to students of black history, and to provide inspiration to black writers. His collection became a valuable resource for students and writers during the Harlem Renaissance—that period of new ideas by leading black writers and artists in the 1920s. This was typical of Schomburg, for he had always been very generous about sharing his books.

In 1927, Schomburg received the William E. Harmon Award for outstanding work in the field of education. In 1929, he retired from his job on Wall Street and became the curator of a collection at Fisk University in Nashville, Tennessee. He built up the Fisk collection to include every kind of information from Ashanti customs to Zulu nursery rhymes.

In 1932, another gift from the Carnegie Corporation made it possible for the New York Public Library to hire Schomburg to be reunited with his collection. He became the curator of the Division of Negro Literature,

History, and Prints. He remained there—doing the work he loved most—until his death in June, 1938. After his death, the division was renamed the Schomburg Collection of Negro Literature and History. In 1973, it became the Schomburg Center for Research in Black Culture.

Today the Schomburg Center—which is located at 135th Street and Lenox Avenue in New York City—has the world's largest and most complete collection of material about the history, writings, and art of black people.

Arthur Alfonso Schomburg had started out looking for "missing persons" in black history. He found and collected proof that black people had made great achievements. Then he shared his findings.

On a more personal note, Schomburg was widowed twice. His first wife, the former Elizabeth Hatcher from Virginia, died in 1902. His second wife, Elizabeth Marrow Taylor from North Carolina, died in 1909. He was survived by this third wife, Elizabeth Green, one daughter, and seven sons.

Arthur Schomburg's legacy is stated in the essay he wrote in *The New Negro:* "History must restore what slavery took away, for it is the social damage of slavery that the present generation must repair and offset."

SOJORNER TRUTH

Peter Krass

*In her mid-forties, Truth began her crusade as a traveling preacher.
Asking God to give her a new name to use as she went about doing His work,
she received a message to change her slave name of Isabella to Sojourner Truth.*

When the first bit of sunlight illuminated the sky over New York City on June 1, 1843, Isabella was already awake, stuffing a few dresses into an old pillowcase. The day of her departure had come at last. Her employers, the Whitings, were stunned by the news that she was leaving and asked her where she would be staying. "The Lord is going to give me a new home," Isabella told them,

Heading east, in the direction that an inner voice had told her to follow, Isabella took a ferry to Brooklyn. There she disembarked and began walking on a road that stretched eastward, toward Long Island. At age 46, she felt free, as though she were repeating the escape from slavery that she had made nearly 17 years before.

However, something still bothered Isabella. She believed that the name she had been given as a slave was inappropriate for a person who was beginning a new life as God's pilgrim. She wanted a new name, a free woman's name.

Calling on God for help in choosing her new name, Isabella received an answer. She should call herself "Sojourner." She thought that it was a good name for someone who had been called on, she later said, to "travel up and down the land, showing the people their sins, and being a sign unto them." The name also reminded her of the holy people described in the Bible who had traveled to foreign lands to preach the word of God. More and more, she felt as though she was following in the tradition of the great prophets of biblical times.

Proudly bearing her new name, Sojourner continued walking for another few miles, until she saw a woman working in front of a house. Having grown thirsty, Sojourner asked her for some water. As the woman was gladly fulfilling Sojourner's request, she asked the traveler what her name was.

When Sojourner told her, the woman attempted to find out what Sojourner's last name was and asked, "Sojourner what?" Her name was simply Sojourner, the traveler said, and then she continued on her journey. Yet the woman's question continued to nag at her. Why did she not have a last name?

Once again, Sojourner prayed for guidance. And once more, an answer came to her: Truth. Her full name would be Sojourner Truth—a very suitable name for one of God's pilgrims, she thought.

As Truth traveled east across Long Island the white farmers whom she encountered stopped their work to listen to her, finding themselves enthralled by the powerful and inspiring manner in which she spoke. They were amazed that she seemed to know every word in the Bible even though she was illiterate.

Word about the fiery preacher spread throughout Long Island. People began to whisper, "It must be Sojourner Truth" whenever she appeared at a religious meeting in a new neighborhood.

Eventually, Truth decided that she should follow God's call by heading to another area. She took a ship across Long Island Sound and proceeded northward, preaching in Connecticut and Massachusetts. Wherever she went, people flocked to listen to her.

Truth eventually arrived in Northampton, a town located along the Connecticut River in the heart of Massachusetts. There she visited the Northampton Association of Education and Industry, a cooperative community that operated a silkworm farm. The community members shared equally in all of the work but did not participate in any of the religious fanaticism that had existed in Robert Matthew's Kingdom commune. Attracted by the Northampton Association's idealism and spirit of good fellowship, Truth joined the community in late 1843.

While Truth was living at the community, she met many prominent public figures. Among the people who either lived in the community or came to visit the Northampton Association were abolitionists Samuel Hill, George Benson, and David Ruggles, as well as two of the leading organizers and speakers of the antislavery movement, William Lloyd Garrison and Frederick Douglass. Although the importation of slaves into the United States was forbidden after 1801, slavery was still being practiced in most of the southern states. Led by Garrison and Douglass, the abolitionist movement sought to put an end to slavery.

In 1831, Garrison had founded an influential antislavery newspaper, the Liberator, and he had formed the New England Anti-Slavery Society during the following year. Douglass, who had escaped from slavery in 1838, was just beginning to enjoy his reputation as one of the most eloquent abolitionist lecturers. Truth was greatly impressed by the effectiveness of these activists in stirring up antislavery sentiment in the North.

Between 1846 and 1850, Truth became increasingly involved in the antislavery crusade. For the most part, Truth associated more with Garrison's American Anti-Slavery Society than with its rival organization, the less militant American and Foreign Anti-Slavery Society.

Garrison's organization distrusted political parties and stated that slavery could be destroyed only by moral persuasion. The Garrisonians believed that accounts of the cruelties of the slave system printed in abolitionist newspa-pers would eventually compel the slaveholders to change their ways. The American and Foreign Anti-Slavery Society, on the other hand, cooperat-ed with the Liberty party, the Free Soil party, and other progressive political organizations in working for national laws that would outlaw slavery. . . .

By the early 1850s, many slave narratives had caught the public's atten-tion. The most widely read of these books was The Narrative of Frederick Douglass, which was published in 1845, at a time when the abolitionist leader was still a fugitive slave. These books not only presented the unvarnished truth about the brutal slave system, but they also gave stirring accounts of the courage and dignity of slaves who had escaped from bondage. Some of the slave narratives became best-sellers, and they helped to arouse a growing feel-ing of moral revulsion against slavery among Northerners.

Olive Gilbert, a friend of Truth, believed that a narrative of her early life as a slave in the North and her profound faith in God would be uplift-ing to many people. Truth liked the idea, and in 1850, she and Gilbert published The Narrative of Sojourner Truth, which included an introduc-tion by Garrison. Truth, who could not read the account of her own life, was able to support herself by selling copies of the book at abolitionist meetings.

The fight against slavery was not the only cause to which Truth was attracted. During her stay at the Northampton Association, she had heard lecturers who advocated that women be given the same political and legal rights enjoyed by men. Recognizing that she and the women's rights speakers were kindred spirits, Truth decided to join their ranks in yet another battle for freedom.

Not all of the male members of the antislavery movement agreed with Truth and the other women abolitionists on the issue of women's equality. Garrison and Douglass were avid supporters of women's rights, but many of the abolitionists remained unsympathetic to the feminist cause and did not want to allow women to assume leadership roles in antislavery societies. . .

. . . In 1848, feminists organized the first national women's rights conference at a church in Seneca Falls, New York. Hundreds of female activists were joined by a courageous group of men who supported women's equality. Disregarding the jeers of antifeminist men in the audience, the delegates issued a Declaration of Sentiments and Resolutions, a document based to a great extent on the Declaration of Independence. The declaration proposed an 11-point plan for helping women achieve equality with men.

Truth did not attend the 1848 convention, but she went to many other women's rights meetings. In October 1850, she traveled to Worcester, Massachusetts, to speak at that year's national women's rights convention.

At last, Truth was called on to speak. "Sisters," she began, "I ain't clear what you'd be after. If women want any rights more than they's got, why don't they just take them, and not be talking about it?"

However, the problem of attaining equal rights for women was more complex than Truth was willing to admit at the convention. The chief problem was that a sizable number of men strongly opposed equality for women and were ready to fight to preserve the status quo. In addition, the women's rights activists disagreed among themselves about the best way to achieve their goals. Some wanted to pursue their rights in law courts, while others believed that putting pressure on political parties and congressmen would achieve better results. The debates would continue for years at annual conventions held throughout the country.

Yet Truth's defiant message at the 1850 women's rights convention heartened the ranks of the nation's abolitionists and feminists as well as all of the oppressed people who yearned for equality. "Why not just take your rights?" she had asked. Many Americans who were deprived of their rights in their own land were beginning to ask the same question.

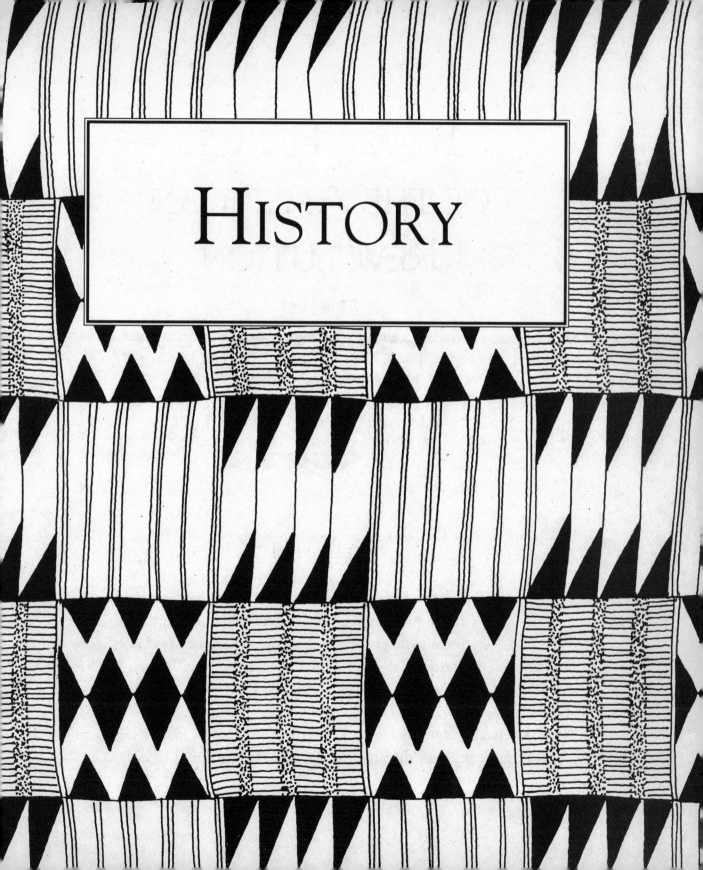

HISTORY

Black Heroes of the American Revolution

Burke Davis

Though their names usually did not appear in the history books, the contributions of countless black Americans during the country's war of independence cannot be overestimated.

William Lee

William Lee, whose name is unknown to most Americans, was by the side of George Washington at almost every minute of the Revolution, sharing dangers, victories, and defeats and was perhaps the general's closest companion before and after the war. Washington later gave William Lee his freedom and left money to care for him in old age. It was probably because of his friendship with his black companion that the general, even though, like Jefferson, a slaveholder, said that there was "not a man living" who wished more sincerely than he that slavery could be abolished by law.

GEORGE LATCHOM

George Latchom was the hero of a short skirmish in Virginia. During the last months of fighting in the Revolution, in 1781, a small British army landed on a sandy shore called Henry's Point, within a few miles of Yorktown. There were no troops of the regular American army to meet these invaders, but there was a band of Virginians, home guard soldiers who were known as militia.

A few of these untrained troops, led by Colonel John Cropper, fired at the British as they moved from their boats to the shore and kept up the fire until the redcoats were only a few yards away, charging with their bayonets. The white Colonel Cropper stood far in front of his men, exchanging shots with the British until the last. By his side was only one man: the slave George Latchom, who was owned by one of Cropper's neighbors.

Cropper and Latchom retreated through a marsh, where the colonel sank to the waist in soft mud, helpless before the oncoming enemy. George Latchom shot and killed the nearest redcoat, and when other enemy soldiers hesitated, he grabbed Cropper beneath the arms, tugged him free, and carried him to safety across the marsh. Men of both armies marveled at Latchom's strength, for Colonel Cropper was a large man who weighed some two hundred pounds.

As soon as the militia band was out of danger, Colonel Cropper bought George Latchom from his owner, set him free, and, as the colonel's biographer wrote, "befriended him in every way he could, as an evidence of his gratitude, till Latchom's death."

Austin Dabney

Austin Dabney, a slave on a Georgia plantation, was given a chance to win his freedom by serving in the American army when his master was drafted and asked Austin to take his place.

The slave accepted and soon became an artilleryman in the Georgia corps commanded by Colonel Elijah Clark. These gunners fought in several battles against the British in the South, including one at Cowpens, South Carolina, where almost an entire redcoat army was killed, wounded, or captured.

Austin Dabney and his companions also fought at the little battle of Kettle Creek, "the hardest ever fought in Georgia." Dabney was shot in the thigh during this heavy fighting. Later the Governor of Georgia said of Austin, "No soldier under Clark was braver, or did better service during the Revolutionary struggle."

Dabney was unable to walk for a time after being wounded at Kettle Creek, but was nursed back to health by a white soldier named Harris. Austin Dabney was so grateful that he spent several years working for the Harris family and insisted on sending the eldest son of his rescuer through college from his own pocket.

Dabney drew a pension like other veterans of the Revolution, but in 1819, when old soldiers were given chances in a lottery for lands in the western part of the state, he was not allowed to take part. Soon afterward, when the Georgia legislature finally awarded him 112 acres for his "bravery and fortitude" in several battles, Dabney's white neighbors in Madison County protested, claiming that it was "an indignity" to white men to have the black veteran treated equally in the awarding of public lands.

But Austin Dabney was not to be defeated. Not only did he win his land grant, he also eventually became a close friend of several wealthy planters of his neighborhood. He owned fine horses and took them to racetracks, where they ran against the horses of his white friends.

Dabney spent his old age in the village of Danielsville, Georgia, where he often went into the judge's chambers after the adjournment of the county court, talking with lawyers and judges about the long-gone days of the Revolution. With admiration one of them said of him: "His memory was retentive, his understanding good, and he described what he knew well."

Prince Whipple

One of the most famous paintings of the Revolution shows George Washington in a crowded small boat, crossing the icy Delaware River on Christmas night, 1776. The general was leading his tiny army across the river in a surprise attack on Trenton, New Jersey.

In the boat, helping to row through the ice floes, was Prince Whipple, a slave who was the bodyguard of General William Whipple of New Hampshire. The tall black man may have been the first to step ashore when Washington's boat landed on the dark banks, and he was certainly near the general during the night and early morning as the patriots marched through snow and sleet to attack the sleeping German troops in Trenton. No one remembered this bodyguard's part in the nine mile march against Trenton, but it was never forgotten that he was one of the leaders on the general's dangerous crossing of the river.

Prince Whipple was born in the African village of Amabou, where he lived until he was ten years old. His father, who was a man of some wealth, then sent the boy with one of his young cousins to America, where they were to be educated. But when they arrived in America, a greedy ship's captain took the boys to Baltimore, where he sold them into slavery.

Prince was bought by William Whipple and taken to Portsmouth, New Hampshire, where he lived as a servant until the Revolution. After the war, in which his master served General Washington as an aide and became a general, Prince Whipple was given his freedom for his faithful service—but this was only after he, joined by about twenty other black men in Portsmouth, had written the legislature of New Hampshire to protest that they had been born as free men in Africa and that, as the Declaration of Independence had told the world, "freedom is an inherent right" of all men and could not be taken away by force. Slavery, these black patriots declared, was hateful to all men who cared for "the equal dignity of human nature." It is not known how soon after this petition that he was freed from slavery, but it must have been only a few months.

This black bodyguard was so highly trusted by General Whipple that he was once sent with a large sum of money from Salem, Massachusetts, to Portsmouth. When two robbers attacked him on the road, near the town of Newburyport, Prince Whipple knocked down one of the highwaymen with the handle of a heavy whip and shot the other with a pistol, saving General Whipple's money.

Prince Whipple, "beloved by all who knew him," as an early historian said, died in New Hampshire not long after the Revolution, leaving behind a widow and several children to enjoy the freedom he had won for them.

James Forten

When offered his freedom and a life of ease in England, the young
black sailor from Philadelphia replied, "No, I'm a prisoner for my country, and
I'll never be a traitor to her."

Just before the end of the Revolution, a fifteen-year-old black youth signed on as a powder boy aboard the American privateer Royal Louis, a small ship commanded by Stephen Decatur, Sr.

The youngster was James Forten, who had been born free in Philadelphia, where he had attended the school of an anti-slavery Quaker. This slender young volunteer was to become one of the wealthiest men in Philadelphia after the war. He was already a war veteran, for he had served as a drummer in the army.

The *Royal Louis* put to sea to prey on British shipping, with the hope of dividing captured prizes among the officers and crew. Of her crew of two hundred, twenty were black. The first cruise was bloody, but successful, and Captain Decatur's ship forced a British Navy brig to surrender. The second cruise ended in disaster. A heavily armed enemy frigate, the *Amphyon*, with the aid of two other warships, battered the Royal Louis so fiercely that Decatur was forced to surrender.

It was a bad moment for James Forten. The British seldom exchanged black prisoners who fell into their hands, but usually sold them in the West Indies to serve as plantation laborers under cruel overseers and the merciless tropical sun. But James Forten was one of the lucky prisoners aboard the *Amphyon*. He met the captain's son, a boy of his own age, and the two became friends at once. The English boy was so fond of the quick-witted black American, and so impressed by his skill at playing marbles, that he persuaded his father to offer Forten a life of ease in England. Forten refused, declaring he would not be a traitor to his country.

Rather than shipping him to the West Indies, the British captain sent Forten to the prison ship *Jersey*, which was anchored off Long Island. "Thus," James Forten wrote later, "did a game of marbles save me from a life of West Indian servitude."

There were days when Forten felt that he had not been so lucky after all, for he was shoved deep into the hold of the ship with a thousand other prisoners, forced to live on wormy meat, crusts of moldy bread and foul water, gasping for breath in the stinking, overcrowded quarters. Each day, fresh bodies were hauled out of the hold for burial in the sand dunes ashore. During the war, more than 10,000 prisoners died on the rotting hulk of this prison ship.

James Forten once had a chance to escape when a patriot officer, who was to be exchanged for a British prisoner, left the *Jersey* with his chest. Forten had planned to crawl into the officer's chest and be carried to freedom, but stood aside to allow a younger white boy to hide instead. Forten helped to carry the chest over the side of the ship into a waiting boat and watched his smaller companion escape.

After enduring seven months in the floating hell of the *Jersey*, James Forten was set free in an exchange of prisoners and walked to his home in Philadelphia. During the next fifty years of his life, Forten was to become one of the best-known men of his city. He began to make sails for ships and was soon the head of a business employing scores of people. James Forten, who became an inventor as well as a manufacturer, gave much of his wealth to aid poor and struggling blacks, and became a founder of the Abolition movement to help end American slavery. Among his friends was the famous white orator William Lloyd Garrison, who befriended many of the country's blacks.

Garrison won Forten's heart in his early speeches attacking slavery when he said, "I never rise to address a colored audience, without feeling ashamed of my own color, ashamed of having been identified with a race of men who have done you so much injustice."

James Forten lived to see his sons and grandsons become leaders in the anti-slavery crusade, but never regretted the years he spent as a drummer, powder boy, and prisoner during the Revolution.

AFRICAN-AMERICAN
INVENTORS

Patricia and Frederick McKissack

James Watt (1736–1819), the well-known Scottish inventor, patented an improvement of a steam-powered engine in 1769, thereby ushering in a new era of industrial development. In turn, inventors throughout the nineteenth century built on or improved upon his steam-powered engine. These improvement were never more evident than in the railroad industry.

ON THE RIGHT TRACK

Between 1865 and 1900, the railroads employed more African Americans than any other industry. Blacks helped lay the tracks, and build and service the cars. They also took care of the passengers on board. The work was steady, but the salaries were poor, and the working conditions were often demeaning and dangerous. Railroad injuries were frequent and often fatal. One of the most dangerous places to work was in the train yards, where the cars were connected, until Andrew Jackson Bear (1859–1921) developed the "Jenny Coupler."

After the Civil War, Beard worked in an Alabama train yard, where men were often seriously injured and killed trying to attach train cars. A trainman had to be ready to drop a coupling pin in place as two cars rolled together, but sometimes a worker was crushed to death or lost a limb trying to do this. Beard studied the problem and developed a solution: an automatic device that allowed train cars to be put together quickly and safely. He patented it in 1897, but 6,500 other people who had designed coupling devices also obtained patents.

How could so many inventors receive patents on the same idea? More than one person can share the same idea, but the unique way an inventor *develops* that idea is what gets patented. Even though Beard had lots of competition, his design was so good, he was paid $50,000 by a company that began manufacturing his coupler. The "Jenny coupler" helped save the lives of countless railroad workers.

The Real McCoy

Another inventor who started his career working for the railroads was Elijah McCoy (1843–1929). Have you ever heard the expression "the real McCoy?" This phrase originated with this inventor and his inventions. His automatic lubricators helped increase the safety and efficiency of engines. When cheap and inferior imitations of his designs flooded the market, customers, before making a purchase, began asking "Is this the real McCoy?" Today the question is synonymous with "Is this the best?"

McCoy was born in Colchester, Ontario, Canada, on May 2, 1843, the son of two runaway slaves. After the Civil War, Elijah's family moved to Ypsilanti, Michigan, where he attended school and worked in a machine shop. He was an alert, inquisitive child who liked to tinker with things. He wanted to attend engineering school, but there weren't too many educational opportunities open to him, so, at great sacrifice, his parents sent him to Edinburgh, Scotland, to study.

After finishing his apprenticeship in mechanical engineering, McCoy returned to the United States. Unfortunately, attitudes about African-American ability had not changed much; the only place that would hire McCoy was the Michigan Central Railroad. As a train fireman, McCoy was responsible for keeping the engine fueled and well-oiled. It was a hot, backbreaking job requiring more brawn than brains.

With lots of time to think on his job, McCoy was always looking for ways to improve his knowledge of machines. He noticed that engines of all types had to be stopped periodically and oiled or they would break down or catch fire. Often very young children were hired to work in factories for pennies a day as "oilers." Some were orphans who slept in the factories on the floor beneath the machinery. It was dirty, dangerous work, and the children were often maimed or killed. Seen climbing around on machines, these children were called "grease monkeys," a term still used today for mechanics.

McCoy knew that lubricating the engine was important, but stopping the train or the machine every time the engine needed to be oiled was costly and inefficient. There had to be a way for machines to be oiled while in operation. McCoy worked on the problem for two years, designing an automatic lubricating device. Finally, in July 1872, McCoy patented a "drip cup," the first of his automatic lubricating devices (patent #129,843). In his patent application, McCoy called his invention an "Improvement in Lubricators for Steam-Engines." It worked in the following way: A cup filled with oil was attached to the machine, and a stopcock regulated the flow of oil—while the engine was still running.

An Ypsilanti company was assigned the rights to manufacture the device, which was used on large, stationary factory equipment.

McCoy moved to Detroit, Michigan, where he worked as a consultant for a railroad conglomerate. During his career, he patented fifty-seven other designs, twenty-three of which were lubricating devices for various kinds of machines, including train engines. Although he worked for the Elijah McCoy Manufacturing Company in Detroit, McCoy didn't own any shares in the company. He died in 1929, but his name is remembered whenever consumers ask for the best—the real McCoy.

While Elijah McCoy was inventing the self-lubrication device, other people were at work in the new field of electricity.

THE HUMAN DYNAMO

Granville T. Woods

In 1900 and again in 1913, the U.S. Patent Office did surveys to find out how many patents had been issued to African Americans. The report stated that there were "more than a thousand colored patents [issued], many of which appear to be of considerable importance." Among those listed as very important were the fifty or more patents issued to Granville T. Woods (1856–1910). Because of Woods's electrical and telegraphic inventions, some historians compare him to Edison. Almost all of them agree that Woods was perhaps the most celebrated African-American inventor of the nineteenth century.

Granville Woods was born free in Columbus, Ohio, on April 23, 1856, a few weeks after Booker T. Washington was born a slave in Virginia. The Woods family was poor, and young Granville had little opportunity to attend school. He apprenticed as a machinist and blacksmith, beginning at age ten as a bellows blower.

While still a teenager, he earned extra money to pay for his education in mechanics. When his family moved to Missouri in 1872, Woods was hired by the Iron Mountain Railroad as a fireman. Beginning in 1878, Woods worked as an engineer on the British steamer *Ironsides*. He returned to the United States and worked for two years on the Danville and Southern railroads. During this time, he learned firsthand how machines operated and how to repair or improve them.

On His Own

Woods applied for jobs as a mechanic, but no company would hire him for anything but lowly positions. Although he had more training and experience than most people, he was passed over for promotions.

For a while, Woods made the most out of these dead-end jobs, but he soon realized that if he was ever going to fulfill his dreams, he needed to take a bold step. He moved to Cincinnati, Ohio, and started his own business.

Woods joined the early pioneers who were fascinated by electricity and all its potential. Opportunities were wide open in this area of science and invention. However, after reading everything he could about the subject, Woods knew he needed to be better prepared to be able to compete in this field. He took night classes in mechanical engineering, with an emphasis on electricity.

In 1884, Woods patented his first two inventions: an improved steam boiler furnace and an improved telephone transmitter. The following year, he developed an "electrical apparatus for transmitting messages." Bell Telephone bought the rights to use it. Woods sold the rights to these early inventions and used the money to finance Woods Electric Company, located in Cincinnati. There, he researched, manufactured, and sold his own products.

One of Woods's telegraph inventions, patented as an "Induction

Telegraph," made it possible for telegraphs to be sent between two moving trains. Another one of his inventions significantly improved the safety and efficiency of railroad transmissions. On the patent application, he described the invention as a "synchronous multiplex railway telegraph." It allowed a dispatcher to know where trains were located at all times. Woods stated that the purpose of his invention was to avert accidents "by keeping each train informed of the whereabouts of the one immediately ahead and following it . . ."

Lucius Phelps and Thomas Edison had also developed a similar telegraph system, which resulted in a patent dispute that had to be settled in court. Twice the courts ruled in Woods's favor because he was able to prove that he held the rights to inventions claimed by Edison and Phelps. His victories earned him wide acclaim. After losing to Woods the second time, Edison offered him a job. Booker T. Washington invited Woods to teach at Tuskegee. Woods turned them both down, preferring to stay independent.

The *Catholic Tribune* of January 14, 1886, stated that Granville T. Woods was "the greatest colored inventor in the history of the race and equal, if not superior, to any inventor in the country." But Woods had only just begun his work.

In 1890, Woods closed down the manufacturing end of his business and moved to New York City. With the help of his brother, Lyates Woods, he became a full-time electrical inventor. Among his major successes were developing and improving devices and systems for the electric streetcar.

His inventions and innovations helped improve the method of transferring electricity to streetcars more safely and efficiently, by means of a third rail. This allows the railroad car "to receive the electrical current while reducing friction." The method is still used in New York City's subway system. In 1901 Woods sold the invention to the Union Electric Company.

Between 1902 and 1905, Woods patented innovations on automatic air brakes, which he sold to the Westinghouse Air Brake Company of Pennsylvania. He also patented fifteen inventions for electric railways, and a still larger number for electrical control systems.

Woods died in 1910. Volume I of *The Journal of Negro History* summarized his contributions best:

> *There is no inventor of the colored race whose creative genius has covered quite so wide a field as that of Granville T. Woods, nor one whose achievements have attracted more universal attention and favorable comments from technical and scientific journals both in this country and abroad.*

STEALING THE PLANTER

Zak Mettger

*During the Civil War, many black Americans, both free and enslaved,
fought bravely for their country. Their actions contributed to the Union victory
and influenced the years that followed.*

Born into slavery on Port Royal Island in South Carolina, Robert Smalls
worked on boats from early childhood. When the Civil War broke out,
Smalls was twenty-two years old and a deckhand on the *Planter*, a cotton
steamer based in Charleston harbor. He earned sixteen dollars a month, but
as a slave was only allowed to keep a dollar; the rest went to his owner.

Late in 1861, the Confederate Army leased the *Planter* and its black crew
to transport ammunition, guns, and food to rebel forts along the coast. Smalls's
knowledge of local waterways impressed the white officers who took command
of the ship, and they soon promoted him to pilot. (Unwilling to give a slave
such an important title, the officers referred to him as the "wheelman."

Even though he held a position of responsibility, Smalls was still a slave.
In the spring of 1862, the Union captured Port Royal and the other Sea
Islands, located just a few miles beyond Charleston harbor. All of the
landowners fled, leaving their slaves the only occupants of the plantations.

Smalls grew restless, knowing freedom was so close—so close, in fact, that as he walked the decks of the *Planter* peering through the captains' field glasses, he could see the Union blockade fleet anchored just outside the harbor. The sight inspired him to plan a daring escape.

For weeks, Smalls and his eight crewmates waited for their chance. It finally came on the night of May 12, when the white captain, engineer, and mate left the ship to attend a ball at Fort Sumter hosted by the wealthy society families of Charleston. They would not be back before dawn.

At three o'clock in the morning, Smalls ordered the men to start the engine and cast off. Even at that unusually quiet hour, they faced a perilous journey. Between the *Planter* and it destination—the Union fleet—were six heavily armed forts. Only by giving the proper signal—a secret combination of short and long blasts from the ship's whistle—would Smalls and his crew be allowed to pass. Danger lurked below the water as well, where deadly mines floated, ready to blow up any invading Union ship. But Smalls was prepared. He had been watching and waiting for weeks, and had learned all the signals and memorized the exact location of every mine.

Smalls expertly eased the *Planter* away from the dock. His first stop was the North Atlantic wharf, a few miles away, where the crew's wives and children were waiting by prearrangement. They picked up the five women and three children without incident and continued on to the most treacherous leg of their journey, past the forts.

To avoid raising rebel suspicions, Smalls raised the ship's two flags—Confederate and state—and kept the *Planter* to moderate speed. He even put on the captain's straw hat and jacket and mimicked his walk as he moved about the deck. As the ship passed each fort, Smalls confidently gave the correct signal.

Once in open sea, Smalls ordered the crew to open the engine full throttle, run a white sheet up the flag pole as a sign of surrender, and make for the nearest Union ship—the *Onward*.

The *Onward's* captain received the *Planter* crew warmly. Smalls had not only delivered him a Confederate ship, but her valuable cargo as well: two hundred pounds of ammunition and four big guns that had been loaded on the ship the night before the men made their escape.

Smalls's remarkable feat marked the beginning of a distinguished career in the service of his country; he piloted Union ships throughout the war and was promoted to honorary captain in December 1863. After the war, Smalls was elected to the South Carolina Legislature and to the U.S. Congress.

THEIR OWN CALL TO ARMS

Countless black women helped the Union Army—and the fight for freedom—in any way they could. Not allowed to serve as soldiers, they worked as teachers, nurses, laundresses, cooks, and also as spies and scouts.

One of the best-known of these women was Harriet Tubman, an escaped slave. Tubman helped more than three hundred slaves reach freedom in the northern United States and Canada during the 1850s via the "Underground Railroad," the secret network of abolitionists who fed and sheltered runaway slaves on their treacherous trip north.

Starting in 1862, Tubman also cared for sick and wounded soldiers in military hospitals in the Carolinas and Florida. Her most important army role was as a scout for Union officers who raided enemy territory to gather equipment and liberate slaves. Wrapping her head in a bandanna and disguising herself as an old slave woman (although she was only in her forties at the time), Tubman moved easily through rebel territory without drawing attention. She collected information on the location of cotton warehouses, ammunition depots, food stores, and livestock, and passed it on to Union officers. Whenever she encountered young slave men, she urged them to run away and join the Union Army.

Another black woman who dedicated herself to the Union cause was Sojourner Truth. Deeply religious, an abolitionist and an early feminist, Truth distributed gift boxes of much-appreciated food and clothing to black troops in northern camps. She raised the money to buy these necessitites by giving lectures and singing songs to northern audiences.

Truth escaped from slavery in 1827, the year before it was abolished in her home state of New York. In the 1840s, she became deeply involved with the abolitionist movement and vowed to spend the rest of her life traveling and spreading the truth about slavery.

One of the most daring black women to aid the Union cause was Mary Elizabeth Bowser. She served as a spy for the North while working for Confederate President Jefferson Davis.

Bowser was born a slave in Virginia but was freed as a young woman. Her employer, Elizabeth Van Lew, was the leader of Union supporters in Richmond, Virginia. When Van Lew asked Bowser if she would be willing to be placed in the Confederate president's house as a spy, she agreed and obtained a job as a servant.

As she dusted and swept, Bowser quickly scanned any telegrams and orders that had been left lying about; no one in the household knew she could read. While serving dinner to President Davis, and his guests, she listened closely for information about troop movements and other rebel plans. Everything Bowser learned, she passed along to Van Lew, who then conveyed it to Union General Ulysses S. Grant.

BLACK SAILORS

The Union Navy offered black men the opportunity to serve their country long before the army did. In fact, free blacks had never been barred from naval service, and former slaves were encouraged to enlist as early as September 1861, almost a year before they were admitted into the army.

The navy also treated black recruits better than the army did. They were paid the same as white sailors of equal rank; they performed the same duties, bunked in the same quarters, and ate at the same tables. The relative lack of discrimination resulted mainly from practical necessity. There simply was not enough room on the ships to house and feed the men separately. The navy was also chronically short of men and could not afford to lose black soldiers because of unfair treatment.

Black sailors served aboard every ship in the Union fleet. Some crews were almost entirely black. They manned the ships that blockaded Confederate ports, the ships that went up rivers to collect supplies and contrabands, the gunboats that fired on rebel forts, and the oceangoing vessels that protected northern merchant ships from Confederate raiders.

As many as twenty thousand black men served in the Union Navy. Many were former slaves who took immense risk to join up, swimming or rowing small boats out to Union ships anchored near their plantations. Some eight hundred black sailors were killed in battle; another two thousand died of disease. Black sailors also distinguished themselves in battle; eight won the U.S. Medal of Honor for extreme bravery.

AFTER THE WAR

After the homecoming parades and celebrations were over, black veterans had to find work. Sadly, their choices were often limited by discrimination and lack of experience. Most ended up in the same low-paying jobs they had held before the war, as day laborers in the North and field hands in the South. But many others obtained an education and trained for a profession or a skilled trade; others opened small businesses.

Private Junius B. Roberts managed to save four hundred dollars from his army wages and bounty. He used the money to pay for his education as a minister. An Ohio veteran used his savings to learn the bricklaying trade, which guaranteed good pay and plenty of work. By saving every dime he could, the former soldier was able to put all four of his children through college.

The dream of most southern black veterans was to own a piece of land on which they could farm. But land cost money—lots of money. One sergeant who served in the 128th U.S. Colored Infantry used his entire army savings of two hundred dollars to buy a small plot of land. When they could not afford to buy property of their own, some soldiers pooled their money and bought one large tract of land on which many families settled.

In the late 1870s, Thomas Wentworth Higginson, former commander of the First South Carolina Colored Volunteers, returned to South Carolina and Florida to revisit scenes of the war. He reported that in his travels he "rarely met an ex-soldier who did not own his house and ground . . . varying from five to two hundred acres."

Thousands of Civil War veterans wanted to stay in the army. They got their chance in July 1866, when Congress created six black regiments as part of the nation's regular army, two cavalry and four infantry (later reduced to two), all under white officers. Although the pay was low, it was equal to what white soldiers got, and it was steady; there was also less discrimination than in civilian life. Most of the 12,500 men who volunteered for these four regiments were Civil War veterans.

The two black infantry regiments, the Twenty-fourth and Twenty-fifth, manned forts along the U.S.-Mexican border and helped to quell violent land disputes between the two countries. The Ninth and Tenth cavalries spent most of their time in the West, where increased migration had sparked fighting between settlers and the Apaches, Sioux, Comanche, and other Native American tribes who were on the land first. Native Americans dubbed the black troops "Buffalo soldiers," because of their dark skin and the courage with which they fought.

Mary Lincoln's Dressmaker

Becky Rutberg

Elizabeth Keckley endured many years of abuse as a slave before buying her freedom. A skilled mantuamaker, a dressmaker able to sew a very difficult style of dress popular at the time, Lizzie set up her own shop in Washington, D.C., just before the outbreak of the Civil War. While sewing for Mary Todd Lincoln, the two women became such close friends that when President Lincoln was shot, Lizzie was the one person Mary wanted by her side.

Some of the women Lizzie had sewn for while working as an assistant dressmaker became her first patrons. One day while she was in the home of Mrs. Rheingold to fit a dress, she met the wife of Captain Robert E. Lee, who was visiting. Mrs. Lee needed a gown suitable for the great event of the season, soon to take place—a dinner party given at the White House in honor of the Prince of Wales. She had purchased silk fabric but hadn't found a suitable dressmaker. She hired Lizzie.

When Lizzie called on her the next day, Mrs. Lee's husband, Captain Lee, handed her one hundred dollars and asked that she spare no expense in purchasing suitable trimmings for the dress. Captain Lee would later be known as the famous General Robert E. Lee, commander of the Confederate troops, in the war that would soon divide the nation.

Lizzie entered Harper & Mitchell's Dry Goods Store on Pennsylvania Avenue and asked if she could look at their laces. When she asked Mr. Harper if she could take the laces for Mrs. Lee's approval, he readily agreed. His trust of her moved her to remind him she was a stranger and the goods were valuable. He remarked that he believed her face was an index to an honest heart. Lizzie never forgot his kind words.

Lizzie finished the dress on time, and Mrs. Lee attracted favorable attention at the event. After that evening, Lizzie received many orders and was soon able to pay most of her bills. On her travels about Washington, she heard that Mrs. Varina Howell Davis, wife of Jefferson Davis, the senator from Mississippi, was looking for a mantuamaker. Lizzie visited her home and left one of her business cards. Mrs. Davis hired her on the spot.

Lizzie spent every afternoon at the Davises' fitting and sewing many outfits. In her presence the Davises freely discussed the prospect of war between the slave-holding South and the abolitionist North. Servants and family members told Lizzie about secret meetings held at the house every night.

Lizzie's fashionable creations drew more and more praise; her business grew rapidly, and patrons included wives of senators, congressmen, and Cabinet members. With the approach of her first Christmas in the nation's capital, she could barely fill all the orders placed with her.

At fifteen minutes before twelve on Christmas Eve, 1860, in the Davis home, Lizzie sat in a room next to the one where the family trimmed their Christmas tree. Lizzie arranged the last cords on a dressing gown Mrs. Davis had ordered as a present for her husband. As the clock struck twelve, Lizzie finished the last stitch, unaware, of course, that Mr. Davis would wear it often as president of the Confederate states during the upcoming struggle between the North and the South.

War became certain before the end of January. While Lizzie was dressing Mrs. Davis one day, her patron invited her to move south with the Davis family. She assured Lizzie that the Southern states would be victorious after a brief fight and that Mr. Davis would be elected president of all the states. She planned to live in the White House and promised to hire Lizzie.

Ever since arriving in Washington and her first glimpse of the White House, Lizzie had nurtured a dream of working for the women there. To fulfill that dream, she was ready to make almost any sacrifice. She refused Mrs. Davis's offer, however. She was vehemently against the South's plan to extend slavery into the new territories, and she had faith in the strength of the North. She would not compromise her beliefs. A few weeks before Mrs. Davis left for the South, Lizzie made two inexpensive plain chintz wrappers for her. Mrs. Davis explained that she planned to stop wearing expensive clothes for a while now that war was inevitable. Lizzie would see those same chintz wrappers at another time in another place, after much of the nation's blood had been shed. Mrs. Davis left some delicate needlework with Lizzie to finish and asked her to forward it to Montgomery, Alabama, where she and her family planned to be.

By the end of February, Jefferson Davis had been elected president of seven Southern states that had formerly seceded from the Union, and Abraham Lincoln had been elected president of the Union. It was about that time that one of Lizzie's patrons, Mrs. John McClean, needed a gown made on very short notice and promised to introduce Lizzie to Mrs. Lincoln and recommend her services as a mantuamaker.

Lizzie was the last dressmaker to be called for an interview at the White House with Mrs. Lincoln. Nervously, she climbed the steps to the Family Room, where she found Mary Todd Lincoln dressed in a cashmere wrap-around morning robe, standing by a window. Mrs. Lincoln turned, smiled, and walked toward her. Lizzie had heard rumors that the new president's wife was vulgar and ignorant. She felt pleasantly surprised when Mrs. Lincoln greeted her cordially: "Mrs. Keckley, you have come at last."

Mrs. Lincoln asked for references and seemed most impressed when Lizzie named Mrs. Jefferson Davis as one of her patrons. Lizzie presented several letters of recommendations from former St. Louis clients and discovered some were friends of Mrs. Lincoln.

When Mrs. Lincoln asked if Lizzie could do her work, she answered almost inaudibly, "Yes." Then, more boldly, she asked, "Will you have much work for me to do?"

Mrs. Lincoln replied, "That, Mrs. Keckley, will depend altogether upon your prices. I trust your terms are reasonable. I cannot afford to be extravagant. We are just from the west and are poor. If you do not charge too much, I shall be able to give you all my work."

Lizzie made her terms very reasonable, and Mrs. Lincoln handed her a bright-colored antique rose silk gown that she planned to wear to the first White House reception that Friday night. It needed altering. Lizzie measured her and took the gown home. Lizzie was hard at work in her rooms finishing the alterations when word came that the affair was going to be postponed until the following Tuesday. Lizzie heaved a sigh of relief now that she had more time to complete the gown. However, Mrs. Lincoln soon sent for her and asked that she change the entire style of the dress. And she also ordered a blue silk blouse for her cousin, Elizabeth Grimsley. Although Lizzie was swamped with other orders, she knew she had to meet these last-minute demands. Mrs. Lincoln had to be pleased no matter how inconvenient her requests.

Tuesday evening Lizzie put the last stitches in the dress, folded and carried it and the finished blue blouse to the White House. When she entered the family quarters, there were several women gathered about Mrs. Lincoln, all talking at once. Above the others, Lizzie heard Mrs. Lincoln's distraught voice, complaining that she could not attend the reception because she had nothing to wear.

She turned, saw Lizzie, and snarled, "Mrs. Keckley, you have disappointed me—deceived me. Why do you bring my dress at this late hour?"

"Because I have just finished it, and I thought I should be in time," Lizzie answered, her hopes and dreams fading before her.

"But you are not in time, Mrs. Keckley; you have bitterly disappointed me. I have no time to dress and, what is more, I will not dress and go downstairs."

Lizzie did not think she was late. In the past her seasoned hands took little time to dress her patrons and arrange their hair. She said, "I am sorry if I have disappointed you, Mrs. Lincoln, for I intended to be on time. Will you let me dress you? I can have you ready in a few minutes."

Mrs. Lincoln sputtered, "No, I won't be dressed. I will stay in my room. Mr. Lincoln can go down with the other ladies."

The women in the room pleaded with Mrs. Lincoln to allow Lizzie to dress her. After more protestations, she finally relented. Lizzie was used to placating high-strung white women. They often aimed their insecurities and nervousness at those serving them. Lizzie calmly dressed Mrs. Lincoln and wove fresh flowers grown in the White House conservatory into her hair. The dress fit well, and Mrs. Lincoln seemed pleased. Lizzie breathed a sigh of relief.

President Lincoln entered the room with two of his sons, ten-year-old Willie and eight-year-old Tad. He threw himself on the sofa, laughed, pulled on his white gloves, and began reciting poetry. He looked appraisingly at Mrs. Lincoln and said, "I declare, you look charming in that dress. Mrs. Keckley has met with great success." Lizzie must have felt deeply satisfied by the compliment, but in her heart she knew it was his wife who had to be pleased.

Just before President and Mrs. Lincoln descended the stairway to the first White House levee—a presidential reception—Tad, as a prank, hid his mother's lace handkerchief. When she became unstrung for the second time that evening, he returned it.

Lizzie was surprised when instead of being embarrassed by her uncontrolled outburst, Mrs. Lincoln took the President's arm and led the party downstairs as if nothing had happened. Lizzie wrote in her memoirs, "No queen, accustomed to . . . royalty all her life, could have comported herself with more calmness and dignity than did the wife of the President. She was confident and self-possessed."

The first reception was a huge success, and Mrs. Lincoln received many compliments on her gown. Lizzie's anxieties turned to joy and relief as she officially became Mrs. Lincoln's mantuamaker.

SLAVERY

INCIDENTS IN THE
LIFE OF A SLAVE GIRL

Harriet A. Jacobs

*Harriet Jacobs was a slave for twenty-seven years before escaping to free-
dom in the North. Her autobiography vividly documents the evils of slavery as
well as her own ability to maintain her spirit and dignity.*

CHILDHOOD

I was born a slave but never knew it till six years of happy childhood had
passed away. My father was a carpenter and considered so intelligent and
skillful in his trade, that, when buildings out of the common line were to
be erected, he was sent for from long distances, to be head workman.

On condition of paying his mistress two hundred dollars a year, and sup-
porting himself, he was allowed to work at his trade, and manage his own
affairs. His strongest wish was to purchase his children, but though he several times offered his hard earnings for that purpose, he never succeeded.

In complexion my parents were a light shade of brownish yellow, and
were termed mulattos. They lived together in a comfortable home; and,

though we were all slaves, I was so fondly shielded that I never dreamed I was a piece of merchandise, trusted to them for safekeeping, and liable to be demanded of them at any moment.

I had one brother, William, who was two years younger than myself — a bright, affectionate child. I had also a great treasure in my maternal grandmother, who was a remarkable woman in many respects. She was the daughter of a planter in South Carolina, who, at his death, left her mother and his three children free, with money to go to St. Augustine, where they had relatives. It was during the Revolutionary War; and they were captured on their passage, carried back, and sold to different purchasers.

Such was the story my grandmother used to tell me; but I do not remember all the particulars. She was a little girl when she was captured and sold to the keeper of a large hotel. I have often heard her tell how hard she fared during childhood. But as she grew older, she evinced so much intelligence, and was so faithful, that her master and mistress could not help seeing it was for their interest to take care of such a valuable piece of property.

She became an indispensable person in the household, officiating in all capacities, from cook and wet nurse to seamstress. She was much praised for her cooking; and her nice crackers became so famous in the neighborhood that many people were desirous of obtaining them. In consequence of numerous requests of this kind, she asked permission of her mistress to bake crackers at night, after all the household work was done; and she obtained leave to do it, provided she would clothe herself and her children from the profits.

Upon these terms, after working hard all day for her mistress, she began her midnight bakings, assisted by her two oldest children. The business proved profitable; and each year she laid by a little, which was saved for a fund to purchase her children. Her master died, and the property was divided among his heirs. The widow had her dower in the hotel, which she continued to keep open. My grandmother remained in her service as a slave; but her children were divided among her master's children. As she had five, Benjamin, the youngest one, was sold, in order that each heir might have an equal portion of dollars and cents.

There was so little difference in our ages that Benjamin seemed more like my brother than my uncle. He was a bright, handsome lad, nearly white; for he inherited the complexion my grandmother had derived from Anglo-Saxon ancestors. Though only ten years old, seven hundred and twenty dollars was paid for him. His sale was a terrible blow to my grandmother; but she was naturally hopeful and she went to work with renewed energy, trusting in time to be able to purchase some of her children.

She had laid up three hundred dollars, which her mistress one day begged as a loan, promising to pay her soon. The reader probably knows that no promise or writing given to a slave is legally binding; for, according to Southern laws, a slave, being property, can hold no property. When my grandmother lent her hard saved earnings to her mistress, she trusted solely to her honor. The honor of a slaveholder to a slave!

To this good grandmother I was indebted for many comforts. My brother Willie and I often received portions of the crackers, cakes, and preserves she made to sell; and after we ceased to be children we were indebted to her for many more important services.

Such were the unusually fortunate circumstances of my early childhood. When I was six years old, my mother died; and then, for the first time, I learned, by the talk around me, that I was a slave.

My mother's mistress was the daughter of my grandmother's mistress. She was the foster sister of my mother. They were both nourished at my grandmother's breast. In fact, my mother had been weaned at three months old, that the babe of the mistress might obtain sufficient food. They played together as children; and, when they became women, my mother was a most faithful servant to her white foster sister. On my mother's death-bed her mistress promised that her children should never suffer for any thing; and during her lifetime she kept her word.

They all spoke kindly of my dead mother, who had been a slave merely in name, but in nature was noble and womanly. I grieved for her and my young mind was troubled with the thought who would now take care of me and my little brother. I was told that my home was now to be with my mistress; and I found it a happy one. No toilsome or disagreeable duties were imposed upon me. My mistress was so kind to me that I was always glad to do her bidding, and proud to labor for her as much as my young years would permit.

I would sit by her side for hours, sewing diligently, with a heart as free from care as that of any free-born white child. When she thought I was tired, she would send me out to run and jump; and away I bounded, to gather berries or flowers to decorate her room. Those were happy days—too happy to last. The slave child had no thought for the morrow; but there came that blight, which too surely waits every human being born to be a chattel.

When I was nearly twelve years old, my kind mistress sickened and died. As I saw the cheek grow paler, and the eye more glassy, how earnestly I prayed in my heart that she might live! I loved her; for she had been almost like a mother to me. My prayers were not answered. She died, and they buried her in the little churchyard, where, day after day, my tears fell upon her grave.

I was sent to spend a week with my grandmother. I was now old enough to begin to think of the future; and again and again I asked myself what they would do with me. I felt sure I should never find another mistress so kind as the one who was gone. She had promised my dying mother that her children should never suffer for any thing; and when I remembered that, and recalled her many proofs of attachment to me, I could not help having some hopes that she had left me free. My friends were almost certain it would be so. They thought she would be sure to do it, on account of my mother's love and faithful service. But, alas! we all know that the memory of a faithful slave does not avail much to save her children from the auction block.

After a brief period of suspense, the will of my mistress was read, and we learned that she had bequeathed me to her sister's daughter, a child of five years old. So vanished our hopes. My mistress had taught me the precepts of God's word: "Thou shalt love thy neighbor as thyself." "Whatsover ye would that men should do unto you, do ye even so unto them." But I was her slave, and I suppose she did not recognize me as her neighbor.

I would do much to blot out from my memory that one great wrong. As a child, I loved my mistress; and, looking back on the happy days I spent with her, I try to think with less bitterness of this act of injustice. While I was with her, she taught me to read and spell; and for this privilege, which so rarely falls to the lot of a slave, I bless her memory.

She possessed but few slaves; and at her death those were all distributed among her relatives. Five of them were my grandmother's children, and had shared the same milk that nourished her mother's children. Notwithstanding my grandmother's long and faithful service to her owners, not one of their children escaped the auction block.

These God-breathing machines are no more, in the sight of their masters, than the cotton they plant, or the horses they tend.

Up from Slavery

Booker T. Washington

Booker T. Washington was approximately six years old when the Civil War ended and all slaves were declared free. His stepfather had already found his way to the little town of Malden in the Kanawha Valley in the new state of West Virginia. He got a job in a salt-furnace and sent for the rest of the family.

Boyhood Days

From the time I can remember having any thoughts about anything, I can recall that I had an intense longing to learn to read. I determined that, while quite a small child, that if I accomplished nothing else in life, I would in some way get enough education to enable me to read common books and newspapers. Soon after we got settled in some manner in our new cabin in West Virginia, I induced my mother to get hold of a book for me. How or where she got it, I do not know, but in some way she procured an old copy of Webster's "blue-back" spelling book, which contained the alphabet, followed by such meaningless words as "ab," "ba," "ca," "da."

I began at once to devour this book. I think that it was the first one I ever had in my hands. I had learned from somebody that the way to begin to read was to learn the alphabet, so I tried in all the ways I could think of to learn it—all, of course, without a teacher, for I could find no one to teach me. At that time there was not a single member of my race anywhere near us who could read, and I was too timid to approach any of the white people.

In some way, within a few weeks, I mastered the greater portion of the alphabet. In all my efforts to learn to read my mother shared fully my ambition, and sympathized with me, and aided me in every way that she could. Though she was totally ignorant, so far as mere book knowledge was concerned, she had high ambitions for her children, and a large fund of good, hard, common sense which seemed to enable her to meet and master every situation. If have done anything in life worth attention, I feel sure that I inherited the disposition to do so from my mother.

In the midst of my struggles and longing for an education, a young colored boy who had learned to read in the state of Ohio came to Malden. As soon as the colored people found out that the boy could read, a newspaper was secured, and at the close of work every day this young man would be surrounded by a group of men and women who were anxious to hear him read the news contained in the papers. How I used to envy this man! He seemed to me to be the one man in all the world who ought to be satisfied with his attainments.

About this time the question of having some kind of school opened for the colored children in the village began to be discussed. As it would be the first school for Negro children that had ever been opened in Virginia, it was, of course, to be a great event, and the discussion excited the widest interest. The most perplexing question was where to find a teacher. The young man from Ohio who had learned to read the papers was considered, but his age was against him. In the midst of the discussion about a teacher, another young colored man from Ohio, who had been a soldier, found his way into town. It was soon learned that he possessed considerable education, and he was engaged by the colored people to teach their first school.

As yet no free schools had been started for colored people in that section, hence each family agreed to pay a certain amount each month, with the understanding that the teacher was to "board 'round"—that is, spend a day with each student's family. This was not bad for the teacher, for each family tried to provide the very best on the day he was to be their guest. I recall that I looked forward with an anxious appetite to the "teacher's day" at our little cabin.

This experience of a whole race beginning to go to school for the first time presents one of the most interesting studies that has ever occurred in connection with the development of any race. Few people who were not right in the midst of the scenes can form any exact idea of the intense desire which the people of my race showed for an education. Few were too young, and none too old, to make the attempt to learn. As fast as any kind of teachers could be secured, not only were day-schools filled, but night-schools as well. The great ambition of the older people was to try to learn to read the Bible before they died.

With this end in view, men and women who were fifty or seventy-five years old would often be found in the night-school. Sunday schools were formed soon after freedom, but the principal book studied in the Sunday school was the spelling book.

The opening of the school in the Kanawha Valley, however, brought to me one of the keenest disappointments that I ever experienced. I had been working in a salt-furnace for several months, and my stepfather had discovered that I had financial value, and so, when the school opened, he decided that he could not spare me from my work. The disappointment was made all the more severe by reason of the fact that my place of work was where I could see the happy children passing to and from school, mornings and afternoons. Despite this disappointment, however, I determined that I would learn something, anyway. I applied myself with greater earnestness than ever to the mastering of what was in the "blue-back" speller.

My mother sympathized with me and sought to comfort me in all the ways she could, and to help me to find a way to learn. After a while I succeeded in making arrangements with the teacher to give me some lessons at night, after the day's work was done. These night lessons were so welcome that I think I learned more at night than the other children did during the day; but my boyish heart was still set upon going to the day school, and I let no opportunity slip to push my case. Finally I won, and was permitted to go to the school in the day for a few months, with the understanding that I was to rise early in the morning and work in the furnace till nine o'clock, and return immediately after school closed in the afternoon for at least two more hours of work.

The schoolhouse was some distance from the furnace, and as I had to work till nine o'clock, and the school opened at nine, I found myself in a difficulty. To get around this difficulty I yielded to a temptation for which most people, I suppose, will condemn me; but since it is a fact, I might as well state it. There was a large clock in a little office in the furnace. This clock, of course, all the hundred or more workmen depended upon to regulate their hours of beginning and ending the day's work. I got the idea that the way for me to reach school on time was to move the clock hands from half-past eight up to the nine o'clock mark. This I found myself doing morning after morning, till the furnace "boss" discovered that something was wrong, and locked the clock in a case. I did not mean to inconvenience anybody. I simply meant to reach school on time.

When, however, I found myself at the school for the first time, I was confronted with two other difficulties. In the first place, I saw that all of the other children wore hats or caps on their heads, and I had neither hat nor cap. In fact, I do not remember that up to the time of going to school I had ever worn any kind of covering upon my head, nor do I recall that either I or anybody else had even thought anything about the need of covering for my head. But of course when I saw how all the other boys were dressed, I began to feel quite uncomfortable.

As usual, I put the case before my mother, and she explained to me that she had no money with which to buy a "store hat." This was a rather new institution at that time among the members of my race, and was considered quite the thing for young and old to own, but that she would find a way to help me out of the difficulty. Accordingly, she got two pieces of "homespun" and sewed them together, and I was soon the proud possessor of my first cap.

The lesson that my mother taught me in this has always remained with me, and I have tried as best I could to teach it to others. I have always felt proud, whenever I think of the incident, that my mother had strength of character enough not to be led into the temptation of seeming to be that which she was not—of trying to impress my schoolmates and others with the fact that she was able to buy me a "store hat" when she was not.

My second difficulty was with regard to my name, or rather *a* name. From the time when I could remember, I had been called simply "Booker." Before going to school it had never occurred to me that it was needful to have an additional name. But when I heard the school roll called, I noticed that all of the children had at least two names, and some of them indulged in what seemed to me the extravagance of having three. By the time the occasion came for the enrolling of my name, an idea occurred to me; and so when the teacher asked me what my full name was, I calmly told him "Booker Washington," as if I had been called by that name all of my life— and by that name I have since been known.

Later in my life I found that my mother had given me the name of "Booker Taliaferro" soon after I was born, but in some way that part of my name seemed to disappear, and for a long while was forgotten; but as soon as I found out about it, I revived it. I think there are not many men in our country who have had the privilege of naming themselves in the way that I have.

THE SLAVE DANCER

Paula Fox

Sometimes young Jessie Bollier plays his fife for pennies on the docks of New Orleans. One night, on his way home from an errand for his mother, he is kidnapped and taken aboard a slave ship. On the voyage back from Africa, Jesse will be forced to play his fife so the slaves can be "danced," the brutal captain's way of keeping them fit enough to be sold.

THE MOONLIGHT

I strained to see the shore we were leaving and when, at last, it melted into the darkness, I was overwhelmed with sleepiness. But it is hard to settle down in the bottom of a small boat. It curved where my back didn't; I was in danger of decapitation from the wooden arm to which a sail was attached, and which swung unexpectedly from side to side. And when I thought: Here is space to stretch out in, I found I needed grasshopper legs to make room for my head, or else a turtle's neck I could pull in to make room for my legs.

I suppose I dozed now and then during that long trip. At times, the water seemed only a dense shadow which we skimmed across to avoid falling through. The men spoke in undertones about nothing familiar to me. The sail, a three-cornered patch of whiteness, swung over my head.

The little boat groaned and creaked. The water tapped ceaselessly against the hull like a steady fall of rain on a roof.

Hours passed with nothing to mark them until in the east the sky paled ever so faintly as though a drop of daylight had touched the black. I wanted to stand up, to stretch. But when I started to my feet, Claudius' voice rang out so loud I was sure he would be heard on every shore. "Sit down, boy!"

We passed a small island. I saw the glimmer of a light in a window—only that solitary, flickering yellow beacon. I felt hopeless and sad as though everyone in the world had died save the three of us and the unknown lamplighter on the shore. Then, as if daylight was being born inside the boat itself, I began to make out piles of rope, a wooden bucket, a heap of rusty looking net, the thick boots of my captors.

"There!" said the big-jawed man, pointing straight ahead.

And there was our destination, a sailing ship, its masts looking as high as the steeple of St. Louis Cathedral, its deck empty, a shape as astonishing on the expanse of dawn gray water as a church would have been. Across its bow were painted the words: *The Moonlight*.

I was hauled up a rope ladder from which I dared not look down, and no sooner had I reached the deck when from being so stiff and tired, I fell flat on my face. At once, my nostrils were flooded with a smell so sickening, so menacing, that it stopped my breath.

"He's not standing well," said Claudius.

"Then we must stretch him," said the other, waggling his chin.

I breathed shallowly. Despite my fatigue, I sprang to my feet and stood there quivering, my head bent back so that I faced the sky. The smell persisted but it was weaker the farther my head was from the deck. Perhaps the two men, who were tall, didn't smell it at all.

"Maybe he swims better than he stands," said Claudius.

"We'll test him in a barrel of vinegar," said the other with a broad grin.

Then he placed my fife to his lips and blew mightily. His cheeks puffed out but he could make no sound.

"You haven't the gift, Purvis," said Claudius.

"Leave him be," ordered another voice, and a third man appeared from out of a little door on the deck. He was much older than my captors, and he was dressed in a thick garment that hung from his shoulders like a quilt. "Purvis, Claudius, leave him be," he repeated. "He's not going to swim away. Give him his instrument and tell him where he is."

The old man hardly glanced at me, and there was no particular kindness in his voice. Purvis, who had taken a hard grip on my wrist, dropped it.

"Thank you," I said, wishing I did not sound so timid.

"Don't waste your breath," said the old man.

"I told you you were going on a sea voyage," said Purvis. "You'll get home. Claudius and I will see to that. But it won't be for a bit."

"Oh, when!" I shouted.

"Not long at all," said Claudius softly, trying to touch my head as I ducked away from him. "With luck, you'll be back in four months."

My knees turned to pudding. "My mother will think I'm dead!" I cried, and ran wildly away from the three men only to collide with a wooden structure of some sort and knock myself to the deck where I curled up like a worm.

I thought desperately of my mother and Betty in the room with that apricot brocade. I cursed the rich stuff and the lady who had ordered a gown from my mother, and the candles I had forgotten from Aunt Agatha. I cursed myself for taking the longest way home.

The old man bent over me. "You've run into my bench," he said peevishly. "Get up now and behave yourself."

I got to my feet. "It's my mother who'll be heartbroken," I said in a low voice, hoping to stir some feeling in him. "My father drowned long ago, and now she's lost me."

Purvis grabbed my arm. "We've taken care of all that, boy!" he insisted. "Claudius and me spoke to your mother and explained we'd borrowed you for a while."

I knew he was lying. But I was afraid to show him that I knew for fear he'd wrap me up in that canvas again.

"The wind's changing," Purvis muttered.

"Indeed, it's not," said the old man.

"What do you know, Ned? You can't tell if you're on land or sea anyhow!"

"I don't require to," replied the old man sharply. Then he turned his attention back to me. "I don't approve of it," he said. "This taking of boys and men against their will. But I have nothing to do with it. We had got a boy, but he ran away in Charleston just before we sailed. Still, it isn't my fault. I'm only a carpenter. You might as well settle yourself to what's happened. The Captain will have what he will have no matter how he gets it."

"Who's on the watch?" inquired Purvis as he pressed my fife into my hand.

"Sam Wick and Cooley," answered Ned.

"I know nothing about ships," I ventured.

"You don't need to, no more than Ned here. He does his carpentering, and can even do surgery if he feels like it. But he can't tell a bowsprit from a topmast. You'll only be doing what you've done before, playing your pipe."

"For the Captain?" I asked.

Purvis opened his mouth so wide he looked like an alligator, and shouted with laughter. "No, no. Not for the Captain, but for kings and princes and other such like trash. Why, we'll have a ship full of royalty, won't we, Ned?" he said.

Misery made my head ache. I wandered away from Purvis and Ned not caring if they threw me in the water or hung me for a sail. They paid no attention to my departure but went back to quarreling about the wind.

I couldn't even feel a breeze. A gull like a puff of smoke flew across the bow. Everything except the dark smudge of shore was gray now, sky and water and dull clouds. It looked like rain. I caught my foot in a coil of heavy chain, and I bumped my shoulder against a mast. Except for the mutter of Purvis' voice, I heard only the fluttering sound of water about the hull of the ship. A man passed me wearing a woolen cap, his gaze on the horizon.

There was no one to save me—and I didn't even know from what I needed to be saved. As quickly as my mother's sharp scissors cut a thread, snip! I had been cut off from the only life I knew. When I felt a hand on my arm, I supposed it was Purvis come to tease me, so I didn't turn around. But a strange voice asked, "What's your name?"

It was a plain question asked in a plain voice. I was startled, as though life had come straight again, and turned to find a tall heavy-limbed man standing behind me. I made no replay at first. He smiled encouragingly and said, "I'm Benjamin Stout and sorry for what's been done to you."

I wanted to ask him why it had been done, but I was so grateful to be spoken to in such a sensible way that I didn't wish to provoke him. I said nothing. He leaned against the bulwark.

"How old are you? Thirteen, I'd guess. I was pressed too, although when I was older than you, and for a much longer voyage than this will be. A whole year I was gone. But then, you see, I got to like it, the sea and all, even the hard life on a ship, so that when I go ashore, I get restless in a few hours. I get half mad with restlessness. Though I promise you, there are days at sea when all you want is to be on a path that has no end, a path you can run straight ahead on till your breath gives out. Oh, I'm not speaking of gales and storms and squalls. I mean the flat dead days without wind."

"I'm thirteen," I said.

"Thirteen," he repeated thoughtfully. "Just as I said, you'll see some bad things, but if you didn't see them, they'd still be happening so you might as well."

I couldn't make sense of all that. I asked him the question that was uppermost in my mind.

"Where are we going?"

"We're sailing to Whydah in the Bight of Benin."

"Where is that?"

"Africa."

For all the calmness with which he said *Africa*, he might as well have said Royal Street. I felt like a bird caught in a room.

"You haven't told me your name," he said.

"Jessie Bollier," I replied in a whisper. For a second I was ready to throw myself off the ship. The very name of that distant place was like an arrow aimed at me.

"Jesse, we'll shake hands, now that we know each other. I'll show you to our quarters where you'll sleep. You'll get used to the hammock in a night or two. I've got so I won't sleep in anything else, and when I'm ashore, I prefer even the floor to a bed."

"Here!" roared Purvis, his heavy steps pounding toward us. "Is this boy bawling up trouble?"

"Shut your great face," Benjamin Stout called over his shoulder, then said to me, "He's harmless, only noisy. But watch out for the Mate, Nick Spark. And when you speak to the Captain, be sure and answer everything he asks you, even if you must lie."

Purvis dropped a heavy hand on my shoulder. "You've met Saint Stout, I see. Come along. Captain Cawthorne wants to see what sort of fish we caught."

His hand slid down and gripped my arm. Half dragging me, for I couldn't match his strides, he took me to a part of the ship which had a kind of small house on it, the roof forming what I later learned was the poop deck.

"Stand, Purvis," a voice ordered, as dry as paper and as sharp as vinegar.

Purvis became a stone. I twitched my arm away from his grasp and rubbed it.

"Step forward, boy," said the voice. I took a step toward the two men who stood in front of the small house.

"What a fearful runt!" boomed the smaller man. Paper-voice agreed, adding a high-pitched "Sir" like a sour whistle at the end of his words. I supposed from that that the short fellow was the Captain.

"Your name?" he asked.

"Jesse Bollier."

"Never heard such a name."

"It used to be Beaulieu but my father didn't want to be thought French, so he changed it," I hastened to explain, recalling Stout's advice to answer everything I was asked.

"Just as bad," said the Captain.

"Yes," I agreed.

"Captain!" roared the Captain. I jumped.

The thin man said, "Address the Captain as Captain, you boy."

"Captain," I echoed weakly.

"Purvis!" cried the Captain, "Why are you standing there, you Irish bucket! Get off to your work!"

Purvis slid away soundlessly.

"So you're one of those Creoles, are you?" asked the Captain.

"It was only my grandfather who was from France, Captain," I replied apologetically.

"Bad fellows, the French," remarked the Captain, scowling. "Pirates all of them."

"My father wasn't a pirate," I declared.

"Indeed!" sneered the Captain. He looked straight up at the sky, an odd smile on his lips. Then he coughed violently, clapped his hands together, grew silent and stared at me.

"Do you know why you are employed on this ship?"

"To play my fife for kings," I answered.

"Did you hear that, First!" the Captain cried.

"That's Purvis-talk ain't it?" I'd know it anywhere. It was Purvis told you that, wasn't it?"

"Yes, Captain," I said.

"Purvis is an Irish bucket," the thin man said reflectively as though he'd only just thought of it himself.

"Well, now, listen, you miserable pygmy!"

"I will, Captain."

Without a word of warning, the little man snatched me up in his arms, held me fast to his chest and bit my right ear so hard I screamed. He set me down instantly, and I would have fallen to the deck if the thin man hadn't yanked me up by my bruised arm.

"He answers too fast, Spark," said the Captain, "but that may teach him!"

The thin man gave me a shake and let me loose, saying "Yes, Captain, he answers much too fast."

"We are sailing to Africa," said the Captain, looking over my head, in a voice altogether different from the one with which he had been speaking. He was suddenly, insanely, calm. I wiped the blood from my neck and tried to concentrate on what he was saying.

We were sailing to Africa, the Captain repeated with a lofty gesture of his hand. And this fast little clipper would keep us safe not only from the British, but from any other misguided pirates who would try to interfere in the lucrative and God-granted trade of slaves. He, Captain Cawthorne, would purchase as many slaves as possible from the barracoon in Whydah, exchanging for them both money, $10 a head, and rum and tobacco, and returning via the island of São Tomé to Cuba where the slaves would be sold to a certain Spaniard. The ship would then return to Charleston with a hold full of molasses, and the whole voyage would take—with any luck at all—four months.

"But what is wanted is strong black youths," the Captain said excitedly, slapping Spark on his shoulder. "I won't have Ibos. They're soft as melon and kill themselves if they're not watched twenty-four hours a day. I will not put up with such creatures!" Spark nodded rapidly like a chicken pecking at corn. Then the Captain scowled at me.

"You'd best learn to make yourself useful about this ship," he said. "You'd best learn every sail, for you ain't going to earn your way just by playing a few tunes to make the niggers jig!" He suddenly sighed and appeared to grow extremely dispirited. "Ah . . .you finish, Spark."

Spark finished, but what he said I'll never know. I had ceased to listen for I was thinking hard upon the one fact I'd understood. I was on a slaver.

Narrative of the Life of Frederick Douglass, an American Slave

Frederick Douglass was born Frederick Augustus Washington Bailey in 1818. When he was seven years old he was sold to Hugh Auld in Baltimore, Maryland. Douglass, who changed his name after escaping from slavery, was a brilliant writer and speaker, a great leader, and the most important black abolitionist of the nineteenth century. The following passages are from his autobiography.

Chapter VII

I lived in Master Hugh's family about seven years. During this time, I succeeded in learning to read and write. In accomplishing this, I was compelled to resort to various stratagems. I had no regular teacher. My mistress, who had kindly commenced to instruct me, had, in compliance with the advice and direction of her husband, not only ceased to instruct, but had set her face against my being instructed by anyone else.

It is due, however, to my mistress to say of her that she did not adopt this course of treatment immediately. She at first lacked the depravity indispensable to shutting me up in mental darkness. It was at least necessary for her to have some training in the exercise of irresponsible power, to make her equal to the task of treating me as though I were a brute.

My mistress was a kind and tender-hearted woman, and in the simplicity of her soul she commenced, when I first went to live with her, to treat me as she supposed one human being ought to treat another. In entering upon the duties of a slaveholder, she did not seem to perceive that I sustained to her the relation of a mere chattel, and that for her to treat me as a human being was not only wrong, but dangerously so. Slavery proved as injurious to her as it did to me.

When I went there, she was a pious, warm, and tender-hearted woman. There was no sorrow or suffering for which she had not a tear. She had bread for the hungry, clothes for the naked, and comfort for every mourner that came within her reach. Slavery soon proved its ability to divest her of these heavenly qualities. Under its influence, the tender heart became stone, and the lamb-like disposition gave way to one of tiger-like fierceness.

The first step in her downward course was in her ceasing to instruct me. She now commenced to practice her husband's precepts. She finally became even more violent in her opposition than her husband himself. She was not satisfied in simply doing as well as he had commanded—she seemed anxious to do better. Nothing seemed to make her more angry than to see me with a newspaper. She seemed to think that here lay the danger. I have had her rush at me with a face made all up of fury, and snatch from me a newspaper, in a manner that fully revealed her apprehension. She was an apt woman, and a little experience soon demonstrated, to her satisfaction, that education and slavery were incompatible with each other.

From this time I was most narrowly watched. If I was in a separate room any considerable length of time, I was sure to be suspected of having a book, and was at once called to give an account of myself. All this, however, was too late. The first step had been taken. Mistress, in teaching me the alphabet, had given me the "inch," and no precaution could prevent me from taking the "ell."

The plan I adopted, and the one by which I was most successful, was that of making friends of all the little white boys whom I met in the street. As many of these as I could, I converted into teachers. With their kindly aid, obtained at different times and in different places, I finally succeeded in learning to read. When I was sent on errands, I always took my book with me, and by going one part of my errand quickly, I found time to get a lesson before my return.

I used always to carry bread with me, enough of which was always in the house, and to which I was always welcome; for I was much better off in this regard than many of the poor white children in our neighborhood. This bread I used to bestow upon the hungry little urchins, who, in return, would give me that more valuable bread of knowledge. I am strongly tempted to give the names of two or three of those little boys, as a testimonial of the gratitude and affection I bear them. But prudence forbids— not that it would injure me, but it might embarrass them; for it is almost an unpardonable offense to teach slaves to read in this Christian country.

It is enough to say of the dear little fellows, that they lived on Philpot Street, very near Durgin and Bailey's shipyard. I used to talk this matter of slavery over with them. I would sometimes say to them, I wished I could be as free as they would be when they got to be men. "You will be free as soon as you are twenty-one, *but I am a slave for life!* Have not I as good a right to be free as you have?" These words used to trouble them; they would express for me the liveliest sympathy, and console me with the hope that something would occur by which I might be free.

I was now about twelve years old, and the thought of being a slave for life began to bear heavily upon my heart. Just about this time, I got hold of a book entitled "The Columbian Orator." Every opportunity I got, I used to read this book. I found in it a dialogue between a master and his slave. The slave was represented as having run away from his master three times. The dialogue represented the conversation which took place between them, when the slave was retaken the third time. In this dialogue, the whole argument in behalf of slavery was brought forward by the master, all of which was disposed of by the slave. The slave was made to say some very smart as well as impressive things in reply to his master—things which had the desired though unexpected effect—for the conversation resulted in the voluntary emancipation of the slave on the part of the master.

In the same book, I met with one of Sheridan's mighty speeches on and in behalf of Catholic emancipation. These were choice documents to me. I read them over and over again with unabated interest. The moral which I gained from the dialogue was the power of truth over the conscience of even a slaveholder. What I got from Sheridan was a bold denunciation of slavery, and a powerful vindication of human rights.

Every little while, I could hear something about the abolitionists. It was some time before I found what the word meant. It was always used in such connections as to make it an interesting word to me. If a slave ran away and succeeded in getting clear, or if a slave killed his master, set fire to a barn, or did any thing very wrong in the mind of a slaveholder, it was spoken of as the fruit of "abolition." Hearing the word in this connection very often, I set about learning what it meant. The dictionary afforded me no help. I found it was "the act of abolishing" but then I did not know what was to be abolished. Here I was perplexed. I did not dare to ask any one about its meaning, for I was satisfied that it was something they wanted me to know very little about.

After a patient waiting, I got one of our city papers, containing an account of the number of petitions from the north, praying for the abolition of slavery in the District of Columbia, and of the slave trade between the States. From this time I understood the word "abolition" and "abolitionist," and always drew near when that word was spoken, expecting to hear something of importance to myself and fellow-slaves.

The light broke in upon me by degrees. I went one day down on the wharf of Mr. Waters; and seeing two Irishmen unloading a scow of stone, I went, unasked, and helped them. When we had finished, one of them came to me and asked me if I were a slave. I told him I was. He asked, "Are ye a slave for life?" I told him that I was. The good Irishman seemed to be deeply affected by the statement. He said to the other that it was a pity so fine a little fellow as myself should be a slave for life. They both advised me to run away to the north; that I should find friends there, and that I should be free. I pretended not to be interested in what they said and treated them as if I did not understand them; for I feared they might be treacherous. White men have been known to encourage slaves to escape, and then, to get the reward, catch them and return them to their masters. I was afraid that these seemingly good men might use me so. But I remembered their advice, and from that time resolved to run away. I was too young to think of doing it immediately; besides, I wished to learn how to write, as I might have occasion to write my own pass. I consoled myself with the hope that I should one day find a good chance. Meanwhile, I would learn to write.

How I might learn to write was suggested to me by being in Durgin and Bailey's shipyard, and seeing the carpenter, after getting a piece of timber ready for use, write on the timber the name of that part of the ship for which it was intended. When a piece was intended for the larboard side, it would be marked "L." For the starboard side, it would be marked "S." A piece for the larboard side forward, would be marked "L.F.," and for the starboard aft, it would be marked "S.A." I soon learned the names of these letters, and for what they were intended. I immediately commenced copying them, and in a short time was able to make the four letters named.

After that, when I met with any boy who I knew could write, I would tell him I could write as well as he. The next word would be, "I don't believe you. Let me see you try it." I would then make the letters I had been so fortunate to learn, and ask him to beat that. In this way I got a good many lessons in writing, which it is quite possible I should never have gotten in any other way.

During this time, my copy book was the board fence, brick wall, and pavement. My pen and ink was a lump of chalk. With these, I learned mainly how to write. I then commenced and continued copying the Italics in "Webster's Spelling Book," until I could make them all without looking at the book. By this time, my little Master Thomas had gone to school, and learned how to write, and had written over a number of copy books. These had been brought home and then laid aside. My mistress used to go to class meetings at the Wilk Street meetinghouse every Monday afternoon, and leave me to take care of the house. When left thus, I used to spend the time in writing in the spaces left in Master Thomas's copy book, copying what he had written. I continued to do this until I could write what he had written. Thus, after a long, tedious effort for years, I finally succeeded in learning how to write.

My Name is Not Angelica

Scott O'Dell

*Raisha is kidnapped from her home in Africa along with others
from her village. After a frightening journey aboard a slave ship, God's
Adventure, they are all sold at the West Indies slave market. Renamed
Angelica by her owner, Raisha toils as a house slave, but reclaims her name,
and her freedom, after the great slave revolt of 1733.*

Chapter 5

Captain Sorensen had decided to sell three of us together, Konje, Dondo, and me. Lenta looked grim and unhappy. She still grieved for her son, so she was kept to one side.

A man rapped his hammer on a stone. He was the auctioneer Captain Sorensen had told me about. "We have three prime slaves of the three hundred slaves *God's Adventure* brought to the island this day," he said. "Here is Konje, chief of the Barato tribe." He put a hand on Konje's shoulder. Konje flinched. "A great breeder of sons and daughters. A magnificent specimen."

Konje did look magnificent. They had covered him with palm oil. He was naked to the waist, and his muscles rippled in the broiling sun. He towered above the black guards standing against the wall and the man with the hammer.

The auctioneer said, pointing to me, "Raisha the daughter of a subchief. Comely, strong, mother of many strong, comely children. She also speaks the Danish language. And Dondo, trained as a slave in a chieftain's family, is the perfect household servant."

He wiped his brow and banged his hammer. He banged it again until the crowd was quiet.

"These three, the finest Africa has to offer, will be sold as one," he said. "And no bid under two thousand rigsdalers will be considered. What do I hear?"

The auctioneer heard silence, then whispers among the planters. A man who stood just below me said to a woman wearing a pink dress and a flower in her hair, "What do you think, Jenna?"

"I think it's a bargain at three thousand rigsdalers," she said. "The man's worth that much alone."

"He's a little overpowering," the man said. "It would take a strong hand to control him."

"You have a strong hand, Jost."

Someone shouted an offer of two thousand four hundred rigsdalers. The auctioneer repeated the offer and gave the stone a blow.

"I like the girl, too," the woman said. "She has a nice smile."

It was the same smile I had learned on the ship, as if I had just received a gift I had always wanted. My face hurt from smiling and I felt like letting out a hair-raising scream. The deep blue eyes of Master Jost, blue as the sky, examined me from head to foot.

Offers were coming fast, a few rigsdalers at a time.

The woman said, "Don't be niggardly, Jost. We will be here all day. The sun is hot. Phillipe Horn is over there writing on a piece of paper. He wants them badly. Get rid of him with an offer he cannot match."

Jost cleared his throat, cupped his hands, and shouted, "Three thousand rigsdalers."

The crowd fell silent. Men I took to be plantation owners, who stood down in front in big straw hats, looked at each other and shook their heads.

The auctioneer shouted, "Three thousand rigsdalers. Do I hear three thousand, one hundred?"

The silence grew. Master van Prok lifted his hat and put it on again. He seemed ready to make a higher bid.

"Three thousand," said the auctioneer, glancing down at the planters, calling each by name. "Gentlemen, what do I hear?"

He heard nothing. His hammer came down with a bang. "Sold, sold to Master van Prok of Hawks Nest for the sum of three thousand rigsdalers."

From the shadows a black man crept out and climbed the ladder to the platform where the three of us stood. He was tall but bent over by some misfortune, so that he shifted crablike from one side to the other as he moved along.

"Come," he said. "I will take you to the boat that will take you to Hawks Nest on the island of St. John. St. John is only four miles away. It will be a pleasant voyage on this sunny day."

He took us past the pen that held the rest of the slaves that *God's Adventure* had brought to St. Thomas that day. Midnight black though they were, they looked like ghosts and were ghostly silent. My heart went out to them.

"What is your name?" Konje asked.

"Nero," the man said.

"What work do you do at Hawks Nest?"

"I am the bomba, Bomba Nero. I oversee what goes on at Hawks Nest. You can also call me Sir Bomba."

He talked out of the side of his mouth. His arrogance and cold, darting glance made Konje clamp his jaws.

At a shack by the wharf, the bomba took Konje inside. Two blacks put manacles on him. I saw them take a red-hot iron out of the fire and stamp a number on Konje's back. He made not a sound. They stamped Dondo, too.

We waited on the wharf for Jost van Prok and his wife. They came with two boys, good for running errands, Master van Prok told Nero when the bomba gave them a surly glance.

"I have two servants,"Jenna van Prok said. "You will be my third. You will like that, I am sure."

"Oh, yes," I said.

It was the task I had worked for from the day Captain Sorensen had told me about it, that it was much better than working in the fields, out in sun and storm. It was why I had learned to be docile, to say nothing unless asked, and to smile even though it hurt.

St. John is a beautiful island, just a few miles from St. Thomas, across pale blue water. At dusk our small boat came to Hawks Nest, the van Prok plantation, and moored in the shallows. From here we all walked ashore, except Jenna van Prok.

She was carried to the beach on Konje's broad shoulders. As he bent to set her down on the sand, Bomba Nero glanced at him. It was a searching glance, little more than the lifting of an eyelid, but in it was hatred.

I told Jenna van Prok that Lenta, my friend, was a good cook and would be very helpful at the house.

"I bid for her," she said, "But the Haugaard brothers outbid me. They have a plantation close to Mary Point. It is near so you'll see her again."

She looked at me from under the rim of her pink hat. "You have a pretty smile, like an angel from heaven," she said. "I'm going to call you Angelica. Do you like that?"

"Yes," I said, though I didn't like the name at all.

The van Proks changed all our names. The mistress called Konje "Apollo." Her husband called Dondo "Abraham." This was a custom, I learned. The planters wanted the slaves to forget they were born in Africa, that they were black Africans.

"Do you understand what I say?" Jenna van Prok asked. "The language I speak?"

"Yes, when you don't speak fast," I said.

CHAPTER 6

Hawks Nest looked down upon the sea. It was neither small nor large among the plantations on the mountainous island of St. John, but half of its land was level, good for the growing of sugar cane.

The rest of the plantation was cut up by gullies, bushy ravines, and by rock-strewn peaks. Here Master van Prok had cleared the land and terraced it for the growing of cotton.

The van Prok house stood on a low cliff within sound of the sea. It was made of stone and timber and looked like a small fort.

The slave huts stood at a distance from the house beside a large pile of boulders, the men on one side, the women on the other. In the middle of the boulders were privies. They were far enough from the house not to be unpleasant for the van Proks.

My hut, like all the others, had stone walls and a roof of palm leaves. One side was open and faced the sea. This was a help because sometimes in the night cool winds blew from that direction.

The first night I slept in my hut, I was told by the van Proks' slaves that for a year now, a terrible drought had settled upon the island. Great white clouds would come up at dawn, spread across the sky, and turn black, but not a drop of rain would fall.

This is exactly what happened on my first night. Dawn broke clear, with a small sea wind. The white clouds came up. The sun burned holes in them. They spread across the sky and turned black, but no rain fell. The clouds disappeared during the night. The heavens were on fire with stars.

Before I went to bed, Jenna van Prok had whispered to me, "My husband has told the bomba to put you to work in the fields tomorrow. This is his habit with all new slaves. He likes to test them. Don't despair. In a week I will have you working in the house."

A tutu horn blew just before dawn, a wild sound from a conch shell. Roosters crowed. The bomba came up the path, banging his ironwood club against everything in his way.

"Out!" he shouted. "This is not Sunday. It is a Wednesday in the month of April. You are not in Africa, dreaming about a breakfast of melons and roasted birds. You're on the plantation of Master van Prok, on the island of St. John in the Danish West Indies among the Virgin Islands. Out!"

We went to the side of a hill in a bushy ravine. There were fifteen of us, all but Konje, who was sent to work at the sugar mill. Before the drought, I was told, cotton grew in the ravine at this time of year and there would be pink flowers on the bushes. Now all was scorched and dry. With long knives we cut down the bushes and stirred up the ground.

In midmorning boys brought our breakfasts—a handful of dried finger-sized fish called poorjack and shriveled chickpeas, but nothing to drink. Already the sun beat down. It burned hotter than it ever did in Barato.

At noon we rested for a while. It was the time when the slaves went off to work in their little plots of land to raise vegetables for themselves. Now all they could do was to scratch at the scorched earth and pray on their knees for rain.

After the sun went down the bomba came and said that we hadn't done much that day, that we didn't deserve even the little fried fish his boys handed out to us.

After three days in the field I found that they ate better food at the van Proks'. Fearing that I would collapse from the work and the heat, Mistress Jenna had made her husband change his mind about testing me for a whole week.

She brought me into the house and I became her body servant, one of three, as she had said. With Amina, a slave she'd had for years, I attended her from dusk until midnight and ate my supper from what the van Proks left over.

We ate salt pork from Holland, salt mutton from New England, and bread baked in St. Thomas. Sometimes the bread had weevils in it, which I picked out before Mistress Jenna was served.

The food was not good. Master van Prok complained about it. "They send us meat that the market has refused," he said. "Meat so tough it bends the teeth. And the salt! You have to drink a firkin of water to calm your thirst. And at this moment there's not much water on the whole plantation."

For the slaves and the van Proks water to drink ran out after the second meal of the day, except for what was needed for the mules that turned the millstones that ground the cane for molasses and rum.

All three of Mistress Jenna's body servants were made to work in the distillery five hours each day. Master van Prok's three male servants hauled water up the hill for five hours, too. Among the three was Dondo. He had worked in the fields for days, until Mistress van Prok discovered that he was good at trimming hair. He then was brought into the household.

From the very beginning, Konje had hauled water up the hill from the sea. He could carry two times more water than any of the other slaves. More weight and much faster. He would put a cask on top of his head and go up the steep hill half running.

The bomba picked up Konje's new name, and when I was working in the distillery I heard him call out, "Apollo, you're a wonder. I, too, was a wonder, like you, but see what the hammer did."

Then he grinned and beat the ground with his club. He was punishing Konje, little by little, to get rid of his arrogance.

GROWING UP

Fast Sam, Cool Clyde, and Stuff

Walter Dean Myers

"Can you stuff?" Fast Sam asked Francis, the new boy on the block.
Though Francis knew he couldn't jump over a basketball rim and stuff the ball,
he said he could—becoming known from then on as Stuff to his soon-to-be best
friends, Fast Sam, Cool Clyde, and Gloria.

Trombones and Colleges

It was a dark day when we got our report cards. The sky was full off gray clouds and it was sprinkling rain. I went over to Clyde's house and Gloria and Kitty were there. Sam probably would have been there, too, only he had got a two-week job in the afternoons helping out at Freddie's. Actually he only did it so that his mother would let him be on the track team again. Sam and his mother had this little system going. He would do something good-doing and she'd let him do something that he wanted to do.

Clyde's report card was on the kitchen table and we all sat around it like it was some kind of a big important document. I had got a pretty good report card and had wanted to show it off but I knew it wasn't the time. Clyde pushed the card toward me and I read it. He had all satisfactory remarks on the side labeled Personal Traits and Behavior. He had also received B's in music and art appreciation. But everything else was either a C or a D except mathematics. His mathematics mark was a big red F that had been circled. I don't know why they had to circle the F when it was the only red mark on the card. In the Teacher's Comments section someone had written that Clyde had "little ability to handle an academic program."

"A little ability is better than none," I said. No one said anything so I figured it probably wasn't the right time to try to cheer Clyde up.

I knew all about his switching from a commercial program to an academic program, but I really hadn't thought he'd have any trouble.

"I saw the grade adviser today. He said I should switch back to the commercial program." Clyde looked like he'd start crying any minute. His eyes were red and his voice was shaky. "He said that I had to take mathematics over and if I failed again or failed another required subject I couldn't graduate. The way it is now I'm going to have to finish up in the summer because I switched over."

"I think you can pass if you really want to," Kitty said. Clyde's sister was so pretty I couldn't even look at her. If I did I started feeling funny and couldn't talk right. Sometimes I daydreamed about marrying her.

Just then Clyde's mother came in and he gave a quick look at Kitty.

"Hi, young ladies and young gentlemen." Mrs. Jones was a kind of heavy woman but she was pretty too. You could tell she was Kitty's mother if you looked close. She put her package down and started taking things out. "I heard you people talking when I first came in. By the way you hushed up I guess you don't want me to hear what you were talking about. I'll be out of your way in a minute, soon as I put the frozen foods in the refrigerator."

"I got my report card today," Clyde said. His mother stopped taking the food out and turned toward us. Clyde pushed the report card about two inches toward her. She really didn't even have to look at the card to know that it was bad. She could have told that just by looking at Clyde. But she picked it up and looked at it a long time. First she looked at one side and then the other and then back at the first side again.

"What they say around the school?" she asked, still looking at the card.

"They said I should drop the academic course and go back to the other one." I could hardly hear Clyde, he spoke so low.

"Well, what you going to do, young man?" She looked up at Clyde and Clyde looked up at her and there were tears in his eyes and I almost started crying. I can't stand to see my friends cry. "What are you going to do, Mr. Jones?"

"I'm—I'm going to keep the academic course," Clyde said.

"You think it's going to be any easier this time?" Mrs. Jones asked.

"No."

"Things ain't always easy. Lord knows that things ain't always easy." For a minute there was a faraway look in her eyes, but then her face turned into a big smile. "You're just like your father, boy. That man never would give up on anything he really wanted. Did I ever tell you the time he was trying to learn to play the trombone?"

"No." Clyde still had tears in his eyes but he was smiling, too. Suddenly everybody was happy. It was like seeing a rainbow when it was still raining.

"Well, we were living over across from St. Nicholas Park in this little rooming house. Your father was working on a job down on Varick Street that made transformers or some such nonsense—anyway, he comes home one day with this long package all wrapped up in brown paper. He walks in and sits it in the corner and doesn't say boo about what's in the bag. So at first I don't say anything either, and then I finally asks him what he's got in the bag, and he says, 'What bag?' Now this thing is about four feet long if it's an inch and he's asking *what* bag." Mrs. Jones wiped the crumbs from Gloria's end of the table with a quick swipe of the dish cloth, leaving a swirling pattern of tiny bubbles. Gloria tore off a paper towel and wiped the area dry.

"Now I look over at him and he's trying to be nonchalant. Sitting there, a grown man, and big as he wants to be and looking for all the world like somebody's misplaced son. So I says, 'The bag in the corner.' And he says, 'Oh, that's a trombone I'm taking back to the pawn shop tomorrow.' Well, I naturally ask him what he's doing with it in the first place, and he says he got carried away and bought it but he realized that we really didn't have the thirty-five dollars to spend on foolishness and so he'd take it back the next day. And all the time he's sitting there scratching his chin and rubbing his nose and trying to peek over at me to see how I felt about it. I just told him that I guess he knew what was best. Only the next day he forgot to take it back, and finally I broke down and told him why didn't he keep it. He said he would if I thought he should.

"So he unwraps this thing and he was just as happy with it as he could be until he tried to get a tune out of it. He couldn't get a sound out of it at first, but then he started oomping and woomping with the thing as best he could. He worked at it and worked at it and you could see he was getting disgusted. I think he was just about to give it up when the lady who lived under us came upstairs and started complaining about the noise. It kept her Napoleon awake, she said. Napoleon was a dog. Little ugly thing, too. She said your father couldn't play anyway.

"Well, what did she say that for? That man played that thing day and night. He worked so hard at that thing that his lips were too sore for him to talk right sometime. But he got the hang of it.

"I never remembered Pop playing a trombone," said Clyde.

"Well, your father had a streak in him that made him stick to a thing," she said, pouring some rice into a colander to wash it off, "but every year his goals got bigger and bigger and he had to put some things down so that he could get to others. That old trombone is still around here some place. Probably in one of them boxes under Kitty's bed. Now, you children, excuse me, young ladies and gentlemen, get on out of here and let me finish supper."

We all went into Clyde's living room.

"That was my mom's good-doing speech," Clyde said. "She gets into talking about what a great guy my father was and how I was like him and whatnot."

"You supposed to be like your father," Sam said. "He was the one that raised you, right?"

"She wants me to be like him, and I want to be like him, too, I guess. She wants me to keep on trying with the academic thing."

"What do you want to do," Sam asked, "give it up?"

"No. Not really. I guess I want people like my mother to keep on telling me that I ought to do it, really. Especially when somebody tells me I can't do it."

"Boy," Sam said, sticking his thumbs in his belt and leaning back in the big stuffed chair, "you are just like your father."

Then we all went into Clyde's room and just sat around and talked for a while. Mostly about school and stuff like that, and I wanted to tell Clyde that I thought I could help him if he wanted me to. I was really getting good grades in school, but I thought that Clyde might get annoyed if I mentioned it. But then Gloria said that we could study together some time and that was cool, too.

For the Life of Laetitia

Merle Hodge

*Laetitia, called Lacey for short, is thrilled to have won a place
in the government secondary school. But to attend, she will have to leave her
familiar Caribbean village, and move to La Puerta to live with her father.*

When we set out down the Trace that morning, I wasn't feeling too joyful.
It was very strange to be going down to Sooklal Trace in a motorcar. People
stopped whatever they were doing in their yards and peered at us. Some
were taking water from their barrels at the side of the road, washing clothes,
or bathing. Some waved, or looked puzzled when they recognized me.

The car was old, and it made a lot of noise over the bumps and holes in
the road. The worst part was that my father kept trying to make conversation with me above the noise.

"So you like plenty books, eh? Well, we will see what we can do. I have
one or two books myself, you know."

He was very impressed with the box of books I had put into the car
along with the suitcase.

"I like a little reading now and then, you know. Although I wasn't so bright as you—I didn't get pick to go to secondary school. I only make it to seventh standard."

He kept turning his head to grin at me, and I thought sooner or later he would run into somebody's barrel. Sooklal Trace had never seemed so long, even though I was traveling in a car. It seemed much longer than when I walked out on mornings with the other schoolchildren, or when I got a bumpy ride on the bar of Uncle Leroy's bike.

"I tell your brother, I say: "Well, you see what your sister do? She come and she pass her exam for secondary school. Well, you know what you have to do now—you can't let the girls beat you!" And with this he laughed from down in his belly, glancing at me again and again to see if I was enjoying the joke.

He was still laughing when he passed Miss Adlyn going down the road with the baby. The boy was all dressed up, and I knew she was taking him to the clinic in La Puerta for his regular checkup. She heard the car coming and put out her hand to beg for a lift. When she realized we were not going to stop, she paused to shift the baby over to the shoulder where the bag was, and the bag over to the other shoulder.

I couldn't even wave at her—I wanted to sink down into the car seat. I could imagine Miss Adlyn making her way down the Trace, changing around the baby and the bulging bag several times before she got to the main road. There she would wait in the shade of Rampie's shop for a bus, maybe give up after an hour and pay the taxi fare to Junction, then in Junction wait again for a bus to La Puerta. And we were going to La Puerta!

"But your Tantie Velma will help you with your lesson. Yes, man, she is the one in the family with education. She was a high-school girl, too, you know!" He glanced over at me again and looked back just in time to swerve away from Mr. Popo's dog, sunning itself in the middle of the Trace. He cursed the dog under his breath, then put on his smile again.

"Yes, man, she just waiting to measure you up for your uniform."

This brightened me a little. I began to feel excited about school again.

The government secondary school was the biggest and most modern thing in La Puerta. I used to look at it with awe when I went with Ma and Carlyle to sell the cocoa. It was not one building, but several, and all of them two storeys high.

I looked at the students with awe, too; the way they took over the streets in their plaid uniforms, talking and laughing gaily, as if they owned the town.

And now I had been given a place at this school!

My name was right there in the newspapers, among all the other children who had passed the Common Entrance Examination: JOHNSON, LAETITIA CHRISTINA. It was a Sunday, and Uncle Jamesie was home for the day with Tantie Monica and the children. Pappy right away sent Uncle Leroy out the road to knock on Rampie's side door for a bottle of rum and some sweet-drinks.

I would be the first one ever, the first one in the family to go to secondary school. Pappy made speech after speech about the new and blessed day that was dawning in the land. The celebration went on until Uncle Jamesie realized that darkness would catch them walking out the Trace if they didn't leave in a hurry. By then even Ma was tipsy, dancing with us one by one.

Two days later my father appeared, out of the blue. He, too, was bursting with pride.

I had never seen much of my father before this. We spotted him now and then on our trips into La Puerta, and if he saw me, he would call me over and begin to fish in his pockets until he found a dollar bill. He would press the money into my hand and say: "Go and buy sno-cone."

Sometimes Uncle Leroy got a few days' road work in Junction, and if my father passed that way and saw him, he might give Uncle Leroy five dollars for me. One Christmastime he sent a present, a doll in a white-and-gold dress, and my mother said it must be the Christmas rum in his head.

Ma, my grandmother, did not have a very high opinion of him. Whenever we met him in town, she would grumble all the way back home on the bus, every now and then stopping to suck her teeth loudly: "*Steups!* Anyhow, the less said about that man the better."

But before a few minutes had passed she would begin to grumble again about how he had no conscience, and how he would meet his Judgment Day. She complained that now he was a big Supervisor, driving a motor car and all, and still wouldn't help his child in a decent and proper manner.

"Sno-cone?" she said. "The child could live on sno-cone?"

And then again she would stop and chide herself: "Look, Wilhemina Johnson, hush your old mouth. Less said, the better. Leave him to God. Hah! He will meet his Judgment, so help me he will meet it."

You can imagine, then, that when my father appeared in front of our house that day, for the first time in many years, my grandmother did not greet him warmly to begin with. He arrived with the back seat of his car full of parcels, which turned out to be presents for me, to reward me for having passed my exam.

At first he just sat out in the car, not knowing what to do, for Ma was standing in the doorway, her two hands on her hips, regarding him with a face of stone.

He grinned nervously and waved a limp hand. "Good afternoon, Ma Willie."

Ma sent Carlyle to invite him in. The other children were only waiting for her to move from the doorway in order to run down the path and swarm all over the car. And quite a swarm we were, for it was August vacation, and in addition to the children who lived here all the time (Ruth and Kenwyn, Carlyle, and myself) we had Uncle Leroy's daughter Charlene, one of Ma's godchildren, Carlyle's little brother, and two of Uncle Jamesie's children who had refused to go back to Petit-Fort with their parents on Sunday. But Ma knew what was in their minds: "All of you, find yourself in the back yard!" she snapped. "Lacey, you come inside."

So the three of us sat in the drawing room. Pappy and Uncle Leroy were down in the cocoa.

My father said he wanted me to come and stay with him and his family in La Puerta, now that I would be going to school there. He'd been walking around with the newspaper in his pocket. He had opened a bottle of whiskey for the fellows on the job. He had shown the Big Boss my name in the paper, and told him that I was his daughter, and the Big Boss had congratulated him.

My father could hardly contain himself.

"Ma Willie," he said, "let me do my duty as a father."

Ma gave a dry laugh that stayed in her throat. But she knew—as I did—that going to live in the town would make life a lot easier for me. La Puerta meant nearly two miles on foot to begin with, and then about four miles to Balatier Junction by bus or taxi, and the long bus ride to La Puerta. It would mean leaving home at some ungodly hour on mornings, and getting back only just before dark.

Also, nobody had as yet counted up what it would cost in fares. Uncle Leroy said that I could get a student's bus pass to ride free on the bus; but the buses along this part of the main road were not very regular, so on mornings I would very likely have to take a taxi to Junction. And we didn't have money to pay taxi fare every day of the week.

Ma questioned my father closely. What did his wife think of my coming to live there? Did he intend to buy my books and uniform? Would he see to it I didn't run wild in the town and get myself in trouble like so many of these high-school girls nowadays?

My father nodded vigorously to everything: "Yes, Ma Willie! Of course, Ma Willie! . . ."

When the interrogation was over, she still didn't give him much of an answer. She told him that we would have to write to my mother first, and I would have to ask my grandfather, and my uncles.

He left, looking a little downcast. Ma told him that Uncle Leroy would bring a message to him at his workplace.

SOUNDER

William H. Armstrong

Though Sounder is not much to look at, he's the best—and most loyal—coon dog in the whole countryside. But when the sheriff comes to arrest Sounder's master, a poor black sharecropper who has stolen a pig to feed his hungry family, Sounder is shot. During the night, the seriously wounded animal drags himself into the woods and cannot be found, but the heartbroken boy never gives up hope that he will see his cherished dog—and his beloved father—again.

The boy moved quickly around the corner and out of sight of the iron door and the gray cement walls of the jail. At the wall in front of the courthouse he stood for a while and looked back. When he had come, he was afraid, but he felt good in one way because he would see his father. He was bringing him a cake for Christmas. And he wasn't going to let his father know he was grieved. So his father wouldn't be grieved.

Now the sun had lost its strength. There were only a few people loafing around the courthouse wall, so the boy sat for a spell. He felt numb and tired. What would he say to his mother? He would tell her that the jailer was mean to visitors but didn't say nothing to the people in jail. He wouldn't tell her about the cake. When he told her his father had said she shouldn't send him again, that he would send word by the visiting preacher, she would say "You grieved him, child. I told you to be perk so you wouldn't grieve him."

Nobody came near where the boy sat or passed on the street in front of the wall. He had forgotten the most important thing, he thought. He hadn't asked his father where Sounder had come to him on the road when he wasn't more'n a pup. That didn't make any difference.

But along the road on the way to jail, before the bull-necked man had ruined everything, the boy had thought his father would begin to think and say "If a stray ever follard you and it wasn't near a house, likely somebody's dropped it. So you could fetch it home and keep it for a dog."

"Wouldn't do no good now," the boy murmured to himself. Even if he found a stray on the way home, his mother would say "I'm afraid, child. Don't bring it in the cabin. If it's still here when mornin' comes, you take it down the road and scold it and run so it won't foller you no more. If somebody come lookin', you'd be in awful trouble."

A great part of the way home the boy walked in darkness. In the big houses he saw beautiful lights and candles in the windows. Several times dogs rushed to the front gates and barked as he passed. But no stray pup came to him along the lonely, empty stretches of the road. In the dark he thought of the bull-necked man crumpled on the floor in the cake crumbs, like the strangled bull in the cattle chute, and he walked faster. At one big house the mailbox by the road had a lighted lantern hanging on it. The boy walked on the far side of the road so he wouldn't show in the light. "People hangs 'em out when company is comin' at night," the boy's father had once told him.

When court was over, they would take his father to a road camp or a

quarry or a state farm. Would his father send word with the visiting preacher where he had gone? Would they take his father away to the chain gang
for a year or two years before he could tell the visiting preacher? How
would the boy find him then? If he lived closer to the town, he could watch
each day, and when they took his father away in the wagons where con-
victs were penned up in huge wooden crates, he could follow.

The younger children were already in bed when the boy got home. He
was glad, for they would have asked a lot of questions that might make his
mother feel bad, questions like "Is everybody chained up in jail? How long
do people stay in jail at one time?"

The boy's mother did not ask hurtful questions. She asked if the boy got
in all right and if it was warm in the jail. The boy told her that the jailer
was mean to visitors but that he didn't say nothing to the people in the jail.
He told her he heard some people singing in the jail.

"Sounder ain't come home?" the boy said to his mother after he had
talked about the jail. He had looked under the porch and called before he
came into the cabin.

Now he went out, calling and looking around the whole cabin. He
started to light the lantern to look more, but his mother said, "Hang it
back, child. Ain't no use to fret yourself. Eat your supper, you must be fam-
ished."

"He said not to come no more," the boy finally said to his mother when
he had finished his supper. "He said he'll send word by the visitin' preacher." He poked up the fire and waited for his mother to ask him if he had
been perk and didn't grieve his father, but she didn't. He warmed himself
and watched a patch of red glow the size of his hand at the bottom of the
stove. He could see the red-faced man lying on the jail floor with blood
oozing out of the corners of his mouth. After a long quiet spell the rocker

began to squeak, and it made the boy jump, but his mother didn't notice. She began to rock as she picked out walnut kernels. She hummed for a while, and then she began to sing like she was almost whispering for no one to hear but herself:

You've gotta walk that lonesome valley,
You've gotta walk it by yourself,
Ain't nobody else gonna walk it for you . . .

In bed, the pressure of the bed slats through the straw tick felt good against the boy's body. His pillow smelled fresh, and it was smooth and soft. He was tired, but he lay awake for a long time. He thought of the store windows full of so many things. He thought of the beautiful candles in windows. He dreamed his father's hands were chained against the prison bars and he was still standing there with his head down. He dreamed that a wonderful man had come up to him as he was trying to read the store signs aloud and had said, "Child, you want to learn, don't you?"

In the morning the boy lay listening to his mother as she opened and closed the stove door. He heard the damper squeak in the stovepipe as she adjusted it. She was singing softly to herself. Then the boy thought he heard another familiar sound, a faint whine on the cabin porch. He listened. No, it couldn't be. Sounder always scratched before he whined, and the scratching was always louder than the whine. Besides, it was now almost two months later, and the boy's mother had said he might be back in a week. No, he was not dreaming. He heard it again. He had been sleeping in his shirt to keep warm, so he only had to pull on his overalls as he went. His mother had stopped singing and was listening.

There on the cabin porch, on three legs, stood the living skeleton of what had been a mighty coon hound. The tail began to wag, and the hide made little ripples back and forth over the ribs. One side of the head and shoulders was reddish brown and hairless; the acid of the oak leaves had tanned the surface of the wound the color of leather. One front foot dangled above the floor. The stub of an ear stuck out on one side, and there was no eye on that side, only a dark socket with a splinter of bone showing above it. The dog raised his good ear and whined. His one eye looked up at the lantern and the possum sack where they hung against the wall. The eye looked past the boy and his mother. Where was his master? "Poor creature. Poor creature," said the mother and turned away to get him food. The boy felt sick and wanted to cry, but he touched Sounder on the good side of his head. The tail wagged faster, and he licked the boy's hand.

The shattered shoulder never grew together enough to carry weight, so the great hunter with the single eye, his head held to one side so he could see, never hopped much farther from the cabin than the spot in the road where he had tried to jump on the wagon with his master. Whether he lay in the sun on the cabin porch or by the side of the road, the one eye was always turned in the direction his master had gone.

The boy got used to the way the great dog looked. The stub of ear didn't bother him, and the one eye that looked up at him was warm and questioning. But why couldn't he bark? "He wasn't hit in the neck" the boy would say to his mother. "He eats all right, his throat ain't scarred." But day after day when the boy snapped his fingers and said "Sounder, good Sounder," no excited bark burst forth from the great throat. When something moved at night, the whine was louder, but it was still just a whine.

Before Sounder was shot, the boy's mother always said "Get the pan, child" or "Feed your dog, child." Now she sometimes got the pan herself and took food out to Sounder. The boy noticed that sometimes his mother would stop singing when she put the food pan down at the edge of the porch. Sometimes she would stand and look at the hunting lantern and possum sack where they hung, unused, against the cabin wall . . .

The town and the jail seemed to become more remote and the distance greater as each day passed. If his father hadn't said "Don't come again," it wouldn't seem so far, the boy thought. Uncertainty made the days of waiting longer, too.

The boy waited for the visiting preacher to come and bring word of his father. He thought the people for whom his mother washed the soft curtains could certainly write and would write a letter for his mother. But would someone in the jail read it for his father? Perhaps none of the people in jail could read, and the big man with the red face would just tear it up and swear. The visiting preacher might write a letter for the boy's father. But how would it get to the cabin since no mailman passed and there was no mailbox like the boy had seen on the wider road nearer the town?

The boy wanted to go to the town to find out what had happened to his father. His mother always said "Wait, child, wait." When his mother returned laundry to the big houses, she asked the people to read her the court news from their newspapers. One night she came home with word of the boy's father; it had been read to her from the court news. When the younger children had gone to bed, she said to the boy, "Court's over." And then there was one of those long quiet spells that always made the boy feel numb and weak.

"You won't have to fret for a while about seein' him in jail. He's gone to hard labor."

"For how long?" the boy asked.

"It won't be as long as it might. Folks has always said he could do two men's work in a day. He'll get time off for hard work and good behavior in it. The judge said it."

"Where's he gonna be at?" the boy asked after he swallowed the great lump that filled up his throat and choked him.

"Didn't say. The people that has the paper says it donít ever say wher' they gonna be at. But it's the county or the state. Ain't never outside the state, the people says."

"He'll send word," the boy said.

THE CAY

Theodore Taylor

*After the freighter Phillip is traveling on is torpedoed by the
Germans, he's rescued by Timothy, an old black West Indian, who pulls him
aboard a raft. Before they manage to reach a deserted island, Phillip is
accidentally hit on the head and loses his sight. Once blind, however, Phillip
is able to see Timothy more clearly, and finally is able to understand,
and appreciate, Timothy's warmth, dignity, and wisdom.*

In the afternoon, Timothy said we'd make a rope.

On the north end of the island, tough vines, almost as large as a pencil,
were laced over the sand. It took us several hours to tear out a big pile of
them. Then Timothy began weaving a rope that would stretch all the way
down the hill to the beach and fire pile.

The rope was for me. If he happened to be out on the reef, and I heard
a plane, I could take a light from our campfire, follow the rope down, and
touch off the big fire. The vine rope would also serve to get me safely down
to the beach.

After we'd torn the vines out, and he was weaving the rope, he said,
"Young bahss, you mus' begin to help wid d'udder wark."

We were sitting up by the hut. I had my back to a palm and was thinking that back in Willemstad, at this moment, I'd probably be sitting in a class-room, three desks away from Henrik, listening to Herr Jonckheer talk about European history. I'd been tutored in Dutch the first year in Willemstad so I could attend the regular school. Now I could speak it and understand it.

My hands were tired from pulling the vines, and I just wanted to sit and think. I didn't want to work. I said, "Timothy, I'm blind. I can't see to work."

I heard him cutting something with his sharp knife. He replied softly, "D'han' is not blin'."

Didn't the old man understand? To work, aside from pulling up vines or drawing something in the sand, you must be able to see.

Stubbornly, he said, "Young bahss, we need sleepin' mats. You can make d'mats."

I looked over in his direction. "You do it," I said.

He sighed back, saying, "D'best matmaker in Charlotte Amalie, downg in Frenchtown, b'total blin'."

"But he's a man, and he has to do that to make a living."

"B'true," Timothy said quietly.

But in a few minutes, he placed several lengths of palm fiber across my lap. He really was a black mule. "D'palm mat is veree easy. Jus' ovah an'un-der . . ."

Becoming angry with him, I said, "I tell you, I can't see."

He paid no attention to me. "Take dis' han' hol' d'palm like dis; den ovah an' under, like d'mahn in Frenchtown; den more palm."

I could feel him standing there watching me as I tried to reeve the lengths, but I knew they weren't fitting together. He said, "Like dis, I tell you," and reached down to guide my hand. "Ovah an' under . . ."

I tried again, but it didn't work. I stood up, threw the palm fibers at him, and screamed, "You ugly black man! I won't do it! You're stupid, you can't even spell . . ."

Timothy's heavy hand struck my face sharply.

Stunned, I touched my face where he'd hit me. Then I turned away from where I thought he was. My cheek stung, but I wouldn't let him see me with tears in my eyes.

I heard him saying very gently, "B'gettin' back to wark, my own self."

I sat down again.

He began to sing that "fungee and feesh" song in a low voice, and I could picture him sitting on the sand in front of the hut; that tangled gray hair, the ugly black face with the thick lips, those great horny hands winding the strands of vine.

The rope, I thought. It wasn't for him. It was for me.

After a while, I said, "Timothy . . ."

He did not answer, but walked over to me, pressing more palm fronds into my hands. He murmured, "Tis veree easy, ovah an' under . . ." Then he went back to singing about fungee and feesh.

Something happened to me that day on the cay. I'm not quite sure what it was even now, but I had begun to change.

I said to Timothy, "I want to be your friend."

He said softly, "Young bahss, you 'ave always been my friend."

I said, "Can you call me Phillip instead of young boss?"

"Phill-eep," he said warmly.

During our seventh night on the island, it rained. It was one of those tropical storms that comes up swiftly without warning. We were asleep on the palm mats that I'd made, but it awakened us immediately. The rain sounded like bullets hitting on the dried palm frond roof. We ran out into it, shouting and letting the fresh water hit our bodies. It was cool and felt good.

Timothy yelled that his catchment was working. He had taken more boards from the top of the raft and had made a large trough that would catch the rain. He'd picked up bamboo lengths on the beach and had fitted them together into a short pipe to funnel the rain water into our ten-gallon keg.

It rained for almost two hours, and Timothy was quite angry with himself for not making a second catchment because the keg was soon filled and overflowing.

We stayed out in the cool rain for twenty or thirty minutes and then went back inside. The roof leaked badly but we didn't mind. We got on our mats and opened our mouths to the sweet, fresh water. Stew Cat was huddled in a miserable ball over in a corner, Timothy said, not enjoying it at all.

I liked the rain because it was something I could hear and feel; not something I must see. It peppered in bursts against the frond roof, and I could hear the drips as it leaked through. The squall wind was in the tops of the palms and I could imagine how they looked in the night sky, thrashing against each other high over our little cay.

I wanted it to rain all night.

We talked for a long time when the rain began to slack off. Timothy asked me about my mother and father. I told him all about them and about how we lived in Scharloo, getting very lonesome and homesick while I was telling him. He kept saying, "Ah, dat be true?"

Then Timothy told me what he could remember from his own childhood. It wasn't at all like mine. He'd never gone to school, and was working on a fishing boat by the time he was ten. It almost seemed the only fun he had was once a year at carnival when he'd put frangipani leaves around his ankles and dress up in a donkey hide to parade around with *mocki jumbis*, the spirit chasers, while the old ladies of Charlotte Amalie danced the *bambola* around them.

He chuckled. "I drink plenty rhum dose tree days of carnival."

I could picture him in his donkey skin, wheeling around to the music of the steel bands. They had them in Willemstad too.

Because it had been on my mind I told him that my mother didn't like black people and asked him why.

He answered slowly, "I don' like some white people my own self, but 'twould be outrageous if I didn' like any o' dem."

Wanting to hear it from Timothy, I asked him why there were different colors of skin, white and black, brown and red, and he laughed back, "Why b'feesh different color, or flower b'different color? I true don' know, Phill-eep, but I true tink beneath d'skin is all d'same."

Herr Jonckheer had said something like that in school but it did not mean quite as much as when Timothy said it.

Long after he'd begun to snore in the dripping hut, I thought about it. Suddenly, I wished my father and mother could see us there together on the little island.

I moved close to Timothy's big body before I went to sleep. I remember smiling in the darkness. He felt neither white nor black.

In the morning, the air was crisp and the cay smelled fresh and clean. Timothy cooked a small fish, a pompano, that he'd speared at dawn down on the reef. Neither of us had felt so good or so clean since we had been aboard the *Hato*. And without discussing it, we both thought this might be the day an aircraft would swing up into the Devil's Mouth, if that's where we were.

The pompano, broiled over the low fire, tasted good. Of course, we were eating little but what came from the sea. Fish, langosta, mussels, or the eggs from sea urchins, those small, black round sea animals with sharp spines that attach themselves to the reefs.

Timothy had tried to make a stew from seaweed but it tasted bitter.

Then he'd tried to boil some new sea-grape roots but they made us ill. The only thing that ever worked for him was sea-grape leaves, boiled first in sea water and then cooked in fresh water.

But above us, forty feet from the ground, Timothy said, was a feast. Big, fat green coconuts. When we'd landed, there were a few dried ones on the ground, but the meat in them was not very tasty. In a fresher one, there was still some milk, but it was rancid.

At least once a day, especially when we were around the hut, Timothy would say, "'Tis outrageous dem coconut hang up in d'sky when we could use d'milk an' meat." Or he'd say, "Timothy, my own self, long ago could climb d'palm veree easy." Or hinting, and I guess looking up at them, "Phill-eep, I do believe you b'gettin' outrageous strong 'ere on d'islan'."

He made a point of saying if he were only fifty again, he could climb the tree and slice them off with his knife. But at seventy-odd, he did not think he could make it to the top.

That morning over breakfast, Timothy said, looking to the tops of the palms, I'm sure, "A lil' milk from d'coconut would b'good now, eh, Phill-eep?"

As yet, I didn't have the courage to climb the palms. "Yes, it would," I said.

Timothy cleared his throat, sighed deeply, and put the coconuts out of his mind. But I knew he'd try me again.

He said, "Dem devilin' coconuts aside, your mutthur would never be knowin' you now."

I asked why.

"You are veree brown an' veree lean," he said.

I tried to imagine how I looked. I knew my shirt and pants were in tatters. My hair felt ropy. There was no way to comb it. I wondered how my eyes looked and asked Timothy about that.

"Dey look widout cease," he said. "Dey stare, Phill-eep."

"Do they bother you?"

Timothy laughed. "Not me. Eeevery day I tink what rare good luck I 'ave dat you be 'ere wid my own self on dis outrageous, hombug islan'.'"

I thought awhile and then asked him, "How long was it before that friend of yours, that friend in the Barbados, could see again?"

Timothy replied vaguely, "Oh, many mont', I do recall."

"But you told me on the raft it was only three days."

"Did I say dat?"

"Yes!"

"Well," Timothy said, " 'twas a long time ago. But 'e got 'is sight back, to be true." He paused a moment, then said, "Now, I tell you, we got much wark to do today."

I noticed more and more that Timothy always changed the subject when we began to talk about my eyes. He would make any kind of an excuse.

"What work?" I asked.

"Now, lemme see," he said. "For one ting, we mus' make another catch-ment . . . an' we mus' go to d'reef for food . . . an'. . ."

I waited.

Timothy finally exploded. "Now, dat is a lot o' wark, Phill-eep, to be true."

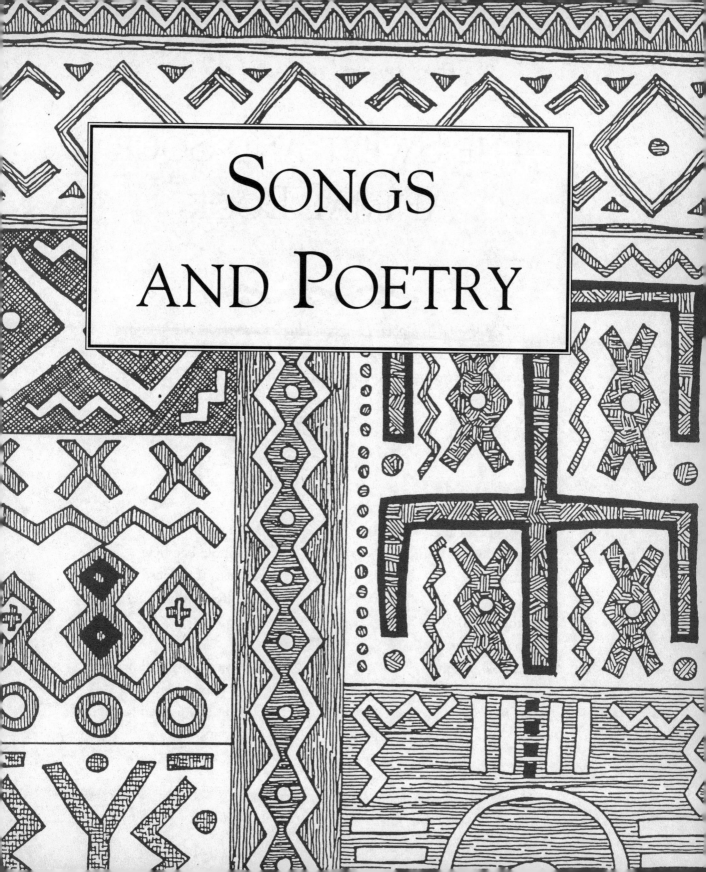

SONGS AND POETRY

THE SWEET AND SOUR ANIMAL BOOK

Langston Hughes

Best known as a poet, Langston Hughes also wrote plays, essays, novels, short stories, and books and poems for children. These enchanting little verses, take youngsters on a captivating romp through the alphabet.

A
There was an ape
Who bought a cape
To wear when he went
Downtown.

The other apes
Who had no capes,
Said, "Look at that
Stuck-up clown!"

B
A bumble bee flew
Right in the house
And lit on a bouquet
Of flowers.

It turned out the flowers
Were papier-mâché—
So that bee looked for honey
For hours.

C
There was a camel
Who had two humps.
He thought in his youth
They were wisdom bumps.

Then he learned
They were nothing but humps —
And ever since he's
Been in the dumps.

D
Rover dog
Is quite brave when
He's chasing Tom Cat
Around the bend.

But when Tom Cat
Scratches him on the nose,
Rover Dog turns tail
And goes.

E
Elephant,
Elephant,
Big as a
House!

They tell me
That you
Are afraid of a
Mouse.

F
There was a fish
With a greedy eye
Who darted toward
A big green fly.

Alas! That fly
Was bait on a hook!
So the fisherman took
The fish home to cook.

G
What use
Is a goose
Except to quackle?

If a goose
Can't quackle
She's out of whackle.

H
Dobbin used to be
A fire horse
Pulling a truck
With pride.

Now the village has
A motor truck—
Old Dobbin's
Cast aside.

I
Ibis,
In case you have not heard,
Is a long-legged
Wading-bird.

Happiest
Where fish are found,
He hates to set foot
On dry ground.

J
Jaybird,
Jaybird,
Do you know
What I would do?
"Naw!"

I wouldn't try
To sing at all
If I were you!
"Caw!"

K
A little white kitten
Got caught in the rain.
The mud and the wetting
Caused him great pain.

When he got in the house
And lay down to dry,
He started to purring,
"How happy am I!"

L
A lion in a zoo,
Shut up in a cage,
Lives a life
Of smothered rage.

A lion in the plain,
Roaming free,
Is happy as ever
A lion can be.

M
Jocko is
A peanut fiend.
He can eat peanuts
Like an eating machine.

When the peanuts are gone
And his fun is done,
Jocko can chatter
Like a son-of-a-gun!

N
Newt,
Newt, newt,
What can you be?

Just
A salamander, child,
That's me!

O
At night the owl
In a hollow tree,
With one eye shut,
Still can see.

But daylight changes
All of that—
By day an owl
Is blind as a bat.

P
There was a pigeon,
A mighty flier,
His friends all called him
Pigeon McGuire.

But he perched upon
An electric wire—
And that was the end of
Pigeon McGuire!

Q
Quail
Are happy,
And fleet on their feet—

Till the hunter
Comes gunning
For something to eat!
B-O-O-M!

R
Peter Rabbit
Had a habit
Of eating garden plants—

Until Mrs. Rabbit
Caught Peter Rabbit
And warmed his little pants.

S
Mrs. Squirrel
Can look so sweet
When she finds
Her nest is neat.

When baby squirrels
Mess up her bower,
Mrs. Squirrel
Indeed looks sour.

T
Turtle, turtle,
I wonder why
Other animals
Pass you by?

Turtles travel
Very slow,
Still I get
Where I want to go.

U
The unicorn
Has a single horn—
Except that there is
No unicorn!

In fairy tales alone
They're born.
Happy unreal
Unicorn!

V
The vixen is
A female fox,
Pleased the woods
To roam.

If a trapper
Puts her in a box
She never feels
At home.

W
A pretty white mouse
Smooth as silk
Made a misstep
And fell in the milk.

When she got out
She was soaked to the skin
And mad as a hatter
Because she fell in!

X
X,
Of course,
Is a letter, too.

But I know *no* animal
Starts with an
X

Do you?

Y
Yaks are shaggy
And yaks are strong,
Happiest where
The winters are long.

But when summer sun
Is bright and bold,
A yak had rather be
Where it's cold.

Z
Zebra.
Zebra.
Which is right—

White on black—
Or black on white?

So with a riddle,
My young friend,
From A to Z,
We come to the end.

AFRICAN-AMERICAN SONGS

African music came to America with the slaves. The societies from which they had been torn were not based on the written word. Rather, tribal history, culture, and religious beliefs were passed through song and dance from one generation to the other.

On the plantations, blacks developed their own musical tradition. Techniques of call and response, brought from tribal villages, continued to be an important element of their music. The coded language of spirituals, which were surprisingly free of bitterness, provided a way for slaves to secretly communicate. "Heaven" and the "promised land" referred to the joy of freedom, "crossing the River Jordan" was a metaphor for crossing the Ohio and Mississippi into abolitionist territory, and references to trains and railroads were reminders of the Underground Railroad and the freedom it represented.

I see glory in the air.
Over my head, I see glory in the air.
There must be a God somewhere.

He's Got the Whole World in His Hands

Traditional

Originally an anonymous black spiritual, this joyful song was made popular in Southern Baptist churches.

Chorus

He's got the whole world in His hands, The whole world in His hands,
He's got the whole world in His hands, He's got the whole world
in his hands.

Verse 1

He's got the wind and the rain in His hands, The wind and the rain
in His hands,
He's got the wind and the rain in His hands, He's got the whole world
in his hands.

Chorus

He's got the whole world in His hands, The whole world in His hands,
He's got the whole world in His hands, He's got the whole world
in his hands.

Verse 2

He's got the tiny little baby in His hands, The tiny little baby in His hands,
He's got the tiny little baby in His hands, He's got the whole world
  in his hands.

Chorus

He's got the whole world in His hands, The whole world in His hands,
He's got the whole world in His hands, He's got the whole world
  in his hands.

Verse 3

He's got you and me brother (sister) in His hands, you and me brother
  in His hands,
He's got you and me brother in His hands, He's got the whole world
  in his hands.

Chorus

He's got the whole world in His hands, The whole world in His hands,
He's got the whole world in His hands, He's got the whole world
  in his hands.

Swing Low, Sweet Chariot

Traditional

In the Carolinas, slaves used a sledlike vehicle called a chariot for carrying things. In spirituals, a chariot "swinging low" from the sky represented a means of escape from slavery in America and a way back to Africa.

Chorus
Swing low, sweet chariot,
Coming for to carry me home.
Swing low, sweet chariot,
Coming for to carry me home.

Verse 1
I looked over Jordan, and what did I see?
Coming for to carry me home?
A tall band of angels coming after me,
Coming for to carry me home.

Chorus
Swing low, sweet chariot,
Coming for to carry me home.
Swing low, sweet chariot,
Coming for to carry me home.

Verse 2
If you get there before I do,
Coming for to carry me home.
Tell all my friends I'm coming too,
Coming for to carry me home.

Chorus

Swing low, sweet chariot,
Coming for to carry me home.
Swing low, sweet chariot,
Coming for to carry me home.

Verse 3

I'm sometimes up, I'm sometimes down,
Coming for to carry me home.
But still my soul feels heav'nly bound,
Coming for to carry me home.

Chorus

Swing low, sweet chariot,
Coming for to carry me home.
Swing low, sweet chariot,
Coming for to carry me home.

AMAZING GRACE

*The lyrics to this simple melody were written by John Newton,
a captain of a slave ship, who became a minister and deeply regretted his
earlier sins as a slaver.*

Amazing Grace! How sweet the sound—That saved a wretch like me!
I once was lost, but now I'm found—was blind but now I see.

'Twas Grace that taught my heart to fear,
And Grace my fears relieved;
How precious did that Grace appear the hour I first believed.

Down by the Riverside

Traditional

The message of gospel music, derived from the New Testament, emphasizes overcoming oppression and hardship through faith.

Verse 1

Gonna lay down my burden, down by the river side,
Down by the river side, down by the river side.
Gonna lay down my burden, down by the river side,
To study war no more.

Chorus

I ain't gonna study war no more,
I ain't gonna study war no more,
Well, I ain't gonna study war no more.
Ain't gonna study war no more,
Ain't gonna study war no more.

Verse 2

Gonna lay down my sword and shield, down by the river side,
Down by the river side, down by the river side.
Gonna lay down my sword and shield, down by the river side,
To study war no more.

Chorus

I ain't gonna study war no more,
I ain't gonna study war no more,
Well, I ain't gonna study war no more.
Ain't gonna study war no more,
Ain't gonna study war no more.

Verse 3

Gonna put on my long white robe, down by the river side,
Down by the river side, down by the river side.
Gonna put on my long white robe, down by the river side,
To study war no more.

Chorus

I ain't gonna study war no more,
I ain't gonna study war no more,
Well, I ain't gonna study war no more.
Ain't gonna study war no more,
Ain't gonna study war no more.

Verse 4

Gonna meet my loving Savior, down by the river side,
Down by the river side, down by the river side.
Gonna meet my loving Savior, down by the river side,
To study war no more.

Chorus

I ain't gonna study war no more,
I ain't gonna study war no more,
Well, I ain't gonna study war no more.
Ain't gonna study war no more,
Ain't gonna study war no more.

GET ON BOARD, LITTLE CHILDREN

TRADITIONAL

*When first written, the train probably referred to a "ride"
on the Underground Railroad.*

The Gospel train's a-comin',
I hear it just at hand;
I hear the car wheels movin'
And rumblin' through the land.

Chorus
Get on board, little children,
Get on board, little children,
Get on board, little children,
For there's room for many a more.

I hear the bell and whistle,
A-comin' 'round the curve;
She's playin' all her steam and power
And straining every nerve.

No signal for another train
To follow on the line;
Oh, sinner, you're forever lost,
If once you're left behind.

The fare is cheap and all can go,
The rich and poor are there;
No second-class on board the train,
No difference in the fare.

This Little Light of Mine

TRADITIONAL

The essence of all spirituals is a deep faith that the future will be better.

This little light of mine,
I'm gonna let it shine.
Oh, this little light of mine,
Iím gonna let it shine,
This little light of mine,
I'm gonna let it shine.
Let it shine,
Let it shine,
Let it shine.

KUM BA YA

TRADITIONAL

*This song is believed to have been brought to the United States
by slaves from West Africa. When sung by some congregations,
"Come by here" sounds like "Kum ba ya."*

Come by here, my Lord, Come by here.
Come by here, my Lord, Come by here.
Come by here, my Lord, Come by here.
Oh, Lord, come by here.

Kum ba ya. Ya.
Kum ba ya. Ya.
Kum ba ya. Ya.
Kum ba ya. Ya.
Kum ba ya. Ya.
Kum ba ya. Ya.
Ah, ah. Kum ba ya.

OVER MY HEAD

SPIRITUAL

This song reflects the faith that slaves had in God and their belief that He would hear and answer their prayers.

Over my head, I hear music in the air.
Over my head, I hear music in the air.
Over my head, I hear music in the air.
There must be a God somewhere.

Over my head, I hear singing in the air.
Over my head, I hear singing in the air.
Over my head, I hear singing in the air.
There must be a God somewhere.

Over my head, I see trouble in the air.
Over my head, I see trouble in the air.
Over my head, I see trouble in the air.
There must be a God somewhere.

Over my head, I see glory in the air.
Over my head, I see glory in the air.
Over my head, I see glory in the air.
There must be a God somewhere.

Take This Hammer

Traditional/Work Song

The lyrics and rhythm of work songs enabled slaves to endure their enforced labor.

Take this hammer,
Carry it to the captain,
Take this hammer,
Carry it to the captain,
Take this hammer,
Carry it to the captain,
Tell him I'm gone,
Tell him I'm gone.

If he asks you
Was I running,
If he asks you
Was I running,
If he asks you
Was I running,
Tell him I was flying,
Tell him I was flying.

If he asks you
Was I laughing,
If he asks you
Was I laughing,
If he asks you
Was I laughing,
Tell him I was crying,
Tell him I was crying.

Take this hammer,
Carry it to the captain,
Take this hammer,
Carry it to the captain,
Take this hammer,
Carry it to the captain,
Tell him I'm gone,
Tell him I'm gone.

MISS MARY MACK

TRADITIONAL/HAND-CLAPPING SONG

*When not working in the fields, hand-clapping songs were sung by enslaved
African-American children to amuse themselves.*

Miss Mary Mack, Mack, Mack,
All dressed in black, black, black,
With silver buttons, buttons, buttons,
All down her back, back, back.

She asked her mother, mother, mother,
For fifteen cents, cents, cents,
To see the elephant, elephant, elephant,
Jump over the fence, fence, fence.

He jumped so high, high, high,
He almost reached the sky, sky, sky,
And he didn't come back, back, back,
Until the Fourth of July, 'ly, 'ly.

HAMBONE

TRADITIONAL CHANT

Forbidden to have musical instruments, slaves used their hands, feet, and sticks to beat out rhythms. "Hambone" is a clapping chant.

Hambone, Hambone, where you been?
'Round the world and back again!

Hambone, Hambone, where's your wife?
In the kitchen cooking rice.

Hambone, Hambone, have you heard?
Papa's gonna buy me a mockingbird.

If that mockingbird don't sing,
Papa's gonna buy me a diamond ring.

If that diamond ring don't shine,
Papa's gonna buy me a fishing line.

Hambone, Hambone, where you been?
'Round the world and back again!

ACKNOWLEDGMENTS

From AFRICAN WONDER TALES by Frances Carpenter Huntington. Copyright © 1963 by Frances Carpenter Huntington. Used by permission of Doubleday, a division of Bantam Doubleday Dell Publishing Group, Inc.

"John Henry" from American Tall Tales—Osborne, Mary Pope. American Tall Tales. New York: Knopf, 1991.

From ALVIN AILEY by Andrea Davis Pinkney; illustrated by Brian Pinkney. Text copyright © 1993 by Andrea Davis Pinkney. Reprinted with permission of Hyperion Books for Children.

From ARTHUR ASHE by David K. Wright. Used with permission by Enslow Publishers, Inc., Springfield, New Jersey. Copyright © 1996 by David K. Wright.

From RAY CHARLES by David Ritz. Copyright © 1994 by David Ritz. Used by permission of Chelsea House.

From COLIN POWELL by Warren Brown. Copyright © 1992 by Warren Brown. Used by permission of Chelsea House.

"Arthur Schomburg," "Daniel "Chappie" James," from TAKE A WALK IN THEIR SHOES by Glennette Tilley Turner. Copyright © 1989 by Glennette Tilley Turner. Used by permission of Cobblehill Books, an affiliate of Dutton Children's Books, a division of Penguin Putnam Inc.

From MARTIN LUTHER KING, JR. by Robert Jakoubek. Copyright © 1989 by Robert Jakoubek. Used by permission of Chelsea House.

Excerpts from BLACK HEROES OF THE AMERICAN REVOLUTION, Copyright © 1976 by Burke Davis, reprinted by permission of Harcourt Brace & Company.

AFRICAN-AMERICAN INVENTORS by Patricia and Frederick McKissack. Copyright © 1994 by Patricia and Frederick McKissack, and reprinted by permission of The Millbrook Press, Inc.